88 **MORE** Ways

MUSIC

Can Change

Your Life

"88 MORE Ways Music Can Change Your Life"

Written by Vincent James & Joann Pierdomenico

88 Ways Music
www.88WaysMusic.com
www.Facebook.com/88WaysMusic
@88WaysMusic

ISBN: 978-0998363714

Printed in the U.S.A

Foreword

Once I was a boogie singer...Great intro line for a song, eh? Also interesting when it's the first line of a true story in the first major hit song you wrote. Well, I was and still am that boogie singer who became the white boy that played that funky music. Where does a child first get that inspiration and realization that music is what you're going to do best and good enough in your life to make a living? For me, I had an older sister who was 10 years older than me. She would bring her girlfriends home with a handful of records and they'd dance in our kitchen after school. That was my first awakening to the miraculous reaction music got out of people. I also began to wonder "how the heck do they make that music?"

Early guitar influences like Buddy Holly, Bo Diddley and Chuck Berry would inspire me to beg for a guitar for Christmas and learn to play what they were doing to make that happen. The Beatles came along soon after and I was forever hooked. I worked my way putting many bands together, often learning other instruments so I could help others learn their parts. I hustled many years to draw crowds and compete with other bands until, finally one day, I was able to write what is still one of the biggest songs of all time, Play That Funky Music (white boy).

The world and business of music has been my life, made me a great living and made lots of people happy along the way. Just being a part of the alumni and history of rock and roll, as well as, having created something I know will last long after I'm gone, has left me humbly proud.

When I was asked to provide the Foreword for Joann and Vincent's new book, I was truly honored. Over the last several years, I've been greatly inspired by their many efforts to help more kids reap the benefits of playing music. All too often, the value of music and music education is taken for granted by the powers that be. The stories within these pages will help us all remember why music is so incredibly important in our lives.

Rob Parissi – *Founder of the band Wild Cherry, writer and performer for "Play That Funky Music"*

Table of Contents

Table of Contents

Introduction

The stories you will read in "88 MORE Ways Music Can Change Your Life" come from "deep down" in those who have written them. For some, it was painstakingly difficult to put into writing and, even more so, to share. For others, the experience was a form of therapy... writing helped them heal from their own situations and even prompted some to reach out to people they haven't seen or spoken to in many years. Some stories were whipped out in a matter of minutes, whereas, others took hours, days and even weeks to put together. However their stories and quotes came to be, "88 Ways Music" would like to say "Thank You" to each and every contributor for their time, effort and, yes, even tears sometimes. Without you, our contributors, "88 Ways Music" could not be the emotional and inspiring book that it has come to be.

There are stories that will really make you think, some that will make you laugh and, yes, a number of them will having you reaching for the tissues. Our hope, is that they will inspire and help you to remember the beauty and power of music.

Our Mission

Authors Vincent James and Joann Pierdomenico are on a MISSION to help more children and adults reap the educational, therapeutic and social benefits of playing music. To help support this mission, the "88 Ways Music" book series was created to share inspirational quotes and stories relating how music has affected the lives of people around the world. 80% of "88 Ways Music" proceeds are donated to music education and service non-profit organizations.

Acknowledgements

We would like to thank the following organizations that were instrumental in helping us gather stories for this long awaited sequel to the original "88+ Ways Music Can Change Your Life".

Pickleberry Pie – Non-Profit that sends performers into hospitals and other facilities to bring the healing power of music to children who are sick or seriously disabled.

ReverbNation – All-in-one platform for indie, DYI artists for feedback, exposure, performance and promotional opportunities.

Musical U - Community platform helping musicians of all levels become more musical - offering training resources, a friendly supportive community and access to expert help.

NAMM – The National Association of Music Merchants (NAMM) offers biannual trade events that bring members of the musical products industry to network and conduct business for the upcoming year. Top 100 Dealer Awards each year include the Music Makes a Difference Award.

*We would also like to thank the following music schools and stores along with Vincent's childhood friend, **Mark Bloodgood**, for sending in musical instrument photos for the front cover of "88 MORE Ways Music Can Change Your Life":*

A & G Central Music
San Diego Music Studio
The Candyman Strings & Things

Inspiration
&
Motivation

"When I said I love the 'Oldies'
I meant Grandma and Grandpa."

This kid doesn't know what he's missing…

"What a Feeling"

It was the end of a challenging first year at PITT Dental School and I was ready for summer's reprieve. I was introduced by a mutual friend to Randy Mims, who was producing 14 year old Michael Jackson's concert that night and was just starting the sound check at the Civic Arena. It was the beginning of a memorable weekend being on stage with MJ and opening act, Mandrill. That led to an invitation to spend a month on Randy's farm in Chapel Hill, NC. While visiting him there, he got a call from Hanley Sound, which provided sound for the Newport Jazz Festival and Woodstock. Randy was asked to set up the sound system for the 1973 Hampton Jazz Festival and made me a "roadie" for a weekend...my responsibility: set up the microphones for each group, putting me around a series of musical titans: Charles Mingus, Duke Ellington, The Staple Singers and so many more...oh...AND two of my favorites, BB King and Stevie Wonder.

Meeting Stevie Wonder was like meeting GOD. Seriously. With the curtain down, they brought him out to one of his three keyboards and left him with me as I was finishing up. After exchanging a few words, I backed up. They raised the curtain, and I took a few shots of him at close range as he performed his first song. Snapping those few shots was life-changing, in a sense, altering the course of my life. I was on a professional track with dentistry at the time, but photography was my passion. And now, I'd just had a taste of something too exciting not to deal with it. I'd already attended many concerts, but now I wanted to go with my Nikon, which was generally not permitted. TRUE CONFESSION: I developed a sure-fire way to smuggle my F2 and one telephoto lens in with me. I shot undetected for years, without flash, using high speed films and never shot before the fourth song. By then, they discovered any unauthorized shooters. Just not me.

In time, my prowess and portfolio was sufficient enough to become involved with a classic rock radio station on Grandview Avenue, decorating it with a commission for 30 framed photos. That led to my first STONES concert, shooting a memorable photo of Mick Jagger and so many more. Having compelling images got me in with the WXPN radio station and various music festivals, which has satisfied some of my needs for shooting live performance artists. I have gone on to shoot performances in many musical genres including classical, opera and musical theatre including members of the Pittsburgh Ballet, some of whom appeared in "Flashdance", the movie filmed in Pittsburgh at the time I was working with them. From that fateful day, having a brief interaction with Stevie Wonder, my path in life was forever altered. "What a feeling" to do what I do, and it still feels great!

Alex Lowy
Philadelphia, PA – USA
www.LowyPhoto.com

"A Dream Finally Realized"

Sterline began piano lessons for the first time over 11 years ago. She came into my store, walking with a quad cane with tears coming down both cheeks from behind her black wrap-around sunglasses. She said she had always wanted to take piano lessons, and needed to start right away, because she was 85 years old and didn't know how long the Good Lord was gonna let her stay here. She'd recently had her cataracts removed, and was able to take off the glasses next week and see the page.

Sterline has, occasionally, shown up with a walker and oxygen for lessons and is our most faithful student. Her adult grandchildren have called me to say how profoundly piano lessons here has changed their grandma's life for the better.

A few years ago, we bought Sterline a tiara and cake for her 95th birthday and I took her out for lunch to celebrate. Sterline proudly wore her tiara to lunch and it was such a special day for all of us. To top it off, NAMM (National Association of Music Merchants) President Joe Lamond and the NAMM office staff all signed a birthday card for her and made sure she received it on her special day.

Very few kids had musical opportunities growing up during the Great Depression, least of all a little black girl from a poor family. I'm so grateful to have helped Sterline with her lifelong dream to play the piano!

Alice Alviani
Niles, Illinois - USA
www.FamilyPiano.com

"Music in the Time of Corona"

I can offer a few varied reflections on my experiences during the infamous Corona pandemic, which left thousands sick and millions without work. This was an especially difficult time for "gig workers," such as musicians and DJs. Unemployment insurance required a cleverly-worded appeal and proof of prior income, as small business loans ran dry. My Irish-American grandfather passed during this time, from complications due to various cancers that had ravaged his system. He was 93.

My grandfather and grandmother loved music, especially Irish music, and gifted me with a special violin about 10 years ago. The violin had belonged to my grandmother's brother, who had raised her. It was one of those classic, Stradivarius models (a copy), made circa 1920 - a sturdy German make. FYI...violins are like men and wine; they get better with age. I repaired the violin and then gave a big house concert for my grandparents and family. My family often fought with great vitriol over religion and politics, but this was the ONE event that seemed to bring everyone together. IRISH music, in particular, was so loved by my family, including my Irish-by-association grandmother. I played "Danny Boy", "Irish Eyes", "Goodnight Irene", "I'll Take You Home Again, Kathleen", and various uplifting church tunes. My Princeton-educated cousin, Shannon, crooned in a beautiful soprano timbre and my Uncle Larry strummed some of his original tunes on the guitar. By the end of the night, my family was one, finally.

We lost my "Mom-mom" some years ago, and as previously mentioned, we recently lost my grandfather at the beginning of this traumatic pandemic. I knew my grandfather was dying when he was no longer able to sing in his silky Irish baritone "The Irish Lullaby." The last time I visited him, his voice was at a whisper and he prayed for death. When he passed, I was happy to know he no longer suffered and was with my grandmother in a place far better than 2020.

Now, let me tell you about "Music in the time of Corona." Churches were closed. Even when they started to re-open, singing was banned. However, you better believe that we sang for my "Pop-pop's" burial at Holy Cross Cemetery in Delaware County, a county in which he lived a great deal of his life. I hired a bagpipe player, a fellow member of the local Irish Community, to play the classics such as "Amazing Grace", "Danny Boy", and "The Wearing of the Green", which were all tunes that my grandfather would sing again and again. My sister would be responsible for "How Great Thou Art" on guitar and I was asked to perform the classic hymn "Love Lifted Me", which was playing when my grandfather died. His last words were: "I'm going home."

After the burial, I ceased playing the violin altogether for a few weeks. My life became like a scene out of Groundhog Day, and I started to experience some Quarantine-related depression. I needed a remedy fast! So, I began piecing together set lists and found the appropriate backing tracks - I re-arranged my pedalboard and microphone. To paraphrase Darwin, it's not the most physical or intelligent creature that survives, but the most adaptable...and I was certainly willing to adapt. I posted a few advertisements on Facebook and prepared to launch a virtual show: the new music performance paradigm "in the time of Corona."

I didn't have a fancy stage on which to perform... my tacky, vintage, DelCo house would have to suffice. I fluffed my hair, painted my lips and warmed up ye olde vocal cords. I picked up my fiddle, clicked on my computer and began to serenade my virtual Facebook audience. I performed everything from Sinatra and Joplin to Celtic and Boccelli. Comments and donations poured into the feed. Fans from my bands Barleyjuice and Jamison were watching, even a few family members. By the end of the show, which was a straight two hour jaunt, I had over 1,000 views...not bad for a girl from Havertown! I received so many compliments and appreciative comments, that I proceeded to play multiple virtual shows during the pandemic.

Recently, my band Jamison - with whom I just released a Christmas album (An American Celtic Christmas) - performed a major, virtual show that included a production team and staging... we received over 10K views and counting! So, indeed, life goes on "in the time of Corona" and, fortunately, so does music. I feel blessed knowing my grandparents are smiling down upon me as I continue to play the Irish music that meant so much to them.

Alice Marie
Philadelphia, PA – USA
www.AliceMarieViolin.com

> # *Music has the power to know exactly what we're feeling...*

"Late Bloomer"

My mom likes to say that I was a late bloomer during the first few years of life. Although I was a very loving and affectionate child, running up to everyone, hugging them and saying "I love you", I was not hitting my milestones such as feeding myself or interacting with others and had some early learning disabilities. Throughout those early years and despite doctors urging to send me away to permanent institutions (for lack of a better word), my mom stood fast - knowing that there was a personality inside of me that was just waiting to get out. She stayed firm with her motherly instincts and kept working with me, with the hopes that the person that I was, would eventually immerge. When my basic milestones were finally reached, I was still locked away inside of myself and had difficulty communicating and interacting with others. I wasn't at all motivated to learn and, as a result, was placed into special education classes. The truth was, that teachers simply didn't know what to do with me. I have copies of my early report cards showing the dreaded "N" for Needs Improvement on so many areas, accompanied with the teacher's notes of concern.

And then, during the first day of a new school year (I think around the 5th grade), I, along with other young children, was led into my first music class. And the rest was history. It was as if my brain turned on for the very first time. This was MY language. This was MY way to interact that I never knew existed. And perhaps, with music, something magical fired in my brain that made me literally come cognitively alive. I quickly discovered that I had a talent for singing and, especially, for singing harmonies. I remember driving my music teachers crazy, because they wanted me to sing in unison to the songs. It was as if my brain was finally completing the last re-wiring it needed to open myself up to the world around me. Although I can't find it now, I remember my report card DRASTICALLY changing that year and for all years beyond that. Very soon after, I recall being taken out of the special education class and put back into the regular classroom.

I would go on to be an almost (darn math!) straight A student throughout junior and senior high school, became an active member of our school choirs and placed 11th in my state for All State Choir. This, ultimately, provided me with a music education and vocal performance scholarship to college. I've gone on to perform professionally with the Opera Colorado, Opera Philadelphia and several musical theatre companies around the region. By discovering my passion, a world of opportunities have, literally, opened up to me.

I often wonder what would have become of me, had that music class not been available in the curriculum. How much further would I have coasted through life or, possibly, declined even further. Finding one's passion at an early age is an amazing gift; whether it be music, sports, science, writing or almost anything. A school should provide ALL of those opportunities, as they all have value. Music literally saved my life and my wish to the world is that every child be given the same chance to unlock their life's true potential.

Amy Armstrong
Philadelphia, Pennsylvania – USA
www.instagram.com/divaisinthedetails
www.OperaMouth.wordpress.com

"Even in the most beautiful music there are some silences, which are there so we can witness the importance of silence."

Andrea Bocelli
www.AndreaBocelli.com

"Somewhere Around Nothing"

There is no simple way to tell my story. When I look back at everything that has happened in my life, what led me to this point can only be described as a chain reaction. And the events always seem to be connected to the one thing that has been my passion since I can remember- music.

Ever since I was a kid, I knew that I wanted to play music. It was always somewhere within me, but I never quite knew how to get it out. I am not a natural born singer. Any attempts to sing would always turn into a desperate need to cover ears, including my own. So, I knew that it had to be playing an instrument. But how to pick one when you are just a kid and have no idea where to start? My parents never wanted me to play music. They interpreted my interest as nothing more than a passing whim and thought that I would soon switch my focus to something else. I can't blame them; I never really spoke much about my true desire and, instead, I carried it inside me till my teenage years.

As they say, every dream begins with a dreamer and, one day, my patience finally paid off. I can remember it as if it was yesterday. I didn't have cable TV at home, so I'd always ask my friend to record movies on a tape for me (yes, tape! I am that old!). Quite often, she would forget to switch the recording off and I would end up with a tape full of TV commercials & music videos. Imagine the look on my face when I found a selection of niche rock music on one of the tapes. 'How boring', I thought. Until, I listened to one music video that pushed me onto a completely new life path. It was Apocalyptica 'Somewhere Around Nothing'. I can remember being completely mesmerized by the sound and energy coming from that one song! I stared at the TV screen, playing the song over and over again, wondering how on earth I never knew of this band. I finally went to my parents to tell them, with all the seriousness that a 13-year-old could have, that I will be going to music school and that I will be playing cello. And I did.

It was a bittersweet beginning. I don't think there was a single person who was willing to take me seriously. My parents thought I was mad - 'tell me what a cello is again?'; my friends would laugh at me, comparing my gigantic cello case to a small coffin. Even my music teacher had doubts; I was 13 years old so, in theory, I was about 5 years late to the party. But I didn't care. All I had in my head was the music, the energy and the determination that, one day, I will be able to play that one song that meant so much to me. It was then, that I experienced what true passion is and how I can build on it. Within a few months, I had transformed from a shy and quiet girl who always did as she was told, to a proud little person who simply stopped giving a damn about what others had to say. I now held a desire deep inside, knowing that my passion would carry me far.

As life went on, I met a number of people with similar passions and began to understand that this was only the beginning of my journey. I soon began listening and reading more about niche rock music, including Apocalyptica of course, and learned a lot about different cultures and inspirations for those bands. There was one common theme that kept coming up; Scandinavia. Scandinavian culture soon became very close to my heart, so when an opportunity came along to participate in a student exchange program in Finland, I jumped on it without any hesitation. Looking back, I am not even quite sure how I did this. I didn't know any Finnish and my English was only good enough to enable me to order a coffee. Yet somehow, I managed to get myself to an international music school in Oulu and study there for a year. Not only did I study there, one of my music tutors was a gentleman who taught Eicca Toppinen who was the lead cellist in Apocalyptica! WOW, what a small world!

I have had a wide range of different experiences in life but I still think that my student exchange was one of the most important ones so far. In just one year, I learned two foreign languages, met a bunch of wonderful people and discovered things about myself that I never knew before. It scares me to think that I could have missed all of this if I hadn't heard that one music video a few years earlier.

And the journey continues. While I never became a professional musician, I don't regret a single minute spent in music school. My cello is now my remedy; my music creates a bubble of safe space where I can always go when I want to forget the whole world. I love my job, and what I do is hugely important to me, but I don't think I would be as successful if I wasn't able to decompress every now and then with my 4 strings and a bow. And playing music pushes me to do more; it unleashes all the wonderful emotions and turns them into a creative power that lets me write songs, lyrics... who knows, perhaps they will fly out of my drawer one day.

I consider myself extremely fortunate to have the gift of music in my life. Through music, I have met some amazing people who pushed me on to the right track. I am more than confident that I could never be anywhere near as happy and fulfilled if I didn't have the joy of music in my life.

While I would love to say more, I'll just say that I am back to playing my cello. You can be sure to find me *Somewhere Around Nothing.*

Aneta Robak
Bournemouth, Dorset, United Kingdom

"Acoustic for a Change"

While away at college, I remember seeing Dan Fogelberg at Red Rocks in Colorado. I was touched by the stories his lyrics told, but even more moved by the acoustic guitar. How beautiful those arpeggiated melodies were. The music truly touched my heart. I wanted to learn to play that way. I wanted to play, in such a way, that people were emotionally impacted. I came home to Florida for Christmas break and told my parents I wanted to learn guitar. My cousin was there at the time and said she had one I could have. It was a classical guitar with strings about an inch off the frets – really hard to play. I struggled for a few weeks and just gave up on the whole idea.

After graduating college, I started the business that I still own today. We currently employ over 250 people and are one of the largest in our industry. When I started out, there was only me, my creative ideas and a lot of anxiety – my work/life balance was way off. Work, work, work and no play! After 15 years of that, I basically burned out. I became less and less interested in the business. I began having panic attacks and eventually lost my confidence. It was a difficult time. Fortunately, by this point, the company could afford my absence with other key people in place to run the day to day. My wife Susan, however, could not understand what I was experiencing and was concerned the business and our marriage would not last. I went to counseling and discovered what I needed was a more balanced life. Go to church, exercise, get a new hobby, make friends, eat better, etc. were my mandates. One of the first things that came to mind was "learn to play guitar".

So, at 36 years old, I started lessons with the lead guitarist for UFO (Paul Chapman). UFO was a 70's English rock band that became quite popular in the U.S. I wanted to learn instrumental fingerstyle/classical and Paul was a shredding metal guitarist. Not a perfect combination, but to my surprise, he was an amazing teacher. I soon discovered that playing soothing melodies on the guitar brought me peace I had not felt in years. There was a meditative "losing of myself" reaction. Balance was beginning to enter my life.

After years of lessons, I was ready to play out and focus on providing an instrumental musical backdrop for events. As a way to give back, I decided to play free for worthwhile charity events. While playing these events, audience members would often come up to talk about their instruments at home and how they would love to find a new home for them. Since I had played events for Boys & Girls Clubs and YMCA's, I offered to place their instruments with one of them. As I played more events and continued connecting with charities, I noticed a pattern - the strong need for donated instruments. After brain storming some ideas, "Acoustic for a Change" was born. I would play free of charge at events for the opportunity to make an announcement to the audience about our ministry. It was amazing!!! We were overwhelmed with donated instruments. It felt awesome to give back and change lives. Balance was now even more entrenched in my life.

One day, we received a call from the mother of an 11 year old boy, who had been fighting Leukemia for a few years. After sharing that her son Levi has always wanted a black drum kit, we unfortunately had to let her know that we did not have one available. Exactly one week later, I received a call from a donor who had a drum kit they wanted to donate. The donor shared that he had this drum set for years, but recently felt led to donate it. He further told us about his grown son who had struggled with depression and committed suicide 7 years earlier. As I lift the sheet off the drum kit, it was a beautiful black color. WOW! I immediately shared Levi's story with our donor and you could see his spirits lifted by the power of his gift.

12 year old Iris was living in foster care, when we received a request. Her case worker described how Iris had left her battered home due to her father's violence and mother's addiction. One night, her father was so enraged that he stepped on her cherished guitar and destroyed it. Iris was crushed, but we were able to quickly provide her with an even better guitar and more.

Another child we assisted, came from a family with severe financial hardships. The child's mother suffered from Multiple Sclerosis and the cost for the medications alone was $60,000 a year. This financial strain made it impossible to afford instruments for the children to play in the school band. We were thrilled to purchase a brand new sax and trumpet for them.

After almost 15 years, Acoustic for a Change has donated thousands of instruments. For me, it wasn't financial success that brought balance and peace... it was the power of music and using that power to change lives.

Arturo Echarte
Acoustic for a Change
Lakeland, Florida
www.AcousticForAChange.com

"You Just Have to Believe"

I am convinced you will become what you think about most of the time. If you have the courage to walk away from security, change your position in life and be willing to sacrifice, you will do well.

How does a kid from Tarpon Springs, Florida make a gold record? Before I got the gold record for the Paradise album (Just Another Day in Paradise), I had been doing a thing called alpha thinking, which is imprinting on your subconscious mind what you want to happen. Believe me, it works, because it scared the hell out of me.

I had a nice, comfortable job and a good size following where I was. I made good money playing 4 shows a night, 6 nights a week with my Martin guitar. I realized, that the opportunity of a producer walking through the door or a publisher taking a shine to me, was not going to happen to me in Clearwater. So, I moved to Atlanta – it was very difficult and I nearly starved for 18 months. No one there really knew me and it was hard to find work, but I refused to go back to Florida until I got that gold album. I worked every day, all day, at the craft of songwriting with my producer Sonny on some of it. I was also blessed with some natural songwriting talent, thanks to my great-great grandfather, Johann Wolfgang von Goethe. 18 months later I got the gold album and a top 10 hit with "Key Largo"! "Casablanca" from the same album became Song of the Year in Pacific Rim countries including China and Japan. Shortly thereafter, I was knighted and received an honorary doctorate degree in music from Hannover University in Germany. *You just have to believe!*

Bertie Higgins
Los Angeles, California - USA
www.BertieHiggins.com

"My Battle and Victory Against MS"

I come from a family with no musical background, but music has been a major part of my life since I began playing the cello in the third grade. In seventh grade, I began playing the guitar and quickly became quite serious about it. But, in 11th grade, I went back to the cello for good and committed to making it my profession. I was able to join the Juilliard Preparatory Division as a scholarship student and later enrolled in the Juilliard School, where I earned my Bachelor and Master of Music degrees. After graduating, I began playing chamber music full time and served on the faculty of the University of Virginia until 1983, when I began playing full time with the Metropolitan Opera Orchestra. I later joined the Baltimore Symphony and, since 1985, have been a member of the Philadelphia Orchestra.

In February 1999, I was stricken with a virulent case of Multiple Sclerosis, which left me nearly blind and without the use of my hands. Imagine being a cellist all your life and being told by doctors you would no longer be able to play your cherished 1816 Giancinto Santagiuliana cello – being told that you would spend the rest of your life on permanent disability. The disease progressed rapidly over the next six months and, in August, I was hospitalized for extreme dehydration from a viscous third MS attack. This was the lowest point of my life, as my hands and eyes were severely affected and I could no longer even attempt to play the cello.

Instead of succumbing to a prognosis of permanent disability, I searched for my own answers to the disease to fight my way back to the life I once knew. I began researching a chronic illness where western medicine offered little hope. After discovering the simple Water Cure, I began adequately hydrating and, after studying worldwide rates of MS, I switched to an organic plant-based diet. I also spent many hours studying people who accomplished seemingly impossible feats to better understand their mindset.

My MS-Yoga and weight training program became a daily regimen, and I began meditating extensively to discover how to apply the secrets of the placebo effect to my condition. Possibly my biggest step taken during that time was to return to the Philadelphia Orchestra, just six short weeks after I was given a prognosis of permanent disability. Rejoining the orchestra was a nearly insurmountable challenge, as I could barely play my instrument and the vision in both eyes was seriously impaired from optic neuritis.

The refusal to give in to the disease was without a doubt, one of the best decisions of my entire life. At this point, regaining the use of my hands was priority number one, so I began my own physical therapy program by relearning the cello from ground zero. I also practiced the piano daily to help regain motor skills required to play a musical instrument.

Over the next few years, those efforts were rewarded, as my body cells were gradually replaced with new and healthy ones. As a result of the modifications to my lifestyle, my immune system was also changed . Dr. Robert Sergott, the esteemed Director of Neuro-ophthalmology at Wills Eye Hospital in Philadelphia, believes my immune system was altered by adopting an organic plant-based diet, which changed the microbiome in my gut. He is also convinced that I received high levels of Vitamin D, while cycling outdoors in the sun, on a daily basis. In addition, I exposed my body to lower temperatures with cold showers, and cold weather cycling with minimum protective clothing. I also began intermittent daily fasting as well and weekly fasts of 36 hours.

As the use of my hands gradually returned, I set the highly ambitious personal goal of winning a principal cello audition. The preparation involved 6 - 7 hours of daily practice, on top of my orchestra and teaching responsibilities; I devoted extensive time to the fundamentals of scales and etudes to relearn my cello skills. Four high-level auditions were taken in the following order: Principal Cello of Los Angeles Philharmonic, Detroit Symphony, Baltimore Symphony and Associate Principal of The Philadelphia Orchestra. While I did not win any of those auditions, I felt a great sense of success, as the many hours of arduous practice over several years resulted in the complete return of my ability to play the cello.

To this day, I feel a great sense of vindication for my decision to battle a disease that has an unwelcome record of success. The amazing people I studied and used as my personal guides accomplished many feats in the areas of survival, sports, chess and music including:

* Nando Parrado, who survived the famous 1972 plane crash in the Andes Mountains against impossible odds,

* Baseball legend Nolan Ryan staved off the aging process of the human body with a highly disciplined lifestyle, and he pitched his unprecedented 7th no-hitter at age 44.

* Chess genius Bobby Fischer, who won the Chess World Championship by defeating not just the standing world champion, but by defeating an entire nation and part of its culture.

* Jascha Heifetz, the greatest violinist who ever lived, not only played the violin at a level few can even imagine, he did so for 60 years!

A great deal of knowledge was gained during my fight against an incurable disease and much of that is related to music. Prior to my MS battle, I never gave much thought to the function of the brain while playing music. When we play a musical instrument, our brain multitasks at unbelievable levels. Consider all that the brain is doing when a musician plays: the hands move independently and each of the ten fingers must be controlled with exact independent precision. And that only addresses the mechanics of playing the instrument. Imagine what the brain is doing when a musician performs complex musical pieces from memory. If that is not enough, there is also the artistic or the interpretive side of music. Here, the brain is communicating to listeners and other musicians in an unwritten language. Then, there is phrasing, which is a musical version of poetry reading. Varying dynamic levels and moments of timing are also imperative to keeping the listeners' attention.

I am convinced that a lifetime of devotion to playing musical instruments proved invaluable to the lifelong development of my brain and ultimate success over MS. Music also gifted me with the confidence, discipline and analytical ability needed to confront and defeat an incurable illness.

Bob Cafaro - Author
When the Music Stopped: My Battle and Victory against MS
Collingswood, New Jersey – USA
www.BobCafaro.com

> ## *Playing MUSIC is one of the few activities we humans do that uses both sides of the brain*

"The Music Box"

In elementary school I was put in a box, so to speak, by the adults in my life. I was pegged as the hyper, disruptive student who wasn't very smart and had trouble making friends.

As early as the second grade, I knew I wanted to be a teacher. I remember my second grade teacher constantly putting me down, because of my inattentiveness and poor behavior. Back then, "BAD" meant "STUPID", so I was put in the low groups. This only added to my boredom and misbehavior. My teacher even had a wooden partition built, so that my desk had walls on all three sides. That was when I decided that I was going to become a teacher, so that I could be a nice teacher. That one elementary school teacher did a lot of damage to my self-esteem. I felt like teachers and students didn't like me. I remember her telling me that I would never amount to anything good. Her hatred of me was very apparent; it took seven years for me to overcome what she had done to me.

About the same year, my parents gave me a little toy piano for Christmas. It came with a color-coded songbook. They soon noticed that I would take entire songs and play them in higher and lower places on the keyboard. The next year, they put me in piano lessons. At first, I enjoyed the lessons and did okay. Then, I found out that there was a prize for the student who had practiced the most for the year. I have a very competitive nature, so, of course, I won the prize the next year. As I got better at the piano, relatives began giving me old song books. Playing and singing those songs gave me great joy in my life!

After fifth grade, we moved and couldn't bring our piano. I ended up having to practice at the house of a neighbor I didn't care for. I also had a new piano teacher who was very serious, so I stopped taking piano lessons. I do remember organizing Christmas concerts in the neighborhood. I would play piano and teach other kids to play some or all the piano part, while everyone else sang. The seed of becoming a teacher one day, was alive and well.

When I hit middle school, I was still socially awkward and did the minimum to keep my parents off my back about my grades. My mom talked me into joining band, even though I was two years behind everyone else. Reasoning that it would be easier to mask my potentially poor playing, the band director put me on the clarinet. I discovered the band director never seemed to notice if I was actually playing or not, so I spent half a year faking it in last chair. Then, one day, he gave me second part instead of third. At that point, my competitive streak rose again, and I became motivated to try harder. By the end of the year, I was first chair out of about ten students. As I got better, I gained more confidence.

The summer after ninth grade, I attended Lutheran Summer Music Camp. It was a month long and far enough away, that no one else knew me. Perhaps, because of that, I was able to make some friends and finally began to feel some self-worth. It also worked out well that, in tenth grade, I went to a high school where only a couple of people knew me. Once again, I made friends, mostly in band. Suddenly, I had a passion and a talent, along with some self-esteem and everything else fell into place. I went from getting C's and D's to nearly straight A's the last three years of high school.

This success carried on into college, where I graduated Cum Laude. After graduating from the University of North Texas, I began my career in 1992 at a school district in East Texas. I immediately had trouble fitting into the "music teacher" box (again with the box). After one year, the elementary school principal decided not to renew my contract. He told me I was "too innovative". Instead of forcing my students to sit in chairs and sing songs from books, which was the expectation of music teachers 20 years ago, I taught them to play instruments and incorporated games into my lessons. Because of my ex-husband's military duty, I bounced around school districts and even did a four-year stint in Hawaii, where I picked up the ukulele. My teaching style is constantly evolving. I'm a very different teacher now than I was 20 years ago, or even three years ago. I only have my students in class once a week, so my goal is to make the most of it. In elementary school, I don't believe in spending a lot of time teaching students to read music. You wouldn't teach kids to read a book once a week for 45 minutes. It's still a semi-controversial teaching philosophy, but I make no apologies. I believe it's completely appropriate for students to learn to read music when they are in middle school. My students leave me with the ability to keep a steady beat and to play their part against other parts. I want them to love *making* music.

Every year, I watch my students transform into kids who take pride in their skills and perform with confidence in front of large audiences. However, I don't just teach kids music; I use music to build kids who know how to work together as a group to do something bigger than they could do alone. The success of the group depends on the success of the individual. It is vital for every member to feel like a necessary part of the group. Once one person learns their part, it is their job to help others learn their parts. They must learn how to be both a leader and a follower and to rely on each other. This teaches them to strive for personal excellence as they learn teamwork, discipline and problem solving. This knowledge and understanding, can then be applied to other classes and to real life.

I have a very satisfying career teaching elementary music. I've been a semifinalist (Top 25) for the Grammy Music Educator of the Year three times, and in 2016, I was a finalist (Top 10). I won the HEB Lifetime Achievement Award for Excellence in Education in 2018, which came with a $50,000 prize. Music totally changed my life and there's no doubt in my mind that I wouldn't be the person I am today, if it hadn't been for music. I really hate to think what would have happened to that little girl who felt stupid, that nobody liked, if she hadn't found music. The passion I have for my job comes from the desire to introduce the power of music to others – to give them the opportunity to benefit from playing music as I have. What has music done for me? It *literally* helped me get out of my box. I wish my second grade teacher could see me now.

Bonnie Anderson, Judson ISD
Converse, Texas – USA
www.judsonisd.org/Domain/3832
www.facebook.com/MojoRimba

"Live Music, Love Music"

For George and me, as with countless others, whether we be creators or appreciators, music has always been at the heart and soul of life. It has nourished and kept us company on every level, in ways we can scarcely quantify or qualify... through joy, sorrow, confusion, celebration and every shade of emotion or circumstance life presents. In so many small moments there is a song or piece of music running through my head, running alongside me as I go about my day, my constant companion.

It should have come as no surprise that, when George and I found ourselves teetering on the precipice of separation and divorce, music showed up to rescue us from despair and steer us away from our worst human tendencies. It allowed us both to make the leap of faith across the frightening abyss between marriage and friendship as we, day by day, wrote and recorded our way through the turmoil, grief, disappointment, anger, confusion and devastating earthquake... the dissolution of a marriage.

Song by song our strengths emerged as individuals defining new trajectories, as well as songwriting partners forging deeper furrows in the soil of an as yet undefined future. Our lyrics gave expression to things we could not say to one another; the music spoke for our wildly swinging emotions that needed a safe, energetic way forward in the alchemy of change.

"The Way Moves" is an ancient saying from the Tao Te Ching. For George and me, music was The Way, the humbling, healing force that moved us - step by step - from a dark period in our lives into a brighter day. We called that collection of songs The Wonderground, because music had opened our eyes to the full wonder and depth of life and the miracles that happen every day - all around us - when we allow ourselves to be moved at our very core.

As the group Boy Meets Girl, George and I continue to write and record, to share friendship, to share parenthood and to live our separate lives with gratitude for the music that made this journey possible.

Music is sound, sound is frequency. Let that frequency course through your veins, bringing life to you, bringing you to life. Live music, love music, let it touch you, inspire you, connect you, speak to your soul, move you, encourage you, light you up and take you places you've never been before. Hop on board!

Shannon Rubicam & George Merrill, a.k.a. Boy Meets Girl
Northern California - USA
www.BoyMeetsGirlMusic.com

"The Journey Home"

The Journey Home is, actually, a song on my Passions Collide album. This song has become a part of people's healing journey when a loved one has passed on. Grief is something we all must experience in life and the array of emotions can last a lifetime. The writing of the song was a very cathartic process for me, so let me share my story with you. Hopefully, it will be a healing agent in your life.

My mom suffered from many illnesses in the last decade of her life; she suffered with Rheumatoid Arthritis, COPD, Scoliosis and she even had to have her leg amputated. It was truly tortuous for my family to watch her go in and out of the hospital repeatedly and, towards the end, the ICU. It's painful to watch someone you love in chronic pain. My mom and I had a special connection. She would always ask me to pray with her at the end of most of our hospital visits and late-night phone calls. We both believed and had hope, and there were indeed times when she actually got better. Unfortunately, those moments were short-lived and she would go right back into the hospital. We never gave up on God though, no matter how dire the situation had become.

It was an early spring Saturday morning and I was getting ready to leave to go visit her in the hospital. I remember walking down the hallway, when this melody popped into my head. I ran to my guitar and recorded it on my phone for later examination. In my heart, the melody was one of hope and, later that evening, I started to compose the song. The song itself is a musical journey starting off with rain, signifying a difficult journey ahead. The verses and choruses are in contrast to each other, with the verses sounding rigid and tense, whereas the chorus offers hope and relief. The song builds musically halfway through to that hopeful melody and the sound of wind. I artistically interpreted this as my mom breathing her last breath and being carried by angels to Heaven. The song closes with an altered version of that hopeful melody and, at certain points, you can hear the melody giggling with great joy that she is now at home with the Lord. If you haven't already surmised, The Journey Home is an instrumental song and I am glad that it turned out that way - Now listeners can create their own healing journey.

I told my mom on her deathbed, that if Jesus would allow her to, I wanted her to let me know that she got to Heaven. I am sure that was a bold request on my part, but something amazing happened one afternoon as I was driving back from New York. Before I left my hotel that morning, I cried out to God, "Lord please allow this for me." It was about an hour after I prayed and I was going through a tollbooth. There had to be twelve tollbooths open that morning, so I just randomly picked one. As I got to the booth, the toll worker was yelling something to me. I stopped, rolled down my window and he said, "Go on through." I said, "Excuse me?" He replied, "The lady in the car in front of you paid for your toll." I said, "What did you say?" He repeated it again. So, not thinking anything of it, I sped up to beep and to say thank you.

I saw the car off in the distance, but then some tractor-trailers merged together, blocking my view. When it cleared, her car just seemed to vanish. I sped up, and for the life of me, could not find the generous driver's car for the life of me. And, then, I heard my mom's voice inside my soul saying, "I love you". I immediately pulled over, cried and thanked God. My mom never knew I was writing this song and she never heard it with human ears. Perhaps The Journey Home will one day help you heal from the loss of a loved one as it did me.

Brady Novotny
Cranberry Township, Pennsylvania – USA
www.BradyNovotny.com

"In my off-time, I do record. Once in awhile, I'll just go into the studio if there's a really good song that I have in my head and want to do. As artists, I think you're constantly in creative motion. If I stopped writing songs, then that's a part of me that would stop in my life and I need constant motion."

Britney Spears
www.BritneySpears.com

"Don't Shoot - Educate, Not Incarcerate"

Way back in 1996, a family friend asked if I would be interested in teaching music to kids who had run afoul of the law. These were kids currently being housed in detention centers and who had often been abused and neglected by family and society. While I was a bit hesitant at first, the extra $50 a week sounded good to a working musician, so I agreed. It wasn't long before I realized how much of a gift it actually was for me to mentor these kids, whose future was clearly in jeopardy. You see, teaching music is rarely just about music. In the process of learning to play an instrument, kids also learn many other important life skills like discipline, patience and teamwork. As their musical abilities grow, their confidence also builds, enabling them to have a more positive outlook on life. One year later after I started the program, I was up to almost 20 classes a week making this my prime music activity.

After eight years of teaching music at juvenile halls, clean and sober high schools, group homes and probation camps, another opportunity came knocking. One of the teachers I worked with asked if I would be interested in teaching a music class at San Quentin State Prison. After some soul-searching, I again agreed to take on the challenge, not having any idea what I was getting into. I thought that, if I could bring some real prison stories back to the at-risk kids I teach, maybe some of them wouldn't be so keen on joining their gang friends in prison. If I could help keep just one kid from continuing down that path, it would be worth it.

For the next three and a half years, I made an almost weekly trek to the prison, going through strict entry and exit procedures, in an effort to ensure my safety. Keep in mind that in prison, there are no guarantees, as one can never predict when a riot might break out and you find yourself caught in the middle. While I did witness the beginnings of a few lockdowns, the worst fortunately never came to pass while I was inside. What I did learn, was how powerful these music classes were to the inmates who signed up for them. For a few hours each week, the guilt, shame, fear and abuse these men often continue to suffer is forgotten...simply by picking up a guitar and living in the moment. For many, it was also a rare opportunity to experience joy and happiness within the prison walls as they accomplished learning new songs, playing and singing them together as a group.

I had many emotional experiences teaching guitar at San Quentin, but one that really sticks with me happened one night when an inmate came in to clean the music room before the class started. An older black man, he confided in me that he's 72 years old and that today is his birthday. He is a lifer and never leaving these four prison walls alive. And then he says to me, "Would you sing 'Happy Birthday' to me son? Would you do that for an old black con?". So, I pull out my guitar and start to sing... his eyes begin to tear up and so do mine. The simple gesture of having someone sing him Happy Birthday is a such a rare gift, that he can barely comprehend.

I believe that everyone, no matter their circumstance, deserves to be educated and find something to bring a little joy into their lives, especially if they are imprisoned for life. I've been gifted the talent of guitar playing and have deep compassion for those less fortunate. It's seems only right to share these gifts with those suffering behind the cold, barren, concrete walls and steel bars of a building many will never walk out of. I've provided music education to hundreds, if not thousands, of inmates and have helped many in society today become better citizens with a life free of crime. There are so many stories, both in my book and outside of it, of how music changes lives, but there simply isn't the space for it here. So, I will offer a snippet of an experience I had while onset of the filming of the movie Guitar Man, based on my book *"Don't Shoot, I'm the Guitar Man"*.

My wife and I were on the movie set watching the filming of Guitar Man, when 3 actors dressed as gang members with tats everywhere, walked up to us - smiling. As they got closer to us, their smiles got bigger and I'm thinking "WTF". When they reached us, one of the actors leaned in and whispered to me, "I was one of your juvenile hall students" and then the other 2 actors told me that they, too, were former juvenile hall students of mine and that they are all real brothers from the same family. They told me, that when they were young and incarcerated, it felt like I was the only person that cared for them and how much they looked to me as a mentor. They explained that it was me, Buzzy the music teacher at Juvenile Hall, who helped them understand that, in life, others will help you if you help yourself. I'm still crying over the fact that I'm moving young people's hearts to do the right thing in life. Dreams come true if you dare to dream!

My motto is "Educate, not incarcerate".

Buzzy Martin, Author
"Don't Shoot, I'm the Guitar Man"
Sebastopol, California – USA
www.BuzzyMartin.com

"Changing Lives, One Child at a Time"

Music for Minors II (MFMII) is a non-profit organization providing music enrichment programs to pre-school and elementary school classrooms in California's East Bay region, since 1988. Many years ago, MFMII used to serve Milpitas Unified School District in California. Thankfully, since then, the school district committed to hiring music specialists in children's classrooms, in part due to MFMII's successful efforts in raising awareness about the essential need for music in a child's educational and emotional development. Therefore our program moved on to other schools in need of music education. At that time, a talented MFMII docent was sharing a multicultural music lesson one day and near the end of the lesson, she shared a dance called "Pata Pata". The MFMII curriculum is broad-based and multi-cultural, as our classrooms often include children from around the world coming together to learn in America.

One of the children began to cry during the docent's teaching of the dance, especially as the music started and the children began to try out the dance steps. The classroom teacher went over to comfort the child, and the docent carried on, thinking maybe the child had felt sick or was possibly upset about something. Finishing the lesson, and as the children left for recess, the docent went over to the child and teacher and asked if the student was not feeling well.

The teacher explained that the child was not ill, but had recently come to the United States from Ethiopia and had only been at the school for a short while. The child told her that "Pata Pata" was danced in her homeland every Saturday night, and she feared that she would never dance it again.

Another wonderful MFMII story comes to mind, and is about music breaking through barriers. One of our Music Docents was also a retired teacher, and was teaching a MFMII class to a kindergarten class at Newark Elementary School in Newark, California. One day, an autistic child was mainstreamed for the first time into her regular classroom for music. The docent was teaching some poetry and demonstrating how poetry, like music, has rhythm, and that songs are really poetry put to a melody. She began clapping the rhythm of the lines using the Kodaly method of ta and ti ti for the beat and rhythm of the lines. She drew symbols on the board for the ta and ti ti patterns, and had the children echo her by saying the patterns and then clapping them. By the end of the lesson, the children were reciting the poem while clapping to the rhythmic beat.

When the autistic child returned to his special day classroom, the teachers said that he went straight to the white board and began drawing the rhythm pattern symbols and then clapping them and saying ta and ti ti. What this meant, was that the child was able to learn in a regular classroom setting of 24 children, not just with the usual 5-8 children in his special day classroom. His teachers decided to try and mainstream him into the regular classroom for another subject area to see how he would do. He was able to learn there as well. This MFMII experience eventually led to a complete class schedule change as his potential was more fully discovered – all thanks to the power of music!

Carol Zilli, Music for Minors II
Fremont, California - USA
www.MusicForMinors2.org

> # *Music and the Arts are the magic that makes us Human*

"Just a Closer Walk with Thee"

My dad gifted me the love of music. Throughout his lifetime, he was a first chair trombonist for many bands. Swing and Sway with Sammy Kay was a household term in our home. Guy Lombardi. Chicago. The Spinners. Anything with brass was revered and loved.

We were always going to dad's concerts. Dancing on the boardwalk, while dad played on the grandstand. Marching with the Sousa band, while dad pelted out his solo parts. We spent countless summer nights, listening to my dad play.

The King brass trombone my dad played was a part of him; they were rarely apart. And how I loved hearing him play...it never got old. How I wish I could turn back the clock and appreciate it even more, knowing that someday, I wouldn't be able to listen to him play any longer.

One of the many types of occasions my dad and his brass quartet played for were funerals. The song most requested was "Just a Closer Walk with Thee." The beautiful arrangement they performed included a trombone solo by my dad. To this day, I can still hear the soulful sound of his trombone playing that solo.

When he passed away in 2014, I thought my world would end. He was my best friend, my confidant, my biggest fan. At his funeral, the band got together to play "Just a Closer Walk with Thee." My dad's King brass trombone was proudly displayed on his trombone stand, taking dad's place in the band. At the point where dad would have played his solo, the band went silent in tribute to him.

I have never felt such strong emotion - tears, joy, love and peace - all at the same time. I could hear dad playing. I know he was smiling. And I knew he wanted me to move forward and love life, as he had.

Music is a language we all understand. I'm thankful my dad taught me that.

CarrieVee (Verrocchio), In memory of William C. Berger, Sr.
Binghamton, New York - USA
www.CoachCarrieV.com

"Never Walk In a Straight Line"

Music is: my passion, my soul, my gift and my weakness. As it is, the world and its inhabitants, all too often, charge themselves with taking advantage of this weakness. We are led down a path and, regardless of our fortifications, we find ourselves awaiting professed glory. As children, we are taught to respect, trust and share our fervor with our music educators. However, disheartening, it seems not even they prove exempt from this egocentric ideology. While many, if not all, of my mentors fall far beyond the scope of this accusation, the story I will share shall be one of a man whose failure as a mentor also became my path to success.

Music was ever-so-effortlessly thrust into my life from a very young age; I was three. Coming from a loving family filled with talented singers, it seemed only appropriate I be indoctrinated with a strong love of music. My earliest memories of singing were filled with days at my Aunt Helena's house, whom I've always lovingly called only by her first name "Helena," with a karaoke machine. She has, always will and rightfully so, assumed credit for the inception. As my gift and passion grew, my family continued to offer their support and due diligence in nurturing it.

Although it was not until 8th grade that I joined school choir, I quickly ascertained music as my completing factor. Music was not only meant to be my passion and hobby, but my profession. Many ask, "What took so long?" My answer: jump rope. I began jumping rope, competitively, at the age of 10. Jump rope consumed my life and I found I simply did not have time for music...until I learned to make time. This sacrifice did not come without reward. I was a featured soloist in each of our concerts and was named "Baritone of the Year" by my school's music department. My ambition heralded not only validation, but a recommendation for my soon-to-be-high school's nationally recognized show choir.

After a deeper delve into the program's required commitment, I respectfully declined the persistent director's offer, as I was not yet prepared to end my jump rope career. I, instead, opted to be a dedicated member of my high school's choral department, being one of only a few students who auditioned and were admitted into all three of the school's ensembles: Men's Chorus, Concert Choir, and Chamber Choir. As the year came to a close, I was, again, approached by the director of the choral department, asking me to be a member of the school's show choir. After countless meetings, email correspondences between him and my jump rope coach, and my second audition for the program, we came to an agreement. All responsibilities would be satisfied and I could continue jumping rope and be a member of the show choir. The indescribable amount of joy I had was quickly smitten by unkept promises. The director decided he was no longer willing to "...give up everything..." and that I would be required to quit jump rope if I wanted to be in show choir. I said, "No."

The choral director had gone out of his way to create a sense of safety and possibility by filling my head with stories of pending greatness that would allow a continued commitment to my sport. With all other descriptions null, he lied to me. Someone I had trusted and entrusted with my gift, had lied to me, in hopes I would simply surrender. I quickly learned that I was not the first, last, nor only student that had fallen victim to his schemes. Although it was the first blow, it was certainly not the final. The remaining three years of my time in the choral department were filled with enduring determination met by unwavering malcontent and mistreatment by the director. Hours of preparation for solo and musical auditions were rewarded with misappropriation of his favorite show choir students, always haphazardly selected above all others.

These events that transpired, were the greatest proponents of tension between me and my parents during high school. While concerns of drugs, sex and alcohol befall many parents, it was my yearning to be given the chance to shine and wanting, so badly, to give in to my director's insurmountable pressures, that created a continuous strain on our relationship. These moments drew countless, needless tears. Great parents often are forced to make difficult decisions *for* their children when they are incapable of understanding the truly audacious circumstances they've fallen prey to. To this day, although

I've never expressed it, I am truly indebted to them for protecting the bright future that has come to pass and continues to bloom each and every day.

My music director's actions not only cut into my soul, but bore a scar. Not a scar of deformity or defamation, but a scar of learning and empowerment — after finally receiving a chance to scale over in our final moment together. The last concert of my senior year in high school, I was finally given a solo: "In the Still of the Night." To this day, I fail to understand the entailment of his pivot, although I speculate my graduation and his migration to a collegiate program may have played their parts. It is our final moment together that has forever engrained itself into me. As I said my distant goodbye, he wrapped his arms around me and through misty eyes said, "That song was meant for you." I was overwhelmed with tears, as he had seemingly admitted his wrong-doing. He offered his best and it was then, that I found it in my heart to bid my farewell, not with ill will, but with "Thank you."

A dozen years have passed since that day and I've allowed the masochist-driven determination he created to be at the forefront of my life and career. In 2010, I became a World Champion jump roper and have made appearances on MTV's America's Best Dance Crew, MTV's MADE, The Ellen DeGeneres Show, Disney's Shake It Up, La Grande Cabaret du Monde and Broadway's Cirque Dreams Jungle Fantasy. After 15 years of being a competitive and professional Jump Roper, I've since retired from the competition aspect of the sport to focus on my music career, but still perform when given the opportunity. My music has been downloaded over 4,000,000 times worldwide, featured on ESPN and awarded me two nods on the 2015 Official Grammy Ballot for Best Pop Solo Performance. I've since signed with Spectra Records, the largest independent record label in the US.

I've replaced each of those tears my former director caused with an accomplishment he could never undermine. While my experience was devastating, this process, above all else, has been the most healing. My goal in sharing this story is not to condone distrust, but to promote self-empowerment and self-driven determination, for this is not a story of victimization, but of perseverance. We are often not the cause of our own misfortune, but we alone have the power to choose who we become as a result.

"Never walk in a straight line — for the things we cherish the most, are often found off the beaten path." - Chaz

Chaz Robinson
Orlando, Florida – USA
www.ChazRobinson.com

"Piano with Parkinsons"

After studying the piano and keyboard for over 20 years, I thought I'd reached a reasonable standard in playing. But to be honest, I was frustrated. I could play the keyboard quite well using left hand chords and auto accompaniment, but I was hopeless attempting a piano piece with any type of real movement with my left hand. The funny thing is, years ago, I taught my son to play keyboards. It wasn't long before he progressed far ahead of me and now he performs professionally in pubs and bars. It was kind of irritating in a way, because I can remember me teaching him.

My Parkinson's symptoms began 8 years ago and quickly made walking difficult. My left arm and hand didn't function properly and my coordination suffered. It took almost 2 years for a diagnosis and the drugs now help enormously. Still, I have to be careful when I choose to play the piano, as there are definitely down times with the drugs that I take. You don't want to try and play at the times you just won't be able to play, if that makes sense. But overall, it's no good saying I've got Parkinson's and, therefore I'm never going to improve. That is one thing I wasn't willing to say, so I decided to look for a course that could help.

After some research, I decided to take a course from an organization called Musical U based here in the UK. It's an online program that uses a very different approach to helping musicians and non-musicians become more musical. In a matter of just a few weeks, I was able to breakthrough a period of frustration that's lasted for years. After all the hours of practice I put in, there was this one particular piano piece that I still couldn't master – this resulted in endless frustration. And yet one day... one day I saw my left hand do exactly what it was supposed to do. I was so excited I called to my wife and said, "Hey, listen to this. This is what I've been trying to play for two years and now I can play it." Beethoven's Für Elise AND Handel's Minuet in D Minor! I'm so fired up with enthusiasm now, I sometimes joke that Musical U ruined my sleep. Frequently, I'll start my day at 6 AM by coming down to play the piano.

I cannot quite get over how differently I feel about playing the piano now. I had gotten to the stage where that little voice kept saying "You're never gonna do this. You're never gonna play the piano. Why do you keep going? Why do you put this time and effort in?". But as I said, I don't give up. I just don't give up. But, I was almost to the point of giving up. Just two, three months ago I was thinking about getting rid of the piano. Can you believe that?

People would often say to me, "Chris, what do you do with your time? You know, it must be difficult." To be honest, I suffer a lot of pain. I get very stiff. I have downtimes when it's better to walk away from the piano. When you know you're not going to be able to do it; not because you can't do it, but because your body won't let you do it. But people still question why I continue to try to play and I laugh. Then I tell them that I've decided to make the best use of the time I've got left. I will never give up. I'm still enthusiastic about my interests and my hobbies and what I do. And the new love I have for the piano has rejuvenated me. It's given me inspiration in a way that I didn't have before...I didn't have the passion...I didn't have the fire, but now it's back and I cannot leave the piano alone.

I've spent more time in this room, playing my piano in the last six, seven weeks than I have in the last two years. I'm just so inspired because it feels like I've been given a new lease of life. And it's given me a new a new impetus, a new motivation to practice and to enjoy the work it takes me to progress, despite the challenges. I've got friends who unfortunately also have Parkinson's, and they don't do anything. They make the situation worse, because they sit in a chair and think why did this happen to me? For me, I just get frustrated when my arms lock up and I have to walk away for a bit. I just want to keep on playing as much as I can for as long as I can.

Chris Williams
Worthing, England

"Waiting for Life to Begin Again"

I moved to New York City in the early 90s to try my luck at becoming a Broadway singer. Soon, I was singing for small local opera companies, in the chorus of the New York Gilbert & Sullivan company, performing on cruise ships and international tours. I loved performing, but what I enjoyed just as much, was being in the audience. I loved going to see live theatre. I had several favorite Broadway performers that I would see again and again, whenever they were starring in a show.

The singer LaChanze was among them. I saw her in Company, Ragtime and Spunk, but my favorite was her performance of Ti Moune in Once On This Island. I loved her voice, her honest and earnest portrayals. I considered her a quintessential performer of our time. I still do.

When I got married in 2000, I retired from the theatre world. As newlyweds, my husband and I moved to the Financial District, right around the corner from the World Trade Center. Everything about life seemed new and exciting, full of possibilities. However, just a few months after moving into our new apartment, tragedy struck. On the morning of September 11th, 2001, the first plane crashed into the North Tower, shaking our building upon impact. We ran out, onto our terrace on the 24th floor. We watched helplessly, as the smoke and fire erupted from the towers. To my horror, over my right-hand shoulder-- just 500 feet above us--the second plane flew over our terrace and crashed into the South Tower. The blast was so strong, it blew us back into the apartment and knocked us out on the living room floor. When we finally came to, we grabbed our dog and rushed down the stairs to the exit door. Barefoot and still in my pajamas, we escaped to Battery Park as the collapsing twin towers covered my husband and I with dust and debris and threatened to asphyxiate us. We evacuated Manhattan via a boat to New

Jersey. It was January before we could return to our apartment.

Our dog clung to life; his insides cut up from ingesting glass from the debris he licked off his fur. We were in mourning for our city and for the people who died in the attacks. My husband had a close college buddy who died in the North Tower offices of Cantor Fitzgerald. And, to my dismay, I read that LaChanze's husband had also died there, leaving her with a young child and pregnant with their second.

Eight months later, my husband and I were still picking up the pieces from that tragic day. Each day, we walked around the rubble of the twin towers on the way to our apartment, passing portraits of the missing. We struggled to find new jobs and found it difficult to even discuss the events of that day with each other. We were locked in our own private hell.

I hoped a night out would give us some cheer we desperately needed. That's when I saw an ad in the paper for an Original Broadway Cast Reunion of Once On This Island - a sensitive, yet powerful, Caribbean folk tale and winner of eight Tony Awards. There were only two performances, a benefit for Broadway Cares/Equity Fights AIDS. The show would be in honor of LaChanze and in memory of her late husband, Calvin Gooding. A portion of the proceeds also went to the Cantor Fitzgerald Relief Fund, created to help the surviving family members of this company that had lost more employees than any other that day.

I wanted to support the fund and support LaChanze who, I imagined, must have been devastated. We spent extra money that we didn't really have on good tickets. We were both out of work and still too upset to really work at all, but this was important to me.

The date was Sunday, May 12th 2002. The theatre was packed. Still reeling after the attacks, the atmosphere in the theatre mirrored the emotions of the city - charged, angry and tense. I was so excited to see LaChanze perform her signature role. However, I'm sure everyone was thinking the same thing I was: how would LaChanze get through it? How would any of the actors get through it?

As soon as the curtain rose, the crowd went wild. There was a standing ovation after almost every song. When LaChanze finished singing "Waiting For Life To Begin," the entire audience stood and clapped for five full minutes. There were random exclamations of support and encouragement and yells of approval from the audience that you would never hear during a normal Broadway performance. When the cast members began to cry during "The Human Heart", the whole theatre went crazy - people sobbed, clapped in support, yelled out "You can do it!" and "We love you!". And, throughout, LaChanze gave the most heartfelt performance I'd ever seen.

I had seen this show many times, but never had the lyrics held more meaning. When Ti Muone's parents sang "New dreams are everywhere, choose your dreams with care...," I heard them like it was the first time. Sitting in the third row, my heart - closed and shut off since the attack - cracked and melted and I began to sob. For the first time, I let my heart open up and finally let myself mourn...mourn in a way I hadn't since the horrifying events eight months earlier. I cried so hard, the man sitting next to me shot me alarming looks. When the show ended, the clapping, whoops and yells lasted a full ten minutes. I jumped out of my seat to join in the standing ovation. As we left the theatre, I felt a rebirth, like I was ready for life to begin again.

In my thirty years of living in NYC - seeing over 500 shows and concerts - I have never, in my life, experienced anything remotely like that night at the Winter Garden Theatre. I still cry at the memory of it. The power of music opens your heart and the theatre gives you a place to share that experience with others. It started me on the road to healing after that horrible life-changing event and I'll never forget it.

Christina Stanton
New York, New York – USA
www.ChristinaRayStanton.com

"The Candyman Strings & Things"

Arnold was born with microcephaly, a condition that results in a small-head size and incomplete brain development. On lesson days, he walks into The Candyman Strings & Things with the brightest light surrounding him. He's genuinely the happiest person in the building and ready to dole out the hugs. Arnold's teacher, Andy, says, "Arnold always stays focused and gives drumming his best. His positive attitude is an example for everyone. He demonstrates a very natural musical sensibility, works hard at counting, loves to perform and is a huge fan of Josie and the Pussycats! He reminds us all about the reasons we play music and always has an entertaining story to tell. Arnold puts significant effort into his lessons, as if it's his life's purpose!"

Arnold gets especially excited when he gets to perform at The Candyman student showcases and often performs alongside Andy. When Arnold's father passed away, it really shook him. He expressed his feelings about it to our staff and it was difficult to watch him struggle to process his emotions. When it came time to perform at the next student showcase, we encouraged Arnold to take the microphone to say a few words about his father. It was touching to see him dedicate his performance to his dad. The presentation to the audience was ceremonial for Arnold and the crowd rallied around him with encouraging cheers. This was a truly therapeutic experience that helped to provide closure in dealing with the loss of a loved one and Arnold's family was there to receive him with love and accolades after his performance.

Arnold's mother, Mary, continually expresses that since Arnold has been taking lessons, she and his doctors have noticed remarkable developments in a number of areas. He has become more socially astute, demonstrates better coordination and balance as well as improvements in other medical, mental and physical areas. "Arnold's world has become larger and he's noticeably happier than he was before" she says.

Through this experience, Arnold's case manager, Vanessa, has learned the effectiveness of implementing music in the lives of those with special needs. She has become a devoted advocate for her clients and is helping to change the way her industry views the use of music education and therapy for children with special needs. Arnold's success with music has created a ripple effect that will help to benefit many others over time.

Music is Where Guthrie Lives

When Robin asked her autistic son, Guthrie, if he wanted to take music lessons, she received an emphatic "Yeah!". Guthrie had always shown an interest in music and enjoyed watching music-themed movies such as "Ray", the Ray Charles biopic. At home, Guthrie plays musical DVDs and CDs while dancing and singing along with his microphone and spends hours composing music on his keyboard. Robin had previously tried enrolling Guthrie in musical activities at school, but for some reason, they weren't able to keep him engaged. When she heard about the private lesson programs at The Candyman Strings & Things, she thought, "Maybe something like this might be a good experience for him" and signed him up.

Because Guthrie was so enamored with Ray Charles and had some familiarity with the keyboard, his lessons began with learning how to play piano. However, Guthrie's piano teacher, Doug, soon realized that his inability to focus and follow instructions was hindering progress - traditional piano lessons weren't resonating with Guthrie. So, Doug decided to adapt Guthrie's lessons to a guided experience in recreational music making. He would begin Guthrie's lessons playing piano and, when Guthrie would become restless after 15 minutes, Doug would then move him to a different experience on drums. This switch seemed to work and Guthrie became more engaged in his lessons. When Doug took a hiatus from the program to receive a heart transplant, Marcus became Guthrie's new teacher.

Marcus remembers early on, that Guthrie was very quiet and didn't seem connected with drums. He tried implementing several different instruments in their lessons, "And now, he only wants to sing and play drums! When we first started, he wouldn't look me in the eye, respond to direction or engage in conversation. Now, we not only carry on conversations, but he listens well and does what I ask of him. I have been able to engage Guthrie for the full 45-minute lesson and more! In his second year, he began writing notation, counting and clapping rhythms, and playing drum parts with multiple grooves involved. He comes up with a lot of ideas for cool drum parts at home and, then, shares them with me during his lesson. He also asks if he can collaborate with other kids in our program and now works really well with other students on collaborative performances for our student showcases," says Marcus. At the start of each performance, Guthrie is able to address the audience, beginning each performance with a smile saying, "Hi everybody! How y'all doing out there?!"

Marcus doesn't take the influence Guthrie has had on him lightly and remarks, "Working with Guthrie has been eye-opening and inspiring – the single greatest teaching experience I've had as a teacher."

Guthrie's mother and grandfather, Dean, are always present at his lessons and marvel at the changes they've seen in him. "We tried to implement so many different activities into Guthrie's life, but nothing seemed to reach him. It was only when he became part of The Candyman family, that he truly switched on. He never had a picture of the outside world and, now, he's an integral part of it. He's displaying more conceptual knowledge, he's improved mentally, intellectually and socially. He's gained confidence, self-control and become more verbal with an expanded vocabulary. He's also more observant and conversational...interacting with others like never before." Robin adds, "His emotional range is vastly improved as well. He was very fond of his former teacher, Doug, and when I told him Doug had received his new heart and might return to teaching, I was shocked at Guthrie's reply, "Wow, Mom. Thanks for telling me that. I hope he's doing better." I never knew Guthrie was capable of expressing emotion toward another human being. For him to express that emotion was astounding. His life has truly been enriched."

Robin fondly remarked, "Marcus totally supports Guthrie. With Marcus as part of his world, Guthrie is blooming and coming into who he was meant to be as a person. Marcus encourages him in so many ways and allows Guthrie to be physical, even rewarding him when he breaks a drum stick from playing so hard. Marcus encourages 'sass.' When Guthrie says things like, "I'm on fire!" Marcus comes back with, "Yes! Yes, you are dude. You are on fire!"

To sum up the power of music in an autistic life, Robin states: "With autism, social ability is the most lacking and that's where Guthrie is massively improving. Music is where Guthrie lives and that is where Marcus and The Candyman meet him. Music and Marcus are Guthrie's best friends in the world."

Cindy and Rand Cook
The Candyman Strings & Things
Santa Fe, New Mexico - USA
www.CandymanSF.com

> ## MUSIC & ARTS education give children the best possible chance of success no matter what career path they choose later in life

---

"Chase the Music"

I first met Lauren and her family when she was only three years old. We hosted a chamber music party at our home, outside, in the mountains of Colorado. Lauren's father is a professional horn player and music professor and was one of the performers that night. Lauren's mother is also a musician and plays flute and piccolo in the Colorado Symphony. The family was excited, as they were pregnant at the time, with Lauren's little sister Amanda. Along with performing with the chamber orchestra that night, the father also performed the alpenhorn (think 'Ricola' TV commercials). Amazing sounds rolled through the hills. They were a beautiful young family, very sociable and happy - I truly enjoyed meeting this family immensely.

About six months later, I received a call from a mutual friend, Dr. Karen Gregg, music director for the local high school. She told me that little Lauren had been diagnosed with Leukemia. The family was devastated, as was I. I didn't know them personally, but that sweet little girl didn't deserve this. No one does. I spoke to my wife and suggested that we get her a teddy bear. Not just any bear, but a really special one, like someone had given our younger son. My son's favorite bear had beans in his paws, so they were real floppy. Super cute and hug-gable. However, while trying to locate the manufacturer, we realized kids often have boatloads of stuffed animals and sick kids probably doubly so. No matter how special of a teddy bear we might find, it probably wouldn't be "the one" and we realized we needed to find something else. Something with real meaning.

Not much later, I came upon the idea of having a piece of music composed for Lauren. The perfect idea – something unique, timeless, personal and truly meaningful. I spoke with Karen and asked her thoughts, and if her band would be interested in performing, if we could pull it together. She said "Absolutely"! She took the idea to her book club (mostly other teachers and musicians), and they loved it too. Together, we worked to find a composer. We lucked into Clint Needham, from Ohio. Clint recently had twin boys. When we approached him and told him the story, he stated "I have to do this for Lauren and her family. As a father, I can't imagine what they're going through".

Clint created a beautiful piece of music entitled, "Chase the Morning Sun", just for Lauren. His thought was that, no matter how tough life is, each evening knows that tomorrow is a new day and you have to Chase the Morning Sun.

The piece premiered at the Colorado Music Educators conference, in the Grand Ballroom of the Broadmoor Hotel in Colorado Springs, by the Lyons High School band, who had been invited by blind audition.

I had planned on having Lauren and her family ride with the kids on the school bus. It's about a two-hour drive. One of the parents (a mom!) said, "Clark, are you crazy? What if she doesn't feel well, if they need to leave, if...". "I have a friend with a limo company. I'll have him take care of them." Sounded great! But, that morning, the limo died. The driver, knowing the story, got on the phone and was able to obtain a stretched Excursion. This thing was HUGE! Lauren and her family traveled to the event like ROCK STARS!

Immediately before the performance, I brought Lauren on-stage and Karen introduced her, along with her new little sister Amanda, to the band. More than half the band was crying. They all knew the story, but this was their first time meeting Lauren. I thought, "Oh no! They won't be able to perform..." However, the emotion helped them put everything they had into that performance. It was beautiful. The piece included flute and horn solos, in honor of Lauren's parents. (Lauren picked right up on that!)

After the performance, Lauren looked up at me and said, "Clark, I'm never going to stop smiling!" I was tearful during the performance and could barely hold it together. This little girl had been through so much, was still going through chemotherapy and, yet, was so sweet and appreciative.

This one-time event was the inspiration for creating an organization to do this for as many children as possible. Chase the Music gives children battling critical conditions hope, strength, love and joy through the power of music. Original music - composed and performed just for them.

Thanks to Lauren, I'm never going to stop smiling either.

Clark Hodge, Founder - Chase the Music
Lyons, Colorado – USA
www.ChaseTheMusic.org

"I get the greatest feeling when I'm singing. It's other-worldly. Your feet are anchored into the Earth and into this energy force that comes up through your feet and goes up the top of your head - maybe you're holding hands with the angels or the stars, I have no idea."

Cyndi Lauper
www.CyndiLauper.com

"He's here to hit the high notes."

Security at the zoo has gotten a little lax lately...

"My advice to aspiring musicians is to get up and jam anywhere you can. When I was a teenager, I would dress in a long raincoat, sunglasses and slicked back hair, attempting to resemble Charlie Musselwhite. It did not matter what kind of music the band played - rock, country or blues, I would beg to go on stage and play 'Got My Mojo Workin' with whatever group of musicians would allow me the privilege. You have to be bold, aggressive and impactful. Play anywhere and as often as you can. Also, keep your sax with you wherever possible. Jerry Portnoy, who was Muddy Waters' electrified, amplified harmonica player, worked in New York City as a cab driver. He always had a Mississippi saxophone in his taxi."

Dan Aykroyd, a.k.a. Elwood Blues
www.TheBluesMobile.com

"Lord Howe Island Rockfest"

Lord Howe Island is a tiny island located in the south pacific, 400 miles east of Sydney, Australia. There are just 400 permanent residents living in this beautiful remote paradise, along with one small school serving 30 local children.

During one of my frequent visits to the island, I was shocked to find out that these children had no access to music lessons or instruments. Even more shocking was when I realized that they've never had LIVE music on the island! That's when I decided to send over some staff and teachers from Big Music, along with a bunch of gear and set up concert stages in stunning locations around the island. We equipped all the school kids with ukuleles and our teachers spent time each day in the classroom giving the kids music lessons, introducing them to a variety of instruments and even teaching them some dance moves. And with that, the Lord Howe Island Rockfest was born! Now, in its ninth year, this annual free concert has become the biggest event on the island, with the kids performances always a favorite.

We continue to work with the school children each year and have seen their musicianship develop enormously. Some of the older kids are now learning guitar, bass and drums and put their own bands together on the island. Collectively, the kids have even written a new island song, which they perform at Rockfest. From the time we saw the children's faces light up as they first learned to play the ukulele, to now watching these same children rock out on stage in their own band, music never forgets to remind me of its amazing power to be the human connector in all of us.

Dave Berkman, Big Music
Sydney, Australia
www.BigMusic.com.au

"I'm Not Gonna Be Like You"

I knocked gently on Kirby's open hospital room door. He was watching a movie, so I asked if I could watch with him and he nodded yes. Every ten minutes or so, I'd say something short, like "Now that's a cool car" or "I can't believe she just said that." No response from Kirby. I'd been told that he was probably in no mood to write a song with me, a complete stranger, sent by Pickleberry Pie Hospital Concerts for Kids. After the movie ended, I asked him what some of the words meant that had been used in the movie's dialogue, kinda difficult words. He quickly fired back perfect, succinct definitions. This boy was smart!

I'm sure he saw I'd brought a guitar with me, but I didn't say anything about writing a song. We had just watched a movie together and were almost not strangers anymore. So...I asked him whom he lived with, did he have a sibling or pet and what did he like to do? I noticed he didn't mention his father. We talked a while and I asked about his dad. He said he was a gambler, a drunk and only came around when he needed money.

My heart sank. This kid was in a lot of emotional pain. He was angry. He loudly proclaimed that no matter what, he was NOT gonna be like his father. I said something like, "You say that now, but things happen and sometimes kids do turn out like their... "NO," he yelled, "Never, never, ever will I be like him!" I asked, "So, how are you going to be?"

Kirby then launched into a passionate description of an honorable life. Each time he paused, I waited and kept listening. After several minutes, I picked up my guitar and asked if we could sing that story. Line by line, we hammered it out. It took hours. As we finished up, I could tell Kirby felt empowered by his newfound ability to express emotions directly in a song. I get the feeling this won't be the last time.

"I'm Not Gonna Be Like You"

When things get hard, you walk away,
It's much too inconvenient for you to stay.
I stand my ground and try to do what's right.
And so, my path in life is set.
And, Father, you can bet.

I'm not gonna be like you.

I've got better things to do.
I'll be honest, brave and true.
I'm not gonna be like you.

You sneak around 'cause you're afraid
To face the truth of this big mess you made.
I'm not the victim of the wrongs you do.
I'm strong enough to stand alone,
And my life is my own.

I won't give up, no matter what.
The man I am is the man I'll be,
And no one can ever take that away from me.
© 2007 Pickleberry Pie, Inc.

Dave Kinnoin
Pickleberry Pie Hospital Concerts for Kids
South Pasadena, California - USA
www.SongWizard.com
www.LooseToothMusic.com

"Music Heard on Another Plane"

Songwriting came to me late in life. I grew up with the piano and had a grandfather who played in orchestras. I even played in bands and wrote articles for magazines, but writing music came much later.

My father had dementia and we cared for him in our home. Some days were more challenging than others. You make adjustments. After lunch, he would sit in his wheelchair in the living room while I played the piano, an old Knabe, perpetually in need of tuning.

My first songs will never see the light of day. I would work on ideas, glancing over every once in a while, to see how my father was doing. The image that comes to mind is the early afternoon sun pouring in the front windows, as he slouched over in the chair. His eyes would be closed, his chin touching the front of his flannel shirt.

When I would finish playing the piano, I tried to be quiet so as not to disturb him. One day, as I got up from the bench, the silence must have awakened him. In an uncharacteristic moment, he sat up in his chair and spoke with a mental clarity I had not heard in months, "Dave, I just heard one of your songs on the radio and the kids are going CRAZY for it". "Oh, really," I said. "Do you remember how it goes?" We both laughed.

I'm a level-headed person, not given to sentimentality, nor qualified to put forth ideas of an alternative universe. However, I would like to offer two versions of that witnessed reality. My father had dementia and passed away before I recorded any songs. The cold fact is he never got to hear any of my music or watch any of the videos. It sometimes seems unjust, because, no matter your age, you want a parent's approval. The other reality is that, on that day as sun flowed in, a song came with it that only he could hear.

Great parents have unconditional faith, love and confidence in their children. My father was proving it, once again. In the scrambled scenarios of his mind, he forced it to become a reality. He heard a song so phenomenal, there was no question it was mine.

David Arn
Virginia Beach, Virginia - USA
www.DavidArn.com

"Magic Musical Reunion"

Back when I was a junior in college, I was hired to start a choral program at Dresden High School in Dresden, TN. It was my "dream" job, because it was what I always wanted to do. I labored in that position for nine years and achieved success in terms of awards garnered in state and national competitions. But, after nine years, my career path took a different direction.

Some years later, one of my former choral students contacted me to see if I was interested in directing a group of my former students for an alumni event at Dresden High School. I was both surprised and delighted, but also apprehensive—what would these people sound like 20 years after I last had them as students?

At our very first gathering, after we'd spent some time catching up with each other, I had them stand in sections and gave them four pitches to begin warming up, just the way I used to do it. Next, I asked them to "oooo" a chord. What happened then was nothing short of magic. Suddenly all the years stripped away, and the sound their voices made was exactly how I remembered it all those years ago. My eyes filled with tears, as did theirs. We all stopped and stared at each other in disbelief, then broke into the biggest smiles you have ever seen.

The magic of that first night continued over the next three months as we rehearsed for the upcoming alumni event...the musical gravity pulling us together became so strong, we all decided that we didn't want to stop once the event was over. So, we kept singing, year after year, adding new voices via auditions. We have now been singing together for twenty years and have been recognized by the Tennessee General Assembly and won Silver Diplomas at the World Choir Games. Our musical performances have taken us to Washington, D.C., St.

Louis, Georgia, North Carolina and many Veteran's and Children's Hospitals.

Everywhere we sing, we share the "magic" that we first discovered that one special night and haven't let go of yet.

David Johnson
Dresden, Tennessee - USA
www.DavidJohnsonChorus.com

"Happy Mother's Day"

I have always been close to my parents. I love them dearly and could never thank them enough for all they have done for me through my lifelong musical journey. Albert Einstein famously said, "I often think in music. I live my daydreams in music. I see my life in terms of music." Most of my own memories are remembered through a musical lens.

While growing up, my parents attended every school-age concert and competition, sacrificed and paid for 6 years of private trumpet lessons through 12th grade and often attended post-college performances of various bands that I performed with, including cover bands and big bands.

In 1998, I was invited to join the Eastern Wind Symphony and jumped at the chance to play classical again. At our first rehearsal of the 2002-2003 season, our conductor, Dr. Silvester, announced the concert schedule for the coming year and informed us there would be a special Mother's Day concert. An idea instantaneously came to me. My maternal grandfather was from Venezuela, arriving in the United States in the early 1920s as a concert violinist and composer. Tulio Hernandez had written a lot of music and, although much of his music had a Latin flare, he was also influenced heavily by European composers. In 1920s New York, he formed his own group called "Rudy Hernandez and His Tropical Orchestra" and wrote waltzes and other styles of music fit for violin and smaller ensembles. I approached Dr. Silvester to explain my idea of arranging one of Tulio's pieces for wind ensemble and asked if we could perform it at the Mother's Day concert. He liked the idea and gave his approval.

I explained the backstory to my friend, bass trombonist, composer and arranger Jonathan Schubert, who agreed to assist me with my project. One of Tulio's favorites, Amor Imposible, was an up-tempo waltz that would later become a hit, but unfortunately, he did not get credit. In the mid-1920s, he sent several pieces of his work to a musical associate looking for critique and advice on publishing, but never heard back. The following year, Tulio heard one of his melodies on the radio, shortly before it became a hit from a 1926 movie release. Subsequently, he wrote to this composer to let him know he was aware of the stolen melody, but did not plan legal action. The hit song was titled Charmaine, later included in additional movies in the 1950s and again in the Tom Hanks movie The Green Mile. Approximately eighty years later, I had an opportunity to bring my grandfather's music to life, as it had never been heard – in its original form.

My aunt Sylvia stored all of my grandfather's old manuscripts in a box, in her basement. After explaining my idea to her of arranging, recording and performing Amor Imposible, I drove to Long Island and spent the day sorting through all of his music, finding the original parts and carefully copying them. I drove home that night, very excited, about what was to come. Jonathan and I met several weeks later to sit down and refine my concept – to perform it as written in waltz-style, but to broaden it by incorporating a slow theme that represented the hit it would become. The melody, which was Tulio's, was a big source of pride.

Sunday, May 11th, 2003 arrived and I had to ensure that several things happened. In order to help keep it a surprise for my mom, my dad made sure to arrive to the concert hall just shortly before the show began and it was his responsibility to keep her from seeing the program. This proved most difficult, as she became quite annoyed with him. Whenever she wanted to read the program, he had to pretend to still be reading it.

The concert began and we made our way through several selections, before it was my turn to thank my mom and tell her that I loved her. I stood up from the trumpet section, walked around to the front of the stage and introduced the next piece. I explained to the audience the history behind my grandfather's song we were about to perform. I wished my mom a very happy Mother's Day and told her that I loved her. As I gazed at her in the audience, I could see her begin to cry. I was sure of three things that day... these were tears of happiness to hear her father's music come alive, tears of sadness for missing her father who passed away 7 years before I was born, and finally tears of joy for a Mother's Day gift from a son who loved her tremendously. It was emotional for me to see her reaction and it made sitting back down to play my trumpet an almost impossible task. Jonathan conducted and I struggled to play our beautiful arrangement, but somehow we got through it. It was a beautiful moment for a beautiful day.

As I wrote this essay, the tears flowed - almost as much as I cried that day. My mom is no longer with us after succumbing to cancer in 2014, and I have missed her every day since.

I realized long ago that music has the power to bring emotions to the surface. Music makes these associations with the memories and people in our lives much sweeter and more colorful. Our love is magnified through the power of music, as well as events like the one I pulled off that one Mother's Day, 2003. Our musical arrangement spanned the emotional range of many of our relationships in life. The slower, melancholy sections of the piece reflect the sadness of losing people that we love so much, while the up-tempo waltz of the main body of the song represents the fun, uplifting times in our lives, including the laughter brought on by my dad playing 'keep away' with my mom and the concert program. To not only witness the emotional impact of this life event, but to be an integral part of it, made Mothers Day 2003 one of the most meaningful experiences of my life.

I would never dream of comparing myself to Einstein in any other sense, but I too, see my life in terms of music – that is a lens that will remain with me forever.

David Kershner, The Soul Survivors
Lansdale, Pennsylvania - USA
www.TheSoulSurvivors.com
www.SongsInThePocket.org

"Changing Lives as We Sing and Play Every Day"

It's Monday morning, my bag of musical instruments is ready and I am excited for another week of work. Each day, I have the joy of witnessing the positive power of music by working one-on-one with those developmentally and physically impaired. Though disabled, my students have taught me that music can literally change a life, as it has changed mine.

It all started one day with a friend who was searching for activities for his ten year old son Korry, who is on the autism spectrum. "Why not try to teach Korry some guitar?" Though I worked in finance, I had experience as a part-time guitar teacher. So, I accepted the challenge to connect with this highly distracted boy with a limited attention span.

To succeed, I needed to grab his attention and create songs that were taught with limited explanation. So, I decided to create some fun original songs with easy to play open string patterns and motivational phrasing. Soon, our musical routines increased from mere seconds to uninterrupted minutes. His parents were enthralled with the way holding and playing an instrument could focus his attention longer than his normal tendencies. I realized, if I could use aspects of music to hold the attention of those on the spectrum, that same attention could possibly be directed toward broader skills with physical, mental and social benefits. Korry used his increased focus to practice and learn songs from his favorite shows and movies. He now plays them on guitar, bass, drums and piano.

Fast forward four years and many successes later, I was able to leave the 'rat race' of business behind to focus on using music to enhance lives of the disabled each day. Here are some recent examples from my wonderful clients:

'Rachel' enjoys expressing herself, though the 10 year old was lacking desire to learn an instrument. Because of her braced legs and crimped hands, her movements were awkward. A change in routine, due to Covid, led her to my open-air garage studio where I introduced her to my drum set. Helping her sit on the drum stool, I handed her a pair of sticks. Surprisingly, she seemed in perfect balance. I placed the foot petals comfortably under her feet and a snare drum between her legs. Feeling centered, she gave a boom-boom with her foot petal, a tap-tap-tap on the snare then a pssssh! crash on the cymbal. Soon after, we learned simple beats. No longer feeling disadvantaged, the drums gave Rachel confidence and a new desire to play music.

When 'Brian' started, he would often look distant and confused. Just 9 years old, he was considered non-verbal and often would not respond to questions or even his name. By using the love for his pet dog "LoCo" in a song, he became motivated to hit the drum twice on cue, one for each syllable in the dog's name. Next, I would sing a rocking "Who Do You Love" and he learned to sing back to me "LoCo" in rhythm with the drum. This simple song was the beginning of social communication. Later, in the midst of the song, I would abruptly freeze. I was then able to teach Brian to look at me and count to three as a cue for me to continue. By expanding our variety of song routines, Brian is learning to use eye contact and his voice to express his feelings and desires. From where he started, this is an immense accomplishment.

'Joey' was an enthusiastic guitar player. The 22 year old would watch YouTube videos of how to play chords, then use them in his own song creations. However, his short arms and nubby fingers hampered his ability to play music pleasing to the ear. Each song would have the same raunchy metallic plinking sound. Often, songs and instruments can be adapted to make them more accessible. So, I decided to change his guitar from a standard tuning to an open chord format. With this adjustment, many chords and songs could be comfortably played with one straight finger. Now, it is much easier for Joey to play and he sounds like a real musician. He is so happy and proud to show me his video recordings, some with over 1,000 views on YouTube!

"Robbie" dreams of being a bass player in a rock band, but his social communication disability made this problematic. With prior experience on drums, the 16 year old quickly ascended his guitar skills and can even play by ear. One day, he winced when his mistake prone teacher (me) hit the wrong chord. That look started a social connection. "Why?" I asked. "The chorus" he responded. He was correct. I was supposed to play the progression for the chorus portion. I then talked to Robbie about being in a band, how it is necessary to communicate with the other members about instrument parts and song arrangements. This began an on-going discussion of the structure of each song. At first, I would ask the questions, but eventually Robbie learned to ask me. He is now understanding the need to directly engage another, in order to achieve a mutual goal. This can be a large leap for one on the spectrum and, certainly, one Robbie can take with him as he grows into his rock n' roll dreams.

My goal is to inspire others to find ways to also use music to enhance lives of the disabled. Place yourself in their shoes. Adapt the song, the instrument, the lyrics to motivate communication and participation. If their voices fail, use the sounds, senses and emotions we all feel to connect with them. Music is adaptable and accessible to all. It truly can change your life. I start each day thankful it has changed mine.

David Meyers
Holmes, New York – USA
www.RockOnMusicSchool.com

MUSIC: The magical time machine that never fails to bring us back to that special moment...

"Releasing Hidden Talents"

I don't have the stereotypical backstory of a dynamic vocalist. I didn't grow up singing in church or school choirs, nor did I participate in any singing groups, boy bands or glee clubs as a youth. I always knew I could sing. The only problem was, I was terrified to do it in front of people. I can remember, at the early age of 4 or 5, grabbing my first Casio keyboard and starting to compose music. I was writing and composing music before I could physically write a sentence. It was all in my brain. For 22 years, this fear of public performance plagued me, as I kept my talent hidden.

It wasn't until I read the Parable of the Talents (Matthew 25:14-30) in the Bible, that I gained the motivation and confidence to finally share my musical aptitude. In the parable, Jesus describes a master who gave talents (monetary units) to three servants. "To one, he gave five talents; to another, two; to another, one; each according to his ability." The servant given five talents, traded them and made five more. The one given two talents, made two more. However, the servant given one talent went and hid his talent in the ground. Upon returning to their master, the servants also returned their talents. The one given five talents returned ten, and his master was pleased, stating "Well done, good and faithful servant". The one given two talents returned four, and his master was also pleased, expressing to him also "Well done, good and faithful servant". Lastly, the servant given one talent returned only one to his master. His master was very displeased and answered him "You wicked and slothful servant". He told him he should have invested the talent that he was given and been fruitful.

After reading this, I realized that we are all obligated to share the physical talents that God has blessed us with. Like the servant, I was hiding my talent in the ground and not being fruitful and productive. A short time later, I sang Karaoke for the first time. I was astounded to find that I had no nerves or jitters; no fear to share my musical talents with the world. That night, I received my first standing ovation. It was the first of many. Since then, I haven't had a single butterfly in my tummy prior to performing. The fear was gone, but why? How? I realized I had bought into the Biblical notion of being obligated to share our talents and blessings with others, which glorifies God, if done for the right reasons. I had to change my mindset, my philosophy. Today, I am an award-winning singer, songwriter, composer and producer named D-Bo. I have fans in all 50 states and in 26 countries, released three albums that are available on platforms such as Pandora, Touchtunes, Spotify, Amazon, Apple Music, Google Play and many others. I've consistently been one of the top artists in the world, in all genres, on the online music community ReverbNation. I've had music in the AMC film "An American in Hollywood", been a finalist in Hard Rock Café's Hard Rock Rising Battle of the Bands, received the Touchtunes Breakout Band award and played everywhere from Casinos, Hard Rock Cafes, and NFL Football Stadiums, to headlining festivals.

The lesson to my story is this - you never know what God has planned for you, until you make use of the tools he's given you. Sometimes, we are our biggest obstacle. If you have a fear of public performance or stage fright, give Matthew 25:14-30 a read. It worked for me. It may work for you.

D-Bo
Harrisburg, Pennsylvania – USA
www.D-BoMusic.com
www.facebook.com/musicbydbo

"What keeps me interested is that I have to do it. It's like people wake up and they have to breathe; I have to write songs; I have to make music. That's like eating or breathing to me. It's that simple."

Diane Warren
Los Angeles, California – USA
www.RealSongs.com

"Guitars, Not Guns"

When I was a baby, my grandma would sing me to sleep with James Taylor lullabies and melodies by The Beatles. My grandfather taught me Rolling Stones, Tom Petty, Bruno Mars and his favorite song "Low Spark of High Heeled Boys" by Traffic. My dad taught me every single Michael Jackson and One Direction song and took me to Babyface, New Edition and One Direction concerts, starting when I was about 5 years old. I just loved music! Every kind of music!

While music was the happy part of my childhood, our family was constantly worried about our safety and future. I grew up in an area where guns and violence were common. In just my first year there, my high school had 3 different lock downs for kids bringing guns to school. Police were called in and we would be locked in our rooms until the threat was taken away. In one instance, the gun was loaded and still in the kid's backpack. It was a scary situation. Kids didn't feel safe going to our school. We would often hear gun shots at night, including the time when someone was killed just a block from my house after a drug deal gone bad.

When I was about 10 years old, my grandma took me to a guitar class she heard about called "Guitars Not Guns." This is a program that offers kids a positive alternative to getting involved with the wrong crowd. Each class was held in a little room in the back of our local public library. The teachers, Barbara and Jay, told us they would loan every kid in the class a guitar to use. We could even take them home to practice. We learned the Bob Marley song "Three Little Birds". Something just clicked and I was a lot better than I thought I would be. I really looked forward to those weekly classes. At the last class, we had a party and all the kids got certificates and we played the songs we had learned. Then, Barbara and Jay said we would get to keep our guitars! I mean, they gave every kid a guitar! It was the most amazing thing! So, I took my guitar home and practiced and practiced and got a lot better. The next summer, I went back to class again and, by then, I was getting pretty good. That was 3 years ago. I'm 15 now and, this school year, I was accepted into a music and art school program in St. George Utah. My grandma and I packed up what we could fit in our car (and my guitar of course), and drove from California to Utah where I started 10th grade at Tuachan High School. Now, I take piano lessons, guitar lessons, songwriting and I play in the school's house band.

Guitars Not Guns offered us a safe place and gave us something productive to do with our time. I know it helped me to get where I am today. My dream started to become a reality when I was gifted that guitar and I still play it every day...to me it's proof that music changes lives.

Dominic Medeiros
Richmond, California – USA
www.GuitarsNotGuns.org
www.TuacahnHS.org

"There Are No Boundaries"

I started playing piano when I was 4 years old in Venezuela, and since then music has always been a part of me. It has taken me many places and has bounced my spirit across the universe. I eventually established myself as a music teacher in the U.S. and married the love of my life, Michael. I was a full-time music teacher, active performer and mother of a six year old boy, when we found out we were expecting again. What a joy!

It seemed like forever before we were able to see our baby's first ultrasound. Our initial excitement was out of this world, but short lived...something was wrong. Noah's abdominal wall was missing and his liver, intestines and the tip of his heart were completely out of his body...no skin, no flesh, no muscle. We already loved our little baby boy Noah, so much, that we decided to give him a chance, even when the doctors said he may not survive. The only recommendation given to us, was to make him strong and carry him in utero as long as possible.

On August 18, 2015, Noah was born! They said he barely made it. Everything looked worse than what we could have imagined, but only to the medical staff. We were happily in love with our perfect little prince and he was so full of energy and life.

The doctor diagnosed Noah with arrhythmia – he was a fast breather and needed the assistance of a machine in order to eat. Shortly after being born, Noah was transferred via helicopter to the Children's Hospital. While giving birth, I had refused extra medication, so I could be alert during and after the c-section. I just had to be with Noah, and left the birthing hospital right after surgery. Our loving God Jehova, provided us with all we needed, including emotional support, while we stayed in the neonatal intensive care unit to feed him every day. Each day, I had to help clean his organs, apply medication and wrap him carefully. Changing Noah's diaper was a challenge and breast feeding was nearly impossible...I was still in pain and feverish from standing all day after the c-section. But I was determined to help my son, no matter what. I made sure every time he opened his eyes, he would see me smile back at him. Every time I sang for him, we laughed and Noah looked at me with special attention. I prayed my hardest and asked God to let me help my baby boy.

When we were finally moved out of the ICU to a regular room, I saw an old piano close by...I was so happy! I couldn't take Noah with me to the piano room, but he sure could hear me. I remembered how he used to relax in my belly when I played Mozart for him, so I thought he might like to hear something familiar. The next day I began playing Mozart Sonatas for him 3 hours each day. By the third day, the hospital staff suggested that I record myself playing the piano on my cell phone to play for Noah. I could have played any recording from the internet, but I wanted to feel I was actively helping my child. I played each note with the greatest love.

Noah's specialist had previously predicted we would have to stay at the Children's Hospital for 6 to 8 months. One morning, a panel of specialists and other hospital staff came to see us - they wanted to see for themselves, the amazing improvement Noah had made. They discharged us that day, just 8 days after I began playing music for him. When we left the hospital, Noah's heart rate and breathing were both normal, and was also drinking 8 bottles a day without the support of a machine.

Recently, our miracle Noah turned 5 years old! He is the most wonderful child ever; loving, caring, super smart and a music lover for sure. I thank God for his life every day. He and his brother Itzhak are my all.

Inspired by how music impacted Noah's healing, I wanted to let more people know about the multiple benefits of making music, for both children and adults. Shortly after bringing Noah home, we changed our family's lifestyle and our academy so we could bring in the Celest Music Project. This is a neuroscience based community music program that helps to achieve academic excellence, while having fun and reinforcing acquired behaviors. The program does this by focusing on emotional intelligence skills, personal development and performance. The children in the program receive intensive classical music training and integral support, thanks to partners, sponsors and donors. Together we inspire children to think beyond limitations. I truly believe with the power of music, there are no boundaries we cannot overcome.

Donaylé Sojo Cardenas
Twice As Nice Music Academy
Texarcana, Texas – USA
www.TwiceAsNiceMusicAcademy.MyMusicStaff.com

"40 Years to 45 RPM Flashback"

My story starts in a dusty garage in Chicago, Illinois. The year is 1973 and there is a band called Medusa playing loud rock music inside the garage. I was one of those five musicians, the only female in the band, and I played rhythm guitar. Gary, my future husband, played lead guitar, Lee played drums, Pete was our singer, and Kim played bass.

We played locally for three years, until I decided to leave the band to attend college for nursing. The band split shortly thereafter, and Gary and I married and moved to Colorado, leaving our music far behind, or so we thought. We sorely missed playing music, yet, were involved with our unsatisfying jobs and trying to make a living. Our instruments were languishing and collecting dust in our basement.

Some forty odd years later, I was sitting at home doing boring nursing paperwork, when I received a phone call from out of the blue that turned my world upside down. A music producer, Rob Sevier, from a Chicago record label, Numero Group, found an old 45 record of our music at a record convention. After giving it a listen, he gave me the shock of my life and called me to ask if I could send him the four track reel-to-reel tapes that our music was recorded on. I was incredulous that a record label was interested in the music of those obscure, yet, legendary times. My heart sank when I realized that Gary and I only had trashy cassette recordings of our music. Lucky for us, our drummer Lee had saved the original recordings, and one year later in 2013, our first album *First Step Beyond*, was released. Even more unbelievable, was that the album received WORLDWIDE ACCLAIM! Gary and I reformed the band with new members: Randy, our singer, Phoenix, our bassist, and Dean, our drummer. Gary and I were in our mid-sixties and Randy, Phoenix and Dean were in their late forties and fifties. We went on several tours of the Midwest and west coast, receiving wild fanfare wherever we played! We were even invited to perform at the internationally known music festival, South By Southwest in Austin, Texas.

Our music was so popular, especially with the younger generation, that we went on to record our second album, *Rising From The Ashes*, released in 2017 by a Finnish label, Svart Records. This album also received significant notoriety. The irony of this whole story, is that we were too young at the time to recognize that our music had any redeeming qualities. The turn of events that lead to the discovery of our music finally made us believers some forty odd years later. I firmly believe there are no coincidences in life and that everything happens for a reason that just may not be apparent at the time.

Not too shabby for a bunch of dinosaurs! It just goes to show that you're never too old to rock and roll and make your wildest dreams come true!

Donna F. Brown - Author
"Finding Medusa – The Making of an Unlikely Rock Star"
Pearce, Arizona – USA
www.Facebook.com/WriteOnDonna

"Twelfth Day of Christmas"

It was January 6th, Three King's Day, or what many consider the 12th Day of Christmas. When our church service ended, my friend Katie announced that we had missed Christmas caroling for our "shut-ins" due to the big winter storm earlier in December. She was suddenly inspired to go right then. Would anyone else like to join her?

Spontaneously, about 8 of us met up at the local nursing home and gathered around one of our eldest members, lovingly cherishing the old friendship and familiar tunes. We went to several rooms of people I had known over the years. Then, they went to look for someone I didn't recall and learned that she was in the sunroom. Finding our way there, we discovered this bright room with most people's wheelchairs facing the windows, to enjoy the view outdoors.

We found the last person and invited her to turn around so we could sing those old classic songs together and she was just delighted. Her face lit up and all was well. However, as we sang, I noticed her face begin to change and tears starting to stream silently down her cheeks. At the end of the song, I asked if we should stop? Maybe the emotions of Christmases past were just too much. She looked startled and said, "No, please continue!"

I asked, "But, I thought you were crying?"

She said, "Oh yes, I am, but these are tears of joy. You see, I have sat here in this sunroom every day with this young woman for 4 years...she has never spoken a word. I never knew she could speak. And just now...she was singing!" Our church friend was frail and in her nineties. She pointed to a wheelchair I hadn't noticed before. In it was a young woman in her twenties, curled up and barely able to move.

We quickly asked the young woman, if she would like us to turn her around so she could be part of the caroling. She nodded and we continued with familiar carols, while she and our friend joined in. Our friend continued to weep and smile throughout the whole performance. We later learned the young woman was a college student who was in a tragic car accident that left her almost completely immobile. She has little to look forward to, but the music was still in her!

I was profoundly moved by that experience and was inspired to create the "Healing Circle Singers." We're just a bunch of regular people sitting in circle, listening for a few minutes to any concerns we have for ourselves, for others we know, or for the wider world. Then, we stop getting distracted by words and shift to singing for the healing of ourselves, others and world around us. We allow the music to do its magic, to heal the broken spirits and bodies and planet. We began the first healing circle close to home, and now there are healing circles in Washington, Florida, Texas, New Zealand, Columbia and

Sweden. Just regular people like you and me, releasing the healing power of music - just like we did that day, on the 12th Day of Christmas.

Dorothy Cresswell
Healing Circle Singers
Belchertown, MA and Edgewater, FL- USA
www.DorothyCresswell.org

Let the music take you to your happy place

"Rhythm Heals"

I am an inventor and a graduate of Northern Alberta Institute of Technology and worked at the University of Alberta in Electrical Engineering and Computing Science as a lab technician, primarily involved in high energy plasma physics studies. I also happen to be a drummer. I used to play in a rock band, have run African drumming workshops and done drumming circle performances at the Muttart Conservatory. This is my story and would like to take you on a journey into the deepest levels of the self.

I've always been a drummer, for as long as I can remember. As a child, I was fascinated with rhythm. I remember asking my dad to buy me a pair of drumsticks and me beating on the footstool in my parent's living room. Hour after hour... I don't know how they put up with it. I grew up, graduated, and then one day while at work, I heard about an African Drumming Workshop being put on by David Chiaw, a master drummer from Senegal in Africa. Senegal is known as the "land of the drum." Something spoke to me that day, and I knew I had to attend the workshop.

During the two days of drumming, David taught us African drumming techniques and rhythms and explored this ancient form. We drummed on djembes, which is a traditional African drum, first developed in Africa, perhaps 900 years ago. The word djembe comes from an African expression meaning "A gathering place of peace". The deep connection of the drummers as they listen to that ancient cellular voice from eons ago is a truly healing, deeply nourishing experience. One comes away from a session profoundly refreshed and nourished - physically, mentally, emotionally and spiritually. Joy flows back into the heart.

Drumming is the oldest form of music. The first cave dweller picked up a stick or a bone and began to beat a rhythm. The body resonates and pulsates in rhythm. The baby in the womb listens to their mother's heartbeat for 9 months, and all the while the baby's heartbeat moves in rhythm to hers. Our heartbeat, our breath, walking, running, dancing, speech, laughter, day following night, the orbit of the moon - it's all rhythm.

Drumming is a part of my life. I often find I need to stop work and pick up a drum, just to relax and let it all go. And then one day, drumming saved my life. On December 1, 2001 I was installing a satellite dish on the roof and the ladder slipped on the ice. I fell two stories, landing on my head. I suffered a massive closed-head brain injury, severely damaging the front part of my brain. I went into full amnesia for three months, followed by 9 months of sleeping 20-22 hours a day. Within a few weeks of falling from the roof, it was clear that I was in a state that I might never recover from. My wife was forced to close my business, as she and my two sons rearranged their lives to take care of me.

The experience of the brain injury was very strange. What happened is that I had struck face-first into the ice. The front part of my brain slammed into my skull, severely injuring the frontal lobe. The frontal lobe is the executive processing centre of the brain. Thoughts, decisions, planning, etc. all take place in that region. But with the injury, all thinking processes ceased. Completely. No thoughts, no plans, no analysis; just observation, sensory input, feelings, emotions. But no thoughts, no words - we think in words - this was pure, continuous silence.

Once that first year had passed and I slowly began to function again, I then started down the long road to recovery. I literally watched my brain rewire itself and thoughts began to flow again. I had to learn how to read, write, drive, everything. It took me 7 years of slow recovery to return to normal.

During that first year I went through many, many sessions with doctors, MRI scans, verbal testing, etc. The doctors told me one of several things: Drum! They knew I had been a drummer, so they strongly encouraged me to continue that. Drumming involves most of the senses, in coordination with the frontal lobe in consciously guiding the rhythm. Drumming has the ability to enliven multiple areas of the brain simultaneously, and to coordinate it. The experiences of functioning in silence, watching my brain rewire itself, and the gradual creation of drum rhythms was amazing.

The process of thought gradually started to reawaken and it started with rhythm - a kind of confusing awareness of subtle rhythms, because the rhythm was there, but understanding of it was not. At first, it was awareness of my heartbeat and, then, my breathing. I watched in that conscious silence and gradually, over weeks, began to notice that there was a pattern to it – rhythm! Initially, I couldn't listen to music, because it was too confusing. The part of my brain that is aware of rhythm, gradually began to reconnect with and awaken the frontal lobes. I began to understand music again. Finally, one day, I could pick up the drum and begin to sound out a beat. With that, the awareness of thoughts and the joy of rhythm started to flood in. Slowly at first, and then in a rush. As I played each day, I literally watched my brain rewire itself. I began to be able to read and write again, and to simply listen to music.

The experience of my brain repairing itself changed me. That year of silence, coupled with wordless pure emotion, simple happiness, joy, love, pure sensory experience awakened my heart. I see people differently now. I see music differently now too. I used to just listen to the wholeness of the song, but now, I find I listen to each part individually - yet all at the same time. I listen to what the bass player is doing, how he and the drummer follow each other. I listen to the interplay of the different drums in the kit. I listen to the pauses between the notes. That is where the silence resides, the eternal silence constantly underlying it all.

I am so thankful. My friends, my wife, my children, transcending, drumming... they all saved my life. I am blessed.

Doug Whyte
Edmond, Alberta - Canada

"Every Instrument Has a Story"

One evening, my wife brought home a newsletter from the Appalachian Artisan Center. I couldn't believe what I was reading - a luthier (guitar builder) was coming to teach his methods in my hometown.

Having struggled with addiction to prescription narcotics, I found that woodwork and music soothed my mind and kept me focused on goals. I knew, immediately, this was the program I needed to get me away from my wayward path.

On a September evening, I put my plan in action. I went to a concert at the Artisan Center planning to approach this luthier, Doug Naselroad, I had read about in the newsletter.

"Mr. Naselroad" I said in weary voice, "I would like to build guitars and I think it can change my life." Doug replied, "That is what we do here, come down and join us." "I don't think you understand sir, I can't pass your background check. I am a felon and an addict", I said timidly. "But, if you can find a way for me to join you, I think it will change my life."

Doug invited me to join him at the wood shop where I began to design my first guitar. I wasn't allowed to use machinery or do any woodwork. Doug approached the chairman of the board about my story and, after careful deliberation, they called me into the room where they had been meeting. They sat me down and said, "Earl, we know your history and, against better judgment, we are going to give you a chance to work with us here. Don't let us down". I was beyond elated. After years of broken dreams and bad choices, I now had a chance to show everyone how my life would change by making instruments. My first guitar was by no means a fine piece of art, but neither was I. Doug did not criticize my work, but would instead lovingly show me what I could improve upon in future projects.

Over the next 6 years, I would spend all my time honing my skills in luthiery, building dulcimers, mandolins, ukuleles and guitars. Each instrument I made was better than the last and, with each one, my confidence and self-respect was growing. During my time there, I helped Doug teach the "Kentucky School of Bluegrass" how to build a mandolin and even met Bobby Osborne. The next year, I was the instructor for another class teaching mountain dulcimer construction and my students completed 16 dulcimers.

The director of the Appalachian Artisan Center recognized the growth I experienced in my life while working at the wood studio, and knew our community needed help for the opioid epidemic that gripped our town. We came together to develop the "Culture of Recovery" to offer other addicts a chance to discover what I found in my life.

To date, there have been several hundred addicts given the same opportunity I was. The "Culture of Recovery" is changing the view on addicts and the skills they possess. People like myself, who were once helpless and hopeless, are given a chance at a new life. Many of these former addicts are working with the Appalachian Artisan Center as blacksmiths, pottery craftsman and luthiers, while others apply their new skills at the Troublesome Creek Stringed Instrument Company created out of the "Culture of Recovery".

Thanks to the confidence I built up working at the wood shop, I was able to complete a Masters degree in Network Security. I am now a tax paying, voting, productive member of society with my felony expunged. I'm a proud director of an information technology team for an addiction treatment company. Occasionally, I still like to build my "E3" guitars and ukuleles to clear my mind from the daily stress of work and life. There is also no better feeling than stopping by Troublesome Stringed Instrument Company that grew from a hopeless addict's story.

Every musical instrument has a potential story behind it. So, the next time you see a guitar, mandolin, ukulele or dulcimer, remember... that very instrument could have been *the* difference in someone's life.

Earl M. Moore
Hindman, Kentucky – USA
www.E3Guitars.com

"Save My Trumpet!"

As a young kid growing up in Greenwood, Mississippi, I was inspired by several musicians. I was first influenced by two older kids in my neighborhood, my cousin Terrance Course from down the street, and our neighbor Leo Williams, who lived in the alley behind me. Leo was about 5 years older than me and was a great trumpet player. He let me hold his horn and taught me how to make a sound with the trumpet.

Terrence was also a great trumpet player, and the closest thing to a brother for me. He really inspired me. One day, he took me up to the roof on the back side of the house, where he liked to sit and play. The house was on the smaller side, so the roof wasn't very high up...I could probably have jumped off that roof. While up there, I was playing the trumpet, but not as good as he knew I could. Terrence said to me, "If you don't get it right, I'm gonna push you right off this roof, cause you're better than that!" Of course, I played better, because I didn't want to get pushed off. I became a real trumpet player from that day on, joining the school band in 7th grade. In high school, Terrence was 1st chair in the trumpet section and a soloist; I was third chair. He would tell me, "that ain't gonna work, you better get it together or you're gonna have to deal with me every day!"

The Mississippi Delta is the birthplace of the blues and has a history of producing legendary blues musicians who have influenced music all over the world. I had the privilege of being taught beginner band by Mr. Nathan "Tootie" Jackson, a saxophone player who trained a host of great musicians during his tenure as band director. Mr. Jackson knew that most kids entering the beginner band program could not afford musical instruments, so he would go into the school's room of used instrument parts and put together playable instruments for us. He assembled a trumpet for me, but because the instrument belonged to the school, there was a fee to use it. My mother did not have enough to pay the entire amount, so Mr. Jackson allowed her to pay a small portion of it.

During my middle school years, I played the trumpet at most of the school programs and once even had the opportunity to play at a military funeral when the Army bugler became ill. I earned $15 playing taps at the fallen soldier's funeral. Looking back on that moment, I now realize how much of a big deal that experience was for a young boy.

A turning point in my life came during my junior year of high school. One day, after band practice, I was given a note to take home to my mother. I had no idea what it was about and did not ask. A few weeks later, while at band practice, the band director stopped the band and announced that new instruments had arrived and to come forward when you heard your name called. I was pleased to hear the names of some of the more privileged kids called up to get their brand new instruments. About halfway through the list, he called my name. I was so confused and kept thinking there had been a mistake. I went inside the room where the instruments were located and saw my name on an expensive looking trumpet case. I opened it up and saw a silver Bach Stradivarius trumpet. At the time, this instrument cost over $1,000.00. I immediately found the assistant band director and told him there had been a big mistake, because my family could not afford to pay for such an expensive instrument. He looked at me with a smile and said, "there has been no mistake, it belongs to you."

Watching my mother walk from our one-bedroom house to downtown Greenwood every week to pay whatever money she could raise to pay for my trumpet, motivated me to work harder to become a better player.

In my eyes, she made a monumental sacrifice to promote my education and my family's future.

Later that year, I was walking home from track practice after school and noticed a pillow of black smoke in the air. It was in the vicinity of our house and the first thing that came to my mind was "Oh God, please don't let that be our house...things are tight enough as it is". I was trying to think positive, but something in my gut told me it wasn't good. As I turned the corner onto our street, I could see fire truck lights reflecting off the old houses close to mine. When I saw that, my heart sunk. As I ran a little further down, I saw my mom standing in front of the fire truck and then, my house on fire. First I'm thinking, "where are my sisters?". I then saw my baby sister being taken across the street by a neighbor. When I asked my mom where my other sister was, she told me the school bus hadn't brought her home from kindergarten yet. I felt a huge relief - everyone in my family was safe.

Then I said to myself, "What about my trumpet?". It was a very expensive horn, worth over $1,000. It was not the type of horn people had in my neighborhood and my mother had just begun making payments. There was lots of smoke coming from our windows, but all I could think about was running into the house to get that trumpet. Not thinking about my own safety, I jumped onto the porch just as the fire chief yelled, "Wait! Stop! GET BACK!"

I freeze for a moment, thinking I know exactly where to find my trumpet. I always kept it on the left side of the couch where I slept, right next to the window where I could see fireman throwing flammable items like curtains out the window. The next thing I know, the trumpet case comes flying out the window! I was thinking of how lucky I was, because I was ready to run into the house to get it. I ran over to the case and found it was charred and still smoking. I went to open the metal locks, but they were extremely hot and burned both of my thumbs. But, I just had to open it to see the condition of the trumpet. When I finally got it open, there was a soft hiss, like when you exhale heavily. As I pulled the cloth cover off, I was able to see the trumpet, just as shiny as when I last polished it a few days earlier. I thought to myself "Okay, we're good now!". The people around me were yelling, what are you doing? You gotta get outta there! I flipped the case closed. The handle was burned off, so I put my arms around the case and carried it over to where my mom was. I remember quickly dropping the case down next to me, as it was still extremely hot.

We ended up moving in with my great uncle. I never had a bed, so I went from the couch in our home to my uncle's couch. I received several band scholarship offers to colleges in my state. After graduating high school, I joined the Army Reserves and eventually became a paratrooper. While attending basic training, I experienced sleeping in my own bed for the very first time. It was an army bunk during basic training, but it was better than the old couch back home. I later earned my Bachelor's degree at Alcorn State University in Lorman, Mississippi.

I earned enough in my career to purchase my mother her own home and was also able to move my family into a more stable situation. I retired after nearly thirty years of government service as an air traffic controller. Through my mother's sacrifices and belief in me, I have been able to live a good life. I cannot imagine what my life would have been like without God and my mother.

My gratitude for the gifts I have received led me to establish a nonprofit promoting music and the arts. Successful Inc presents deserving youth with working musical instruments to participate in music and band programs. I like to say that God used my instrument as an instrument to help others achieve success.

I am writing this story on November 26, 2020 which would have been my mother's 81st birthday. She died seven years ago, and I often think about how her sacrifices to influence my life continue to positively influence many young lives today.

I love you mom!

Erskin Mitchell
Memphis, Tennessee – USA
www.SuccessfulInc.org

"A Profound Change of Heart"

Back in the summer of 1985, I had a falling out with a good friend. Not only was he a friend, he was also an important contact in the music business who claimed he'd been my fan for years. He even told my mother he wanted to marry me, so his sudden turnaround was a disturbing mystery - but everything happens for a reason, which would soon unfold.

At the time he stopped talking to me, I felt a knot in my gut that said, "Here's my whole life in a nutshell". Once again, on the receiving end of some undeserved abuse or betrayal, resulting in a good situation being nipped in the bud. In this case, a double whammy - striking me on both personal and professional levels, as he was an A&R man about to sign my band, E-Turn, to a major label. On top of that, a major music publisher told me that my songs were too encouraging and not desperate enough. Crestfallen, I left that office feeling very desperate.

When I got home, I chanted my Buddhist prayers for a major artist to have a big hit with one of my songs. I wrote my prayer down and, right under that, I wrote another prayer for my friend to have a change of heart and talk to me again. With that hope in mind, I wrote *"Change of Heart"* for my friend.

Determining to chant more and share the profound Buddhist principles with more people, brought tangible results. 1986 rolled around - the first week of January my band and I recorded "Change of Heart", but I didn't get to play it for the friend I wrote it for, because he still wouldn't answer my calls. As frustrating as that was, just the emotional release of writing the song was an immeasurable reward in itself. It's like you've worked the magic and, now, it's for the universe to handle. Chanting works like that too. So, I chanted, wrote the song, all the while sharing Buddhism with anyone curious about it.

So things had to turn around, just like the song says, right? Right, but not so fast. Once again, things looked pretty bleak. A tour for our band had fallen through, leaving us with no work for two months. My brilliant cat, Zerkon (the Wonder Cat), who could fetch and jump through a hoop on command, had to be put to sleep and I was down to my last $25. But, I remembered the Buddhist principle about when obstacles arise, the wise rejoice and the foolish retreat. I can't say I rejoiced right away, but I didn't retreat. I kept chanting more and more. I wanted my life to be a source of encouragement to others. I had to break through. I had to show actual proof of my faith and I wanted to do it now!

On May 27th, 1986, while driving to pick up tapes at a friend's studio in rural Pennsylvania, I got lost and chanted until I found my way. Altogether, there and back, I chanted four-and-a-half hours, which was more than I had ever chanted in a single day! I told my friend that I couldn't wait to get home to my answering machine, since I had made a positive cause I'd never made before by chanting for over 4 hours. I was sure I'd get an effect that I'd never received before. Sure enough, when I got home and played back my messages, there was a familiar Brooklynese voice saying, "Hi, this is Cyndi Lauper. I'm a friend of Bonnie's. I'm calling about your tape." Our mutual friend, a Red Cross nurse, had given Cyndi a tape of "Change of Heart".

It all happened very fast. In just a couple days, Cyndi recorded the song, which became the first song on her platinum album, "True Colors" and it was the opening song when she performed in my town, Philadelphia, promoting the album.

I couldn't ask for a better recording of the song. Cyndi's performance was impeccable and the track was brilliant! I couldn't be happier! On top of that, the person I wrote the song for, called to congratulate me! So, both things I chanted for came true! Backstage with Cyndi after the Philly show, while photographers snapped our picture together, it really started to sink in how completely my life had changed. It was, as though, the whole universe had a "change of heart"!

But, my challenges weren't over. No, I didn't walk off into a rosy sunset. The same week that "Change of Heart" was released as a single, my mother was diagnosed with terminal lung cancer and given two years to live. She sold our family home and moved us into a small apartment for her final six months, which my brother and I called "the waiting room". I was my mother's primary caregiver. At the same time, I had to deal with a frivolous lawsuit. An unsavory character had falsely claimed he owned the publishing to "Change of Heart", which meant I was unable to receive any royalties and had to go to court to fight for it. Cyndi's people assured me they had my back, but abandoned me before too long. Knowing the truth, I had to face this challenge head on. So, I went back and chanted...for the best possible outcome. Bless the Lawyers for the Arts who defended me and, together, we had a total victory in Federal Court! BMI released my royalties, and I was able to buy a ranch home for my mother to die in with dignity. But, tragically, she passed away in March of '88 while we were moving in. She was only 66.

There's a Buddhist teaching about "The Eight Winds". "A truly wise man will not be carried away by any of the eight winds: prosperity, decline, disgrace, honor, praise, censure, suffering and pleasure. The heavenly gods will surely protect one who does not bend before the eight winds." Well, I felt like I was being blown in so many directions by multiple winds at once, that it kept me standing straight. Between fighting for my livelihood in Federal Court, caring for my mother (who told me I was better and gentler than all the hospice nurses), buying a home and being congratulated for my hit, I only knew I had to be responsible to all of it, while continuing to write songs.

One day, while my mother lay dying down the hall, I wrote a song with co-writer, Tony Sciuto, that encapsulated what I was going through and hoped it delivered encouragement to anyone going through their own challenges. A year later, Tina Turner recorded our collaboration, *"Stronger Than the Wind"*! Here's the mystical part. I had been chanting for Tina Turner to record one of my songs - she is not only a brilliant artist, but also a practitioner of Nichiren Buddhism, as I am. She told me the song sent chills down her spine! It was to be her album's statement song and I received a fat advance from a publishing company. It all looked good. Then, suddenly, it was dropped from the album and was eventually released as a B-Side, which we nicknamed "Stronger Than the A-Side"! [grin].

I learned from this, that it's important for our prayers to be specific. With "Change of Heart", I chanted for a major artist to have a big hit with one of my songs, which Cyndi did. In February 1987, the song went to #3, whereas with Tina, I had chanted only for her to record one of my songs, which she did. I received the lowest common denominator of my prayer, a B-side! Both of these prayers were written down and chanted for, before coming true. Both songs brought experiences that delivered profound lessons.

Stand up to challenges and obstacles, bending without breaking, and be specific in your prayers - Prayer is so powerful!

Essra Mohawk
Nashville, Tennessee – USA
www.facebook.com/EssraMohawkMusic

"Music Spared My Father's Life"

As far back as I have conscious memory, I have always known that my father traumatically lost his mother, father, two sisters, a brother and other close family relatives who were murdered by the Nazis during World War II. Beneath my joy-filled childhood laughter and smiles, I carried a sadness and pain for my dad's loss of his first family. My beloved, late father was the youngest of four children, born to ultra-Orthodox Jewish parents in Chrzanow, Poland, a small city near Krakow. He came from a long line of Rabbis and Cantors who chanted and studied the Torah 8-10 hours a day. They were poor in finance, but rich in religion, music, and spirituality.

My father was 19 years-old when the Nazis ripped him away from his entire family, arrested and spent five years in concentration camps. While others were tortured and slaughtered, my father's life was spared – he was saved, because he was gifted with a golden tenor singing voice that sent shivers down your spine and could shatter crystal in its' top range. He became the musical entertainment for the camp commanders. They spared him to serve their own selfish desires for musical pleasure and threw him an extra crust of bread every now and then to fortify his stamina.

My father, Cantor Hershel Walfish, came to America with holes on the soles of his shoes, without a penny in his pocket and not speaking one word of English. He lived in Los Angeles for over 65 years and, still, he retained the Cantorial rhythm and inflection of the old-time European Chazan (Cantor). He emerged from the dark depths of the Holocaust to a thriving, vibrant and joyous celebration of Judaism. Many souls could have been forever turned pessimistic, but not my father. He viewed every opportunity as one filled with drive, hope and optimism. He had a marvelous voice and the kind of nasal, guttural, crying Cantorial style you just don't find anymore. For more than 55 years, he sang and taught at Congregation Beth Israel, the oldest Orthodox synagogue in Los Angeles. His melodic tenor voice, compared by admirers to that of Luciano Pavarotti, drew worshippers from across the city.

The New York Times once published an interview with Barbra Streisand in which the journalist writes "Streisand famously has had no serious musical education…". "She says her ability to hold a note can be largely attributed to one quality: willpower". I believe that same willpower Streisand is referring to, musically parallels one's will to survive even the most unthinkable atrocities, and live. Music and willpower saved my father's life. I am truly proud, privileged and humbled to be the daughter of the honorable Cantor Hershel Walfish.

Dr. Fran Walfish, Los Angeles, California – USA
Beverly Hills family and relationship psychotherapist,
author, The Self-Aware Parent, psychologist on The Doctors,
CBS TV, and co-star on Sex Box, WE tv.
www.DrFranWalfish.com

Celebrate LIFE with MUSIC!

"Hope Music Foundation"

As I look back, music has done a lot for my life. Because of music, I was able to go to school and make friends from all around the world. Most recently, music has also enabled me to help others in need.

I lost my mother and father when I was just 7 years old. At that moment, music became my mother and father on earth. Soon afterwards, I began learning to play African drums, the xylophone and tube fiddle in the village where I was growing up. From there, some of the villagers recognized my musical talents and took me to the city of Kampala to further my education.

Acquiring more musical skills was not only a big achievement, but also a huge benefit. Life was difficult without my parents, and I truly believe I am alive today thanks to the healing powers of music. Music reaches deep inside me in ways that no one has ever been able to. Music also enables me to support myself, as it is my main source of income. I am very happy and content with the little I have now, because of music.

I perform and record music for others wherever I can. I feel many emotions when performing and hope, one day, to share my music with more people in larger venues and arenas. Because music has been such a powerful gift in my life, I wanted to do something with music to help other Ugandan children in need. In 2019, I created the Hope Music Foundation, where we teach underprivileged children in the villages to sing, dance and play instruments. I want to utilize music to help children in the same way music helped me all those years ago and continues to fulfill my life today.

Mbaalu Fred
Kibiri, Kampala - Uganda
www.HopeMusicFoundation.org

Is Your Greatest Masterpiece Still Ahead?

I absolutely love opera and I hope you do, too. Opera at its best, is a unique combination of many great art forms: song, dance, drama, costumes, sets and story. And, my favorite opera composer is Giuseppe Verdi, famed for works such as *Rigoletto, La Traviata and Il Trovatore.*

My grandparents, who so influenced me, loved the performing arts and, for many years had Saturday matinee tickets for the Metropolitan Opera in New York – "the Met." The Met is one of our greatest cultural institutions and puts on astounding productions. As an impressionable teenager, I remember taking the train from Philadelphia on Saturday mornings with "Nanny" and "Granddad," having lunch at the now defunct Carnegie Deli (one corned beef sandwich could easily feed four people), then getting to Lincoln Center for the 2:00pm matinee.

The Met is a visual spectacle, even as you approach it from the grand outdoor plaza: visible through five gigantic arches are two colossal oil paintings by Marc Chagall. They flank a grand and sweeping white marble, red-carpeted staircase, above which float eleven glittering starburst chandeliers. In the huge auditorium, the show starts even before the curtain goes up, as the twenty-one chandeliers rise to the ceiling as the house lights go down. When I first witnessed that effect, I thought it was the coolest thing ever – and still do.

One of my first operas was Verdi's *Aida* and it remains a favorite to this day. The music is tremendous and the staging, which at the Met features the "Triumphal March" with live animals parading across the massive stage, was all it took to hook me for life.

Verdi became a world-renowned celebrity and, in many ways, was the embodiment of Italy itself (at least 200,000 people attended his funeral). But, as is true for us today, there are no overnight successes. Verdi's success came through not only talent, but also putting in the time, overcoming challenges and good old-fashioned hard work.

Verdi was twenty-three when he married his beloved Margherita, the daughter of his music teacher, and they soon had two children. He was composing his first opera, when both young children died. Soon after, Margherita passed away as well. Verdi was devastated and this was compounded with the failure of his second opera, a comedy called *King for a Day*. He became despondent and stopped composing - his career seemed over before it had barely begun.

But, Verdi had people who believed in him and he found the courage to get back to composing. His next opera, *Nabucco, was* an immediate success and launched him into the international spotlight and a masterful career, which lasted for over fifty years. He was known for memorable melodies ("La donna e mobile" is, but, one example) and broke new ground with his insistence on portraying real people dealing with real-life situations. His music is intensely passionate, "catchy," stirring, noble and accessible. Verdi is one of us – we, the people.

I love Verdi for his music and how he brought humanity into the melo-dramas he created. I am also inspired by

Verdi because of what he accomplished during his later years. With *Aida*, he had attained his greatest triumph to date. Verdi was fifty-eight and had achieved so much with twenty-five operas and worldwide celebrity. He had taken his art form to new heights and now, perhaps, it was time to step aside in favor of younger composers who wanted to break their own new ground. Puccini and other young bucks were on the scene, sniffing at the Maestro's heels. Time to retire?

Instead, in 1887, he adapted one of his beloved Shakespeare's plays and composed *Otello*, another masterpiece. By now, he was seventy-four years old, an old man, yet this work has all the fiery drama of his earlier operas – but, now, combined with extra measures of sublime beauty and new emotional depths. It was another international sensation and, again, Verdi had every right to retire. He had nothing left to prove. In fact, he fell into a depression wondering if he was done, once and for all.

As it turned out, he had one more opera in him - and this is the piece I take most to heart and find so moving. *Falstaff* – only his second comedy - is also based on his beloved Shakespeare. Verdi is now eighty-years old and, in this final work, he not only reinvents his own musical style, but also redeems the fiasco of the earlier comedy written years ago as a young man.

The quicksilver melodies of *Falstaff* move breathlessly from one to the next, barely finishing an aria before sprinting to the next idea. Verdi seems inexhaustible, his music even more full of life and vigor than ever. He ends his creative life, spent writing tragic masterpieces, with a full-throated laugh at it all; at the very end of the opera, Verdi has his title character proclaim that the world is a jest and *Falstaff* concludes with forgiveness and celebration.

I can't experience *Falstaff* without feeling deep emotion. It's not only the brilliant music that triggers this:

it's the man behind his music who stayed so vital right into old age. I resonate with Verdi's ability to overcome serious challenges and handle change creatively. I especially revel in the fact that, instead of retiring into obsolescence, he reinvented himself and brought forward a work as fresh and youthful as anything he created as a young man. He allowed himself to *play* in a way which, perhaps, you can only do once you've lived a long, full life. Now in his eighties, Verdi has every right to look back and dream, but instead, he looks *forward* and creates.

There have been times where I felt that my best years were behind me, that the future held little hope and my creativity was in decline. Now, in my mid-sixties, I continue to experience an expansion of creativity and new beginnings. I've adopted Verdi as a kind of mentor.

Verdi was resilient. He *had* to create and expressed himself in the fullness of his art. His message to all of us, is that we need not accept the limiting thought that our best days are behind us. When life throws difficulties at us, we can tap our passions, our creativity and, in this way look ahead with hope and anticipation.

I believe that Verdi, in his ninth decade, calls us from the past to live our own "una vita reale" – *a real life*. Will we accept his challenge and continue to sing our own songs?

Is your greatest masterpiece still ahead?

Geoffrey Berwind
St. Davids, Pennsylvania – USA
www.StorytellingSuccess.com

"The Least Musical Person You Ever Met"

I was the least musical person you ever met. Yet, even as I write "met", I realize that you probably wouldn't have met me, because I was invisible.

I grew up in an almost anti-musical household with a father who was, and remained to his dying day, a Drill Sargent. Not being seen, was the best way to stay safe from my father's aggression.

I was also non-musical, because I was born without a socket in my left hip - the tension in my body made it impossible for me to even tap my foot in time. My lack of motor coordination made playing an instrument, or singing, extremely difficult.

During my entire 20s, I felt alienated in a way that I imagine a lot of people experience. And, yet, I always wanted to play music. I first heard The Beatles at the age of 10 and experienced something I hadn't experienced before: happiness. But, music for me was always blocked - it was something created in a whole other time and place and by other people...but not me.

In 1995, I went to a workshop where they asked us to pick a quality we wanted to represent ourselves and to put that on our name tag – that's the name everyone would call us for the rest of the weekend. I thought, "Well, I've got this whole unhappiness thing down so, maybe, I should try to be HAPPY." Each time I introduced myself to someone at the workshop, their faces would light up when I said my name – the name alone created an instant positive vibe between us. It was also a way to have people constantly remind me to be "happy". Since the first 10 seconds of conversation are usually what is most difficult for introverts like myself, this was a way to instantly break through the barriers.

I became obsessed with the word happy and determined to find out what this strange feeling meant and how to generate it in myself and others. Pretty quickly, I discovered workshops on "Finding Your Voice" musically - my personal growth path and my music path were now one and the same. It was then, that the songs I would start to write and sing, would reflect what I was learning.

The word "happy" can be a trap though, as we all experience a wide range of emotions. I didn't walk around with a big smile on my face or write songs about how great life is all the time.

At one songwriting workshop I attended, they put us in groups of three people and told us to come out in an hour with a song to play for the whole group. We started throwing out words, one partner said "Terribly", I said "Happy" and our song "Terribly Happy" was born. It was a sing-a-long. My overly analytical mind thought it was too simplistic, but as soon as we played it for the larger group, it was clear we were on to something. It quickly became my most popular song, my theme song and the title of my album.

I was blessed to find open mics where they welcomed beginners - where I could practice performing, before I felt like I was good at it. This provided a tremendous boost to my social skills. "Terribly Happy" became a staple at open mics throughout the San Diego area, because people loved to sing along.

Biologically, music goes back further than language. It connects us to our core biological selves, the very selves that introverted people are often disconnected from. When we sing together, our brains release the trust hormone oxytocin, creating a feeling of trust, connection and safety throughout our bodies.

When people first get into music, it is often about self-expression, but I believe it's ultimately about communication - to take who you are and what you've learned and translate that into something universal that connects with larger groups of people.

People who know my music, sometimes tell me how "talented" I am. I usually respond by thanking them for enjoying my music and telling them I don't believe talent exists. The only difference between me and people who consider themselves "non-talented", is that I dedicated myself to find the courage and insight to shine a light on the challenges I faced in making music.

I now teach music and have no greater joy than guiding people who *falsely believe* they "just can't do it." I know what it is like to live with pain and frustration and even desperation. If you're drawn to music and think you can't do it, know there is a way - you couldn't be further away from being a musician than I was. We all want to be seen and heard...and, yet, few will stand in the glare of all the possibilities that can happen when you open your heart in public!

The truth is, that among other possibilities, you will find many more hearts that want to hear yours and possibly be opened a bit themselves. As a result, your heart will beat stronger, when it beats along with theirs. My fondest wish is not that you will see me, but that you will find yourself. I hope this is a spark that will aid you in your own musical journey with an ever more open heart.

HappyRon, Author
"Inspirational Quotes with Music" YouTube Series
San Diego, California – USA
www.HappyRon.com

"*Living Retirement In The Pocket*"

As a child of the 60s, music was always an important part of my life. Although I never learned to play an instrument myself, not a day went by without me putting on the headphones and pumping up the volume of my favorite albums to celebrate the good times and help get me through the stressful times. During my high school years in the 70s, I could frequently be found rocking out to the famous bands of the day down at the Philadelphia Spectrum arena. After meeting my future wife in 1979, we began discovering some of the local acts at Philadelphia area clubs. And there was no one more exciting than Robert Hazard and the Heroes! We became big fans and saw them regularly - I still remember the smoky packed bars, the ultra-cool Robert Hazard walking out on stage and the wild crowd singing along to every song. I'll never forget those days!

Then life happened - work, marriage, kids, scouts, Tae Kwon Do, school events and vacations. Our love for music continued, but we no longer had time to go to many concerts or clubs for live shows, other than the rare occasion when a favorite rock band came to town. The radio and our record collection helped fill the void.

Flash forward 30 years. Our kids were now grown and I was ready for retirement. I began thinking about some of the local bands we used to see back in the 80s. We now had the amazing internet and I decided to do some searching. I spent hours surfing the net, reading whatever I could find on some of my old favorites. I came across the name Steve Butler, from another favorite band from the 80s, Smash Palace (formerly "Quincy"). Just for kicks ,I decided to send him an email. I never actually talked to him in person before and I certainly didn't expect a reply. Needless to say, I was thrilled to actually get a response, along with a copy of a CD version of the Quincy album -

one of my all-time favorites. I was beyond excited to learn he had reformed Smash Palace and was playing in the area again. That marked the beginning of my first friendship with a true "rock star" - a guy who I still recall seeing play on MTV, now knew my name. This old guy was in heaven!

It wasn't much later, that Steve mentioned he was also involved in a project called "In The Pocket" - the brainchild of The Hooters' drummer David Uosikinnen and his future wife, Dallyn Pavey. Their goal was to bring together a rotating lineup of Philly's most celebrated musicians to cover classic Philadelphia songs. It sounded exciting, so we got tickets to see In The Pocket perform at World Café Live in Philadelphia. And what a show it was! So many incredible musicians, from all the bands I remembered listening to when I was young - The Hooters, The As, The Soul Survivors, Smash Palace, Beru Revue and Tommy Conwell. The list went on and on. But, without a doubt, the highlight was when In The Pocket introduced their version of the late Robert Hazard's song, "Change Reaction", with former band member John Lilley on guitar. The memories of dancing to the song so many times 30 years earlier, brought tears to my eyes. Here we were again, a 50+ year old couple dancing and singing along, like we were 20 again. I will never forget that night.

Shortly after that, we went to see Smash Palace again at the Tin Angel. I was returning from a trip to the men's room when a woman called out to me, saying "I like your In The Pocket shirt!". I smiled and said "thanks". She then confided that she was the one who had mailed the shirt to me. Here it was, Dallyn Pavey. David was now playing drums for Smash Palace and she was with him at the show. Around this time, I discovered "Facebook", so I became friends with David and Dallyn and began following In The Pocket and all of the musicians in the band. In our "golden years", we now had time to go out more and enjoy live music, once again. Through "In The Pocket", we got to meet and become friends with so many great musicians and their fans. At that first In The Pocket show, my wife and I knew no one. Now, when we see them play, half the people in the audience are our good friends. We stay in touch, hang out, talk about what shows we're going to next and share in our joys and sorrows. In the past few years, we have sadly lost several dear friends, but we are there for each other to help us get through the rough times. When my best friend Adrian was in his final days, many of our musician friends visited and sang to him at his bedside. It was truly touching and even the hospital staff was deeply moved.

The term "In The Pocket" is defined as "When two or more people play musical instruments together and are perfectly on-beat, never missing a note or going off tempo in any way." As for me, this 60+ year old on social security, is living retirement "In The Pocket" - perfectly on beat, in tempo with an incredible group of friends, all brought together through our love of Philadelphia music. To quote a favorite song from The Hooters - "I'm looking older now than when I was a kid, but I'm feeling younger now than I ever did."

Jack Leitmeyer
Philadelphia, Pennsylvania – USA
"Play It Forward Philly"
www.Facebook.com/groups/PlayItForwardPhilly

"Musical Raspberries – Earning My Bronx Cheer"

While most of my work is obviously public, some is very private. I've visited about a dozen different children's hospitals in California, Ohio, Illinois, Maryland, Virginia and Washington, D.C., under the auspices of Pickleberry Pie Hospital Concerts for Kids. Those engagements often include bedside visits with children who can't join the group shows. These are very delicate, unpredictable opportunities to build a bridge to a child who might be very hard to reach. I'll use my best intuition for what to pull from my bag of songs and fingerplays. Things in the room might give clues as to what the child is interested in and, sometimes, the child is able to tell me. I try to read and follow any cues, stay aware of what is working and what isn't, and adjust accordingly. While this work can be trying and unsettling, it can also be very gratifying and heartwarming.

It can be especially challenging when I'm not even allowed to get close to the child, let alone touch him or her. Hospitals require that I be, and have been, in good health before I'm allowed in, and that my hands are sanitized before I enter each room. The concern about infection goes both ways.

I remember one boy who was very wired, literally and figuratively, with monitors all over his scalp. I was reaching him; he was responsive and talkative. Then, he signaled quietly for me to come closer. I intuited that he wanted to whisper something privately to me, while his mother sat nearby. I put my ear close to him. He leaned into me and planted a loud, slobbery raspberry on my cheek. It was certainly not what I was expecting. The nurse and mother were mortified, but I laughed and said I would take that as a love buzz. When his mother told me this was a playful ritual he had with his uncle, I knew I had interpreted it correctly. I consider that intimate "Bronx cheer" an ovation.

As I do after all my performances, when I leave a hospital, I make a point to think about what I might do differently to improve connections. Making myself actually write down these critical "reviews" helps me be better prepared in the future and deepen the minstrel tool bag I carry with me and continually refine. It is a very different kind of toolkit than a visiting doctor's bag, but it's well documented how therapeutic smiles and laughter can be.

I've left many a bedside visit feeling that I've "done good," but usually, no one other than the child knows for sure. So, it was a delightful surprise when I just happened to come across a blog entry, written by Kelli Thomas, that documented such a visit very sweetly. I had not even been aware that the grandmother, Kelli, was watching or taking photos. What touched me most in an email exchange afterwards, was her telling me that it was the first time her grandson had smiled during her visit. With Kelli's permission, below is an excerpt from her blog entitled Quietly Blogging. It captures why I will continue to seek opportunities to brighten a child's hospital stay, always learning as I go.

"Once a stranger and now fellow traveler on this ride with our special one. Jackson gave Aidan his first smile of the day, as he sang silly songs and used Aidan's body as a musical instrument. Tapping on his fingers, playing his ribcage, knocking on his knees. Jackson used Aidan's hands to tell a story, using each finger as a member of a family who ended up living in Aidan's heart. This was music therapy at its storytelling best! What a wonderful human being. I'm so glad we crossed paths."

Jackson Gillman
Onset, Massachusetts – USA
www.JacksonGillman.com

"Pay It Forward"

Having received a great deal of support when we first opened Day Violins, we promised ourselves we would pay it forward in any way we could. There have been many opportunities to keep that promise.

First, there was Bethlehem, who had a great talent. However, it's very difficult for beginning string students to build their confidence and skills playing an inexpensive instrument. When we offered her the use of an expensive viola, she was overwhelmed and asked if we would accept payments. We said yes, but please pay it forward to someone else someday. There is always someone else less fortunate than you, and if you make their lives better through music, then you've fulfilled your financial obligation to us. Bethlehem's talent continued to flourish - she recently got into The Juilliard School on a full-ride scholarship. "Oh my gosh", she wrote, "I couldn't have done it without you!"

Another pay-it-forward moment that took place was with Eddie, a homeless cello student studying at George Mason University. When the string professor from the university came into Day Violins, she expressed how she wished the university had a nice cello for Eddie, instead of the cheap model he currently played. Right away, we knew what we had to do. We asked Eddie and his teacher to come into the shop to get a better cello and, once again, we told them to pay it forward someday. Eddie recently won the university concerto competition on the cello we had given him. We strongly believe this one act of kindness will resonate throughout Eddie's life, positively affecting Eddie and the myriad of people he will connect with throughout his lifetime.

The concept of pay it forward is something we do any chance we get. It's sometimes hard to toot your own horn, but it isn't hard to shout praises for these amazing youth, who thrive when given the chance.

Jason Day, Day Violins
Chantilly, Virginia – USA
www.DayViolins.com

"The Magic Harp"

At Hungry for Music, our mission is putting musical instruments in the hands of underserved children who otherwise would not have the opportunity. Throughout the year, we receive a variety of instrument requests from school and after-school music programs, as well as from social workers. The majority of these requests are for guitars, keyboards, drums, brass, woodwinds, strings and percussion.

But at a recent musical instrument donation drive at the Ace Hotel in Los Angeles, sponsored by the D'Addario Foundation, we received a rather unique request. Several Los Angeles-based music programs performed at this event, including the Young Musicians Foundation (YMF). One of the YMF instructors inquired about the possibility of receiving a harp. To be honest, I wasn't sure. So I asked, "How much is a harp"?

"Eighteen," the instructor said. I told her that between Hungry for Music and a couple of other organizations, we could probably raise that amount. I asked her to give me a couple of months and to reach out again in the fall, after our school-year request period ended.

When fall arrived, the YMF instructor submitted her request on our website. But after reading it, I was stunned. It was only then that I realized she wasn't requesting an eighteen-*hundred*-dollar harp — she was requesting an eighteen-*thousand*-dollar harp!

I had made a promise I couldn't keep. I called one of the organizations that had planned to contribute to the harp fund and explained the misunderstanding. They said not to worry about it and that YMF would understand the miscommunication. Still, it still bothered me. I felt like I had gotten their hopes up.

I was distracted with shipping out beginning-of-school-year instruments, but I remember sending an intention out to the universe or a prayer to God — however you want to look at it, and then just letting it go. About a week later, we received a donation form from a woman in New York City. It said she'd like to donate a $20,000 Lyon & Healy pedal harp to our organization — all we had to do was pick it up! I just couldn't believe it, although my faith in these prayerful intentions continues to grow.

The following week, a Hungry for Music volunteer and I drove to a Manhattan condo overlooking Central Park, rode the elevator to the top floor and met the owner out in the hallway. She was happy that her beautiful harp was going to a good home. Then, we drove it to the folks at the Virginia Harp Center in Midlothian, Virginia, who graciously and safely packed it up and shipped it to YMF in Los Angeles!

"We had been looking for a pedal harp for more than a couple years," says YMF artistic director Lauren Wasynczuk. "This unbelievable gift to YMF means more than we can say. Our harp scholarship student, Melissa, was over the moon to see the harp in person and was thrilled to finally play on a pedal harp after years of patience. She can finally play in all 12 keys!"

I believe in miracles. In my 26 years of working on Hungry for Music's mission, I've witnessed many — and they always seem to come at a time when I need a lift. I believe we all have the power within us to manifest positive change. If we have a creative idea that's beneficial to the world, the universe will comply. We just have to be clear, focused, not forgetting to ask, and open to receiving. Just believe it.

Jeff Campbell
Hungry for Music
Mt. Jackson, Virginia - USA
www.HungryForMusic.org

> ## *What if every child had access to Music Education from birth?*

"I'm a firm believer in starting them young."

Who's ready for a Marching Band stroller parade??

"Mandolin Bookends"

When I got my first job after leaving school long ago, I used to walk past a second-hand shop on my way to work. On that first day, I looked in the window and saw a beautiful, bow-backed mandolin with light coloured wood and an ornate design around the sound hole. With its 8 strings, it was a bit mysterious to me. I had a 6 string acoustic guitar at the time, but couldn't really play it.

As I walked past the shop each morning, I would look in at that mandolin with greater curiosity each time. At the end of my first fortnight at work, I received my first ever pay packet and went into the shop and bought it. I can't remember how much it was, but I do recall spending my entire wage – fortunately, I was still living at home.

Sadly, not having musical aptitude or sufficient motivation at the time, I never learned how to play it. This beautiful instrument ended up as a household ornament that I kept for years. The strings eventually became tarnished, and the back of the instrument dried out and cracked open. During one of our house moves, I reluctantly decided to get rid of it.

As I approached retirement years later, I began to wonder how I would spend my free time. I got to thinking about that mandolin and told my wife that I'd like to give playing it another go. She encouraged me to get one as a retirement present to myself. So, on a trip over to Berlin to visit my son, I suggested we visit a large music store in the city. I just wanted to have a look at what was available – with us planning to travel back home by plane, I had no intention of buying just then.

The store had a beautiful display of mandolins, mostly F hole style with scroll tops in sunburst colours. But as I picked up the instruments and began to handle them, the old doubt of ever being able to play a mandolin rose up inside me. I was quite downhearted, all set to walk out and give up on the idea, when my wife pointed out a very dull looking mandolin I had overlooked. It was a teardrop style Seagull S8 in burnt umber. As soon as I picked it up, something rather special happened. It seemed to have been made from a single piece of wood. It was so beautifully tactile, I couldn't put it down. I decided I wanted it, even if I never managed to learn how to play it.

That was in 2016, and since then I've worked steadily to master the instrument, although "work" is probably the wrong word - it wasn't a chore, I just love it. And nowadays, the internet provides a fantastic resource for learning. A key factor is being able to find the music for the kind of songs I wanted to play, either as expressly for mandolin or as guitar pieces that provide the chord sequences.

In September 2019, I plucked up the courage to join in on a monthly acoustic session at a local pub where everyone present gets to perform 3 songs. After a frankly terrifying first outing at the inexperienced age of 69, I've been back every month. I'm convinced that playing an instrument to any kind of audience is crucial for one's development. On each occasion, I find myself performing more demanding songs and, although I say it myself, getting better and better. Until it all came crashing to a halt with the lockdown for the coronavirus pandemic.

To cut a long story short: I bought a mandolin with my very first pay packet, and I bought a mandolin with my very last pay packet.

Jeff Lewis
Ashton, Northamptonshire - UK

"Baa, Baa Black Sheep for Baby"

One New Year's Eve, my husband and I visited UVA Children's Hospital to sing for kids through the nonprofit Pickleberry Pie Hospital Concerts for Kids. We never know what to expect when we sing for kids in the hospital, but we go with the flow and try to help each child, however they're feeling. At one point that morning, we went to the room of a baby who was hooked up to a multitude of machines. We weren't allowed to go in the room, so we stood at the doorway. His parents and grandparents were there and a lot of doctors and nurses. We sang "Twinkle, Twinkle" and "Wheels on the Bus." As the baby looked on peacefully.

His mother then asked if we would sing his favorite song, "Baa, Baa, Black Sheep." When we sang it, everybody joined in and the baby smiled. This made all the parents and grandparents cry and we knew it was a very emotional moment.

Several months later, the family tracked us down to let us know that their baby J.R. died the very next morning, but that our visit and J.R.'s smile were a precious memory for the family. We had no idea what had been happening, but she filled us in and told us how much it meant.

"For us, that day was particularly stressful. Our son was almost 11 months old and had been battling congenital heart disease since birth and was very ill. The hospital can be a very stressful environment and is no place for kids, though that is what was needed. So, when there are treats that make things feel less like a hospital, that is a God-send.

When you are battling a disease that can shorten your little one's life span, it becomes even more important for sweet memories to be made every day to hold onto - some sunshine for those dark moments.

For us you were all of that on that day. It is the most precious memory for me and my family. And J.R. graced us with a smile - he didn't give many those days, because he wasn't feeling good. I cannot thank you enough for that moment of sweetness and beauty. I will carry it forever.

God bless you two and your music. Thank you for offering comfort, it mattered big time."

There are so many stories of how music makes a difference. For me, knowing that we can help turn someone's day around, through the simple act of sharing songs, makes me proud. I always strive to improve the world and this is one small way I can do my part.

Jenny Heitler-Klevans
Pickleberry Pie Hospital Concerts for Kids
Cheltenham, Pennsylvania - USA
www.PickleberryPie.org
www.TwoOfAKind.com

"How Long Will Your Footprints Last?"

Have you ever walked on a beach and noticed the footprints in the sand? If you walk close to the water, especially as the tide is moving out, you can make footprints that can be seen for hundreds of yards. Or maybe you've seen a picture of footprints on a beach that seem like they connect into the sunset. No matter where or when you've walked on a beach, your footprints are no longer there. They've either washed away or been blown flat by the winds.

But what if our footprints could last forever? I liken this image to how there are many people in the world that we will never forget. Their legacies have resisted the winds of change and the waters cannot flatten out their footprints. Martin Luther King Jr, Abraham Lincoln,

Wolfgang Amadeus Mozart, Mahatma Gandhi, just to name a few, were people who created, inspired and led others in a way that their legacies will last forever. We still study their lives, their works of art, their words and their actions. Each new generation studies these luminaries and are inspired by what they accomplished and what they stood for.

Sadly, "everlasting footprints" can also conjure up a negative image. There have been many who have walked our planet leaving an everlasting legacy of destruction and human suffering. And whether we like it or not, their footprints will be seen forever. But, let's not focus on these people. Let's still acknowledge that our legacies can last forever and, I hope, we would all agree that it is better to be known for doing good works, than bad.

Have you ever had an educator leave a "footprint" imprinted on your life? What was it that they taught you? Perhaps a life lesson? Maybe a character trait that you try to emulate in your life? What makes learning lessons from a teacher special, is that, whatever they taught you, now lives within you and you are, hopefully, passing this along to others you connect with. These are "footprints". This is how someone's legacy can live much years longer than their actual life span. How amazing it would be to have impacted other people's lives and see your footprints help others for generations!

Music educators create everlasting footprints every day. They have the ability to teach lifelong concepts by instilling in their students the values of commitment, discipline, hard work, dedication and leadership. Lessons are learned through difficult rehearsals, amazing performances and from rough performances. These experiences will all become the building blocks for a young person's journey that will stay with them forever.

Music educators are notorious for opening doors into a world that a child didn't know existed. They teach students to not settle for mediocrity. They provide hope when it can often feel as if there is none. They can point to a failure, but use it as a building block instead of defeat. These types of educators will demand a lot from their students. They will ask them to give 110% towards a team goal so that everyone can achieve their highest potential. These lessons have long term positive effects on their students and they will never forget where the lessons were learned. These teachers are creating "footprints" that live and breathe inside their students, providing value and being passed on to others for many years to come.

As young adults begin to make decisions about what they want to do in life, I hope they remember the importance of leaving "footprints". There are a number of vocations that inherently mentor the future leaders of our world. The question we should be asking the younger generation is "how do you want to make your mark?" By removing the focus on financial security for a moment, and moving the discussion towards making the world around us a better place, we will all benefit in the end.

Our footprints might not last as long as Abraham Lincoln or Mahatma Gandhi. Our footprints might not make us rich. But, if our actions are positive and meaningful, we will know that these footprints have made a difference in our homes, our schools, our communities and our nation... possibly even the world.

How long will your footprints last?

Jeremy Bradstreet
Director of Bands, Dublin Coffman High School
Grammy® Finalist, Music Educator of the Year, 2019
Facebook: @jbradstreet10

"Social Justice Through Music"

In January 2020, I began meeting with the leadership of SAGE Magnet, a first-of-its-kind middle school named for promoting Sexual and Gender Equity and residing inside the larger Millikan Middle School in Sherman Oaks, California. We were meeting to explore the concept of a teaching artist residency to teach 6th grade students about social justice through making music. SAGE's mission is to provide opportunities for all students to become self-motivated and life-long learners in a safe environment where students are encouraged to become self-reliant and disciplined citizens. The school promotes academic and character development and fosters individuality, creativity and teamwork.

Joseph Porter, the SAGE Magnet Coordinator, had an inspirational vision to teach students how social change can be brought about in different ways. He wanted students to understand how working towards social justice can go beyond attending rallies and protests in the streets, chanting and carrying signs. He wanted these sixth graders to discover the power of music to move hearts and minds toward justice. Once we met, there was no turning back. My organization, Guitars in the Classroom (GITC), has been sharing music from the Civil Rights Movement with teachers and students for 20 years. There couldn't have been a more natural partnership to share the social power of music to young minds.

We began planning these music integration classes for the students at SAGE seven weeks before the Coronavirus began turning life, as we knew it, into a fond memory. The plan was to teach voice, ukulele, songwriting and group music to encourage students to use their own voices to become agents for social change. Little did we know, we'd need to overcome technical hurdles galore to make it happen. But, everyone hung in there - parents, teachers and students. And with leadership from Mr. Porter, we figured out how to create inclusive, authentic, student-centered instruction, despite being physically separated with our only connection being the small rectangular boxes on our computer screens.

The project had been set to take place in person at the school, but when schools closed and teachers and students went home to shelter in place, we immediately pivoted the project to conduct the classes online over ZOOM. GITC sent instruments for students to Los Angeles, where participating families safely picked them up from the porch of the SAGE parents foundation's president. The project included 10 weekly group music lessons that spotlighted social action for civil rights that included music and instruction in singing, playing and writing additional lyrics. This format allowed sixth grade students to connect current advocacy for justice with the history of change.

These classes began well before the tragic murders of Breonna Taylor and George Floyd, which sparked international uprisings to protest police brutality against Black Americans, bringing the Black Lives Matter movement to the forefront of public conversation and into the heart of vibrant, widespread social action. When people began taking to the streets, SAGE students were already studying the power of music to change hearts, minds and policies when they began seeing civil protest in action on their screens. The project became more real and important to students, as they began coping with the complexity and seriousness of the situation.

"This Little Light of Mine" was chosen as a focus song for the class, because of its simple yet powerfully positive message – it is widely recognized as one of our nation's most jubilant and effective civil rights anthems. Today, demonstrators still leverage its message to push back against injustice.

Mr. Porter's guidance and direction to students to study the history of the song and its role in civil protest, was critical to the success of the project. In fact, highlighted in the SAGE video is footage of Reverend Osagyefo Sekou, who used "This Little Light of Mine" to curb passions during a counter-protest before a crowd of white supremacists and alt-right supporters gathered for the Unite the Right rally in Charlottesville, Virginia. One student, Sabin Park, spoke about the use of song to combat violence with compassion and unity in a video SAGE students created with GITC to share and celebrate their learning.

Mr. Porter explains the heart of this collaboration between GITC and SAGE. "For this specific project, I wanted to teach SAGE students how songs and singing have been used as successful tools for voicing specific needs for change throughout the history of social justice," he says. "I feel it is important for them to know about the history of the traditional protest songs - who wrote, led and sang them and when, where and how they have been most effective in promoting non-violent movements for justice. To top it all off, I wanted the students to actually learn how to play and sing those same songs."

In addition to teaching the traditional lyrics, GITC's hallmark approach to teaching collaborative student songwriting was woven into the class. Students composed their own verses of resilience to "This Little Light of Mine." This allowed students to use the song to reflect on where resilience in their own lives comes from. Students identified positive activities they could engage in to uplift and encourage themselves, despite the risks and losses caused by the spread of the Coronavirus. Each student created a personal line or verse to the song. Together, the old and new lyrics provided SAGE students with a way to help themselves and others.

Thanks to their own determination and a supportive learning environment, SAGE students found learning about social justice through making music to be an engaging experience. Their online attendance was excellent and the end result was a team process involving the classroom participants, GITC staff, SAGE leadership and family members who supported the students to practice and to make their own videos.

"We truly witnessed a village all joining hands to lift up its children," Mr. Porter explains. "Together, the adults worked to encourage these dedicated students to shine their lights with intention and clarity into our world during a pivotal moment in history, ultimately gifting them with a wiser, more musical and empowered future."

Jessica Anne Baron - Founder
Guitars in the Classroom
San Diego, California – USA
www.GuitarsInTheClassroom.org

"How Idina Menzel Helped Me Escape a Cult"

My family has been part of a strict religious cult for multiple generations. When I was just a week old, I was formally inducted and this was my existence for the first 30 years of my life.

Life in the cult was incredibly restricted. Freedom of expression was forbidden...as a woman, I was not permitted to wear jeans, pants, makeup or jewellery, and my head had to be covered at all times. No members were permitted to eat, drink or socialise with those outside the cult. We were also not permitted to be educated outside the home, including college or university. Everyone was employed within the cult, which meant there were a lot of vocations not open to us. If we had dreams of becoming a professional musician, artist, actor, athlete, surgeon or any number of other outside careers, it simply wasn't going to happen. As a result, life was very two dimensional. For 23 years, I also experienced bullying within the cult and was still under house arrest at age 30 for having had a relationship outside the cult 8 years prior.

Growing up in a strict religious cult, also meant I missed out on so much music. There was no radio, no television and we were not permitted to purchase pre-recorded music of any sort or attend concerts, cinema or theatre performances. My only two forms of music were sheet music and the music performed by my siblings. Several of my sisters played guitar, one played piano, another clarinet and I played the violin. Being dyslexic, I had great difficulties trying to read music, no matter how hard I tried. I eventually learned to play by ear. Over time, my love for music grew and grew and the country and western songs I'd been brought up on were my primary love.

However, one day I stumbled upon something that was forbidden to cult members. I'd been using an outside agency to help source some black and white video's for an eye correction therapy business I worked for and had been permitted to use YouTube for research. I saw the words *"Let It Go"*, along with a picture of Idina Menzel on a poster for the movie *"Frozen"*. Something about those three words struck something deep within me. I asked the agency if they could somehow get me a copy of the movie and, when they did, I was able to sneak it into the house. Idina Menzel's rendition of *Let It Go* very quickly became my war cry, as I struggled under the constant pressure to conform to what was expected of me. I had often contemplated taking my own life as a way of finally escaping the cult, but now, something stronger was building inside of me. The lyrics and melody played over and over in my head and began willing me to break out of a life that forced me to be something I was not.

In October 2017, and without being able to tell a soul, I began to plan my freedom. With the help of an external counsellor, I started to smuggle my personal possessions out of my parent's house. 3 days prior to me being due to leave, my parents discovered my plans and was forced to flee one night, as pressure from my family to stay grew unbearable. One can never know what it is like to feel trapped inside a relationship, unless they have experienced a similar situation. Whether being stuck with an abusive partner or being raised in a cult, as I was, the psychological effects run deep, making it extremely difficult to envision what life could be like on the other side.

Over the past few years, I have begun to look back into my past and start the healing process. I am finding more and more songs that speak to my journey. Everything from Idina Menzel's *"Into the Unknown"* to Lea Salonga's *"Reflection"*, from the movie Mulan. And, as I question if I did the right thing by leaving, it feels like Christina Aguilera is speaking directly to me with *"Loyal Brave & True"*. My journey will always have begun with Idina Menzel. She would, once again, ignite my fire when I discovered her performance of "Defying Gravity" at the White House for President Obama. Something, indeed, has changed within me. Idina and her empowering lyrics and vocals, undoubtedly, saved me and gave me a way out, that ultimately saved me from a tragic end.

Jessie Shedden - Author
"Tomorrow's Not Promised"
Cwmbran, Gwent – South Wales – UK
www.JessieShedden.com

> # We can't always choose the music life plays for us, but we can sure choose how we dance to it!

"When Forever Falls Apart"

Unconsciously, we expect things to be a certain way and that the ones we love, will be here forever. For me, forever fell apart. Music has always been my best friend, but it wasn't until I hit rock bottom, that I connected with music on a whole other level.

Has anyone ever told you "I know how you feel" or "I understand" yet, you know for certain they can't possibly understand what you're going through?

On Aug. 20, 2017 my older brother, by two years, took his own life. The moment I found out, the most surreal, indescribable pain filled my body and left me with an echoing void of silence. The world I once knew was gone. I became a stranger to myself. Like a movie, I watched the rest of the world move on like nothing had ever happened and I prayed that everything would just stop. I just couldn't fathom a world without my brother or, the fact that, the sun was still shining. If he was dead, life had lost its purpose. I lost my will to live.

My brother and I used to do everything together. From day one, I followed his footsteps and wanted to do everything he did. Whenever our parents told me I couldn't, I said with a lisp "but Jesper does." Growing up, we were a handful. We used to sneak out of the house in the middle of the night in our PJ's to go to the playground and our mom had to install extra locks on all doors, even windows. We would get up at 3 a.m. to throw eggs on the refrigerator and drink cough medicine, because it tasted so good! Our mom had to put locks on the refrigerator too.

From an early age, we developed a very strong sibling bond and that never changed. Life changed, but our bond remained intact.

I was only 9 years old when I first caught my brother drinking. For as long as I can remember, he was always very self-conscious and alcohol was a temporary solution to his low self-esteem. At 18, he moved to his own apartment and that's when it all went downhill. Nobody knew how bad it was, until it was a matter of life and death. Even then, it was too much for anyone to comprehend. He moved from alcohol to heroin and the chaos ensued. For years, my brother would go in and out of rehab, from one hospital to another - even jail, and I was co-dependent before I could even spell the word. I watched him go from a fun-loving, thoughtful and very smart young man to an angry, withdrawn, ghost-like creature who didn't care about anything. Every day was like entering uncharted territory, a constant feeling of uncertainty, knowing that my brother's life could end at any moment. Years later, my worst nightmare became reality.

During the first three months, my body went on autopilot, sifting out all unnecessary information - protecting my brain from getting overloaded. I was in default mode, exhausted, but still functioning. Days turned into weeks and weeks into months, yet every day was a reflection of the day before. Every minute felt like an hour, every day like a lifetime, yet time stood still. Nothing changed, except the dates in the calendar. The following five months, I thought the initial shock had passed when I fell into a deep depression, thinking to myself that 'this is it!' It couldn't possibly hurt more than it already did. But, I couldn't have been more wrong.

Eight months in, I was gripped by an unspeakable sadness and a venomous rage no one should ever have to experience. I isolated myself. My friends would try to see me, but I didn't feel like getting out of bed. All I did was what I had to do; maintain my status in school, make sure the rent was paid on time and check in with the rest of my family on a regular basis. Occasionally, I hung out with friends, but my mind was always somewhere else.

I guess you could say I had a mental collapse, followed by physical symptoms. I went to the doctor several times with various symptoms and always ended up leaving the hospital without an explanation to any of my illnesses. Some friends suggested that I should go talk to someone, but just the thought of seeing a therapist made me cringe. At one point, I booked an appointment, but canceled it at the last minute. I didn't know where to start. Do I talk about my brother's suicide or the fact that I wanted to follow? Or should I talk about how I'm constantly worrying that someone else in my family will end their life as well? Maybe I should talk about all the years we've lost and all the years he was fighting a drug addiction? All the times he overdosed... all the guilt that would almost suffocate me every time I thought I had disappointed him somehow. What about the years to come that my brother won't be here? It's a lot.

Suicide is a death like no other; it is unexpected and often leaves the closest people to the deceased with extreme feelings of disbelief. It leaves you numb and disconnected with the rest of the world. It's like you're in a bubble, just begging for it to burst. No one, except the people with whom you share the tragedy with, can get in. But, the bubble never bursts. Your pain is definite and the damage cannot be undone. Not only do we mourn our loved ones passing, but we also hold intense feelings about the circumstances of their death.

When someone takes their own life, people often search for answers. Did he leave a note? Was he depressed? Was he taking any drugs? Every question feels like a stab, cutting deeper each time. People usually try to force the "right" answers out of me, so that they can convince themselves that my brother's suicide was expected because, apparently, the expected death is less traumatic.

Suicide is never expected, because if it were, it wouldn't exist. And being suicidal doesn't automatically resolve in suicide. You can't possibly prepare for the amount of pain that comes with such a tragic death and you shouldn't have to.

It may sound cliché, but music really saved my life. Sometimes words just aren't enough. I wanted to die, so I began to play the darkest, most sad chord progression I could find on the piano. It might sound self-destructive or self-defeating, but it made me feel less alone. If the music was as dark as my feelings, we were sad together. My brother can never be replaced and I don't want him to be. I want my brother back. But, at least I have found a way to cherish what we had. I fill the void with memories and turn them into sounds. The sounds fill the silence and the echo is what's keeping me alive.

To me, music is pure altruism - an unconditional love that lets you be who you are, in the absence of judgement.

Jhaye (J Marklund)
Stockholm, Sweden
www.Jhaye.com
www.Instagram.com/JhayeMusic

"Something Magical"

My time as a Pickleberry Pie musician has been full of the amazing power of music to bring joy, even in the saddest of situations, like when a child has an illness and has to spend a long time in the hospital.

Generally, the children who come to my programs are young, probably around ten and under. But, one day, a young teen came. She was clearly very unhappy, and I didn't know whether or not she was also in physical pain, but she looked as though she was. It was the beginning of the program and she was the only one there, so I began playing some "rock and roll oldies" that I knew her mom would know and that she might have heard. She smiled faintly and played along with the shakers I handed her.

I then started what I refer to as a "zipper" song. This is where I ask the children to use their imagination to choose a place they would like to go, any place at all, how they would like to get there, any way at all, and what they would like to see when you get there. I remind them that this is 100% imagination, so unicorns and flying dragons are absolutely permissible. The young teen whispered some answers to me and we added them in to the song. We also added ideas from her mother and other participants who had arrived in the meantime. We kept the song going for a little while, getting everyone's ideas, with lots of laughter and silliness of people putting in truly creative ideas. I noticed that the young teens mom was quietly crying.

When the song was finished, the young teen and her mom got up to go, apologizing that her daughter was tired, but that this had been really fun. The mom bent down to whisper something to the Child Life Specialist who was there, and then looked at me with tears in her eyes and said, "Thank you so much!" The session continued, with me turning my attention to the other children and their families.

At the end of the evening, the Child Life Specialist told me that the mom had asked her to give me a huge thank you. She explained that her daughter had been non-verbal the entire 3 weeks she had been in the hospital. That silly song was the first time her mother had heard her voice since they arrived.

Somehow, music is very helpful to children who might not otherwise talk. Another instance was with a little girl from Australia. Her family had moved to Columbus, Ohio, in order for her to get the treatment she needed for her rare disease at the Columbus Nationwide Children's Hospital. This little girl could not speak at all, but she could sing along, and made requests for songs by singing the beginning of the song to me. It was another case of her mother crying openly, amazed at the level of participation and verbal clarity when music was involved. It seems that every time I visit the hospital to bring music to the children, something magical happens.

Joanie Calem
Pickleberry Hospital Concerts
Columbus, Ohio – USA
www.PickleberryHospitalConcerts.org

"Circle of Giving"

All I know is sound! My universe is sound and I revel in it! Music fills my universe and enriches it in ways I can't even begin to explain!

For me, music is solace, joy, texture, thought, expression and, most of all, an immersive multitude of worlds to explore. It is a language and has no boundaries. It truly transcends the confines of mortal understanding and is a tool through which we can share our humanity with each other.

So, why am I so obsessed with music? Why is it the primary way that I experience all life has to offer? It's simple really. I am blind and have been for most of my life.

I was a very sick child and, at around 18 months old, was diagnosed with a brain tumor. The doctors knew that I had to have surgery if I wanted a chance to live, but they told my folks that I probably wouldn't survive the surgery and, if I did, that I would probably never walk or talk.

Ultimately, the tumor would take my sight and sense of smell and leave me with a host of other health challenges, including nearly dying a few times and, later in life, ending up in a wheelchair before needing to have a complete hip replacement. And, still later, a complete shoulder replacement. The tumor destroyed my endocrine system, which means I have no adrenal function. Some days it is all I can do to stand, but I am triumphant and alive! Hell or high water, I am gloriously alive.

I'm often asked how I continue to overcome all the health issues I am faced with and, still, live a very busy and full life. The answer comes down to music. Yes, I have a career as a musician, recording engineer, producer, music educator and music journalist, but that isn't enough. It is no exaggeration to say that music is my life, through and through, and it provides me with the tools and sustenance I need to live and to assist others to live a life of intention and success.

Music is a good companion and, outside of my family and friends, it is what keeps me going... even when I think I can't keep going.

When I was 7, I was having an especially difficult time with my health. In and out of the hospital that year, I just wanted to go to school, be with my friends and just be a kid. To help cheer me up, my mom bought me my first

Beatles album —"The Beatles Yesterday and Today"— and I played that record day and night! It brought a smile to my face, day after day, and I sang my heart out. The pure joy of that music was a watershed moment in my life, when I really knew that music would bless me for the rest of my life.

Then, when I was about 13 years old, I got pneumonia and almost died. I was so sick, but I still had my BBC TV shows, public television, and public radio, for all the old time radio shows and jazz & classical music. I even had Rock 105 to keep me groovin' all day long. Music gave me hope that my life would get better and gave me the ability to stay joyful.

To understand my need for music to survive, think about this: I get up and start immediately listening to music, before I've even had my first cup of coffee. I, then, go to work and make music all day. I come home to rest my tired mind and, you guessed it, I listen to more music!

As an adult, I have had a few opportunities to pay music, and the universe, back for what I was given through music. One night while performing in a local bar, I was running a high fever and my voice was almost gone. I had the flu, but still did the show. I was in my early twenties, so I was tough or dumb or both, living by the motto "The Show Must Go On". I was at the end of my rope and it was almost time to hit the final song and go home! We were famous for ending with a version of the Allman Brothers song Whippin' Post, but my voice was shot. I knew I couldn't do the usual vocal gymnastics required to perform that song, and instead felt a strong urge to play a song that is very out of place for a bar. The song was the gospel staple *Amazing Grace*.

The band was flabbergasted, but I insisted and we played my arrangement. The crowd responded favorably to this last song of the night, though no doubt, they were perplexed . I was completely exhausted at this point, and just wanted to go home. Suddenly, from out of the crowd, a body collided with mine. A woman I didn't know, put her arms around me and began crying her heart out. I was surprised to say the least and didn't know what to do, so I hugged her back and asked her what was wrong. She told me the most amazing story.

She was in town just for the day. Her uncle, a gospel singer, died and they had his service that day. His favorite song was *Amazing Grace* and it was the main thing he wanted for his service, but for whatever reason, his request wasn't honored. This lady and her husband had come out to grab something to eat, relax and to try and forget that their beloved family member hadn't gotten what he wanted for his service and then this blind guy played the song from stage. She felt like her uncle had finally been honored with music like he would have wanted and I played a small role in giving solace, through music, to a grieving family. Experiences like this remind me how music has the magical ability to perpetuate the circle of giving, and how grateful I am to be part of the journey.

Joey Stuckey
Macon, Georgia – USA
www.JoeyStuckey.com
www.ShadowSoundStudio.com

"Sing on Johnny"

I remember being home in Ireland during the summer of 2015, just a few months before the release of my album, *The Immigrant and the Orphan*. I had a CD of rough mixes from the new record that I was playing for my dad, John (his friends called him Johnny), as we were driving around Wexford, in the south east of the country. A song called *Sing on Johnny* was the fifth song on this sample CD and I was nervous about him hearing it. As track four came to a close, I leaned forward and pushed the button to skip the next track. I wasn't ready. This song represented a lament for the lung condition that Dad had been diagnosed with, but also, a call to arms - a call to keep on singing, to keep on doing the things that he loved. Still, I wasn't ready for him to hear it.

I had written the song the previous autumn. The first line "Sing on Johnny, don't lose a thing" came along as I strummed between an A minor and a G chord and, within a couple of minutes, the first verse and the melody were set. I got that excited feeling you get when you know you are on to something. You know what you are writing about, you know how it goes and you know you have to cancel everything else until the song is done. I wrote verse after verse thinking about my dad. I revisited nights at our home where people would come over and sing. People would be scattered all around the house, in the kitchen, the dining room and the backyard. However, once the singing commenced, everyone gravitated to its source - most often in the living room, and more often than not the source was my dad.

I kept writing until I wrote the line "Sing on Dad, till the work is done." I felt like I was losing him and I was scared. Just like months later in the passenger seat of his little red car, I wasn't ready for that. The song begins with me telling my him in a very "Do Not Go Gentle into That Good Night" way, not to give up, to keep on singing. But ultimately, the reason for me needing him to do this is a selfish one. I needed him, I needed his songs. In the years following his diagnosis of pulmonary fibrosis, he had not stopped singing. It was truly inspiring. He hadn't stopped living either. He had, with astonishing grace, accepted his fate and wrestled it audaciously. With Mam by his side, he had pushed away bad days, succumbed to a few, but ultimately overcame them. He understood the battle, he was a realist. But he fought on believing that one great day could wipe clean a hundred tough ones.

I eventually worked up the nerve to play the song for Dad and he loved it. I don't know if he knew how hard it was for me to play the song for him. I knew it was going on the album, and I knew I'd be telling the story behind it at shows. I still do. Two years after that moment in the car, we made a record together. I'd been bugging him for ages to do this and I really wanted to do it while he could enjoy it to the utmost. My dad always sang, never professionally, but would always sing. He would sing these old Dublin Street songs and they were amazing. He would sing American folk songs too, he loved them. I would look for many of these songs online, so I could learn them, but often there were no versions to be found. So I told my dad that we needed to record them, and eventually he agreed.

My brother, Damien, and I booked a studio, got some musicians and engineers, and sat with Dad to pick the songs and arrange them. It wasn't until we were on the bus going down to the first studio session, that Dad admitted to me that he was nervous. I remember telling him to just sing the songs the way he always did, that was what made me fall in love with them and it would be what would make other people feel the same. So, he put his nerves behind him, and at 78 years old made a debut album which has since been inducted into the National Folk Music Archives of Ireland. His voice pierced through, sounding like something that was so present and full of life, but could have been a thousand years old. It was perfect. It was Folk. He was, at this point, several years into his diagnosis, but he never let the disease define him. There were victories and defeats along the way, but this was a victory we could have only dreamed of.

He died suddenly, but in many ways impeccably, in February 2020, living right up to the last minute. He never let his condition take away the things he loved. It never took away his ability to take a good long walk on Dollymount strand, to sing a song, to lay on the floor coloring with his granddaughters, to have a pint or two in the evening, a nice piece of cheese, a holiday with Mam, a drop of Jameson if the occasion warranted it...it often did.

I was home for a quick visit just a week before he passed. On my last night there, Dad, Damien and I went down to his local, sang a bunch of songs and had a few drinks. We got back to the house around 1 am and had a sandwich, some tea, a drop of whiskey and a bunch of laughs with Mam. If I was, by some miracle, given one more night with Dad, I would do exactly the same thing. I would do it with absolute joy; that's what I learned from him, Shine on Dad, Sing on Johnny.

John Byrne
Philadelphia, Pennsylvania – USA
www.JohnByrneBand.com

"Passing up a Golden Opportunity"

I was 18 years old and had never left Texas. By age 21, I had been to all 50 states and by 28 years old, several countries as well: and it's all because music changed my life. I spent most of my high school years making sure that I didn't spend even one day in school more than the law required. All I wanted was to go through the motions and move on to the part of my life where I could 'get a real job' and enter the corporate world. So, you can imagine how thrilled I was to find out that my school offered an internship program. The program allowed seniors to split their days...half spent in school and the other half spent downtown working. Are you kidding me?! This accomplished both of my goals in life at this time, which were getting out of school and joining the corporate world. Needless to say, I applied instantly and, thankfully, was accepted!

For my entire senior year, I was interning at the worldwide corporate headquarters of the 4th largest software company on earth. This was the 1990's, so all of the this-bubble-will-never-pop trappings were there: cowhide lined every elevator and someone had even commissioned a desk to be made out of Legos. To mitigate the wildly large profits, the word around the office was that our company hired another company to pull out all of the individual stones that lined the bottom of the countless outdoor ponds and fountains on our corporate campus to clean them by hand. This was all resounding confirmation, to me, that corporate life was the good life and it was certainly the life for me. On top of it all, the work was easy! I guess because I was an intern, my managers were going easy on me, but I would fly through my daily duties and constantly ask if there was more work I could help with. I honestly wasn't trying to impress anyone. It was made exceedingly clear to us, many times, that this company does not hire interns. I presumed they preferred to fly in new employees on private jets from the furthest possible locations, in their continued effort to tame those pesky profits. So, even though I'd still daydream about working for this company, I knew that I couldn't; but I also knew that, as quickly as I could, I needed to work at some company just like it. I was, happily, on the fast track to corporate life. Then I discovered Rock Fest.

As the internship and my senior year of high school were coming to an end, I began to look for something fun to do that summer. The first thing I did was type "Peter Frampton tour dates" into Google. I was big into 70's rock at this time and Frampton Comes Alive was a regular in my

CD player. There were no Frampton tour dates in Houston where I lived, so I searched for Lynyrd Skynyrd to check if maybe they were coming to town, and then Sammy Hagar, America and Foreigner. Many of these acts were not touring in our area that summer, but I noticed that every single one was playing in a small no-name Wisconsin town called Cadott. Some of the bands listed the event name next to the city and date. One more Google search and my fate was sealed: "What is Rock Fest Cadott, WI?"

When I realized that there was a four-day rock festival with my favorite bands happening that summer, it wasn't a question of IF I'd be there, it was just a matter of figuring out how. For the next several weeks, my friend and I poured over maps, hustled for cash and budgeted out the whole trip. GPS may have existed in 1999, but it was likely still hundreds of dollars for a unit, so that wasn't even on our radar. We mapped out every route from Houston to Cadott by hand and calculated and compared the cost of each. We also considered which routes would have us reaching towns with a 24-hour Walmart at the end of each days' driving, because with no money for hotels, we planned to park under a security camera and sleep in their parking lots each night. We had thought of everything.

Then, the one thing we could never plan on, happened during the last week of my internship. Against all odds and against company policy, I was offered a job! A corporate job with a salary and benefits, right out of high school. It had never happened before with this company. I remember that a big deal was made about my performance review and the job offer. As people congratulated me, I looked through the window and saw a basket of wet rocks being poured onto the ground, while a team of people scrubbed each one with tiny toothbrushes.

My internship coordinator, my department supervisor, my fellow interns, absolutely everyone thought it was amazing news and a no-brainer for me to take the job.

But, they didn't know about Rock Fest and how music can change everything. I explained to my supervisor that I was incredibly honored that they went through so much trouble to offer me a job, but I had planned a road trip to a rock concert. Looking back, I still can't fully explain why that was an entirely sufficient reason for me to turn down this opportunity; I just knew that no job, not even my dream corporate job, could compare to driving 1,300 miles, worrying about logistics and barely surviving - all in the pursuit of music.

I can still picture the confusion and concern on his face. Over the next few days, I saw that same expression on many other faces. They were, understandably, concerned that I had passed up a great career opportunity. But, here's the irony: that road trip to Rock Fest turned out to be the real work-training that unlocked my future career. I became a tour manager in the music industry! The ability to calculate realistic expenses and drive times came from traveling without steady income. And, as it turns out, because we always included those 24-hour Walmarts in our travel plans for a safe place to camp out at night, I had inadvertently learned to design routing through college towns and major markets - which is necessary when booking concert tours. My experience grew from there.

Years later, as I was managing a musician on tour in India, my life was once again changed by music. It was a cross-cultural experience of such respect and affection, brought about through just a few simple notes of music, that prompted me to found The World Music Foundation, but I think that's a story best saved for another time.

John Gardner – Founder
The World Music Foundation
Chicago, Illinois – USA
www.TheWorldMusicFoundation.org

> ## Sometimes MUSIC is the only thing that can take your mind off everything else.

"Marianne Calypso"

I have been fundraising and supporting local charities for 30 years by playing the accordion in Macclesfield Hospital, East Cheshire Hospice and other local charities. I consider it a privilege to be able to do this, have made many friends and shared many touching moments over the years.

One such moment occurred in 2009, when a lady named Caroline was leaving the hospital with her newborn baby. I asked what was her baby's name was and she replied Marianne. I launched into the familiar calypso 'All Day, All Night, Marianne'. Caroline was absolutely thrilled and said that she would always remember this moment.

Since the Covid pandemic began in March of this year, I have not been able to play in the hospital, but I still play in other areas whenever I get the chance. On the 1st of September, whilst busking a few miles away in Buxton, I had a chance meeting with Caroline and her family. They are now living in London and were on a holiday visit. She was thrilled to meet me again and introduced me to Marianne, now 13 years old. Once again, I played 'Marianne Calypso', embarrassing her slightly, while her mum videoed. Caroline later emailed me and included a photo from 2009 when she was leaving the hospital with baby Marianne. Her note read:

"Dear John, It was so lovely to bump into you yesterday, after so long!

I didn't like to say in front of my daughter, but bringing her home from the hospital was a somewhat difficult moment for me. I was going through a traumatic marriage breakdown during my pregnancy and was very upset to be leaving the hospital on my own that day. But, when you serenaded Marianne (with her own song!) it really cheered me up. I'll always be grateful for how you lifted my spirits.

And as fate would have it, you serenaded Marianne again, yesterday! On a sunny day in beautiful Buxton, on the last day of our holiday. So Wonderful. I shared a photo and video on my Facebook page and briefly explained the coincidence - so many friends found it a lovely story.

I do hope we'll meet again. If you are ever in London, please come and see us. Very best wishes; Caroline, Marianne, Bertie and Alex xxxx

I'm happy to say that we have now formed a lasting friendship through the medium of social media.

John Jones MBE
Macclesfield, Cheshire, England – United Kingdom
www.NorthStaffsAccordionClub.com
www.StockportAccordionClub.org

"Music for Autism"

My wife, Christine, and I are musicians and parents of a son with autism. In 2002, Christine established Music for Autism in the United Kingdom to share our love of music with other individuals with autism and their families. Our journey began by organizing a series of fundraising concerts and producing "Songs for Alexander", a music CD to help fund our charitable efforts.

We designed Music for Autism interactive concerts specifically for individuals with autism and their families. The concerts are held in halls that appeal to people with autism; there is always open space for the audience to react to the music through spontaneous dance and movement. Featuring members of the Orchestra of St. John's, of which I am the Conductor, these unique concerts expose individuals with autism to high quality classical music in an environment designed to make them feel comfortable.

Music for Autism also supports special units and schools for children with autism. The charity's music education and equipment grants have furnished sensory rooms and provided school transportation and school supplies for children. Today, Music for Autism has a well established presence in the United Kingdom.

In 2007, U.S. Founder & President, Robert Accordino, introduced Music for Autism to the United States. Music for Autism has a national presence with "autism friendly" interactives at a number of locations. What follows are just a few of the stories that have inspired us on our journey.

John Lubbock, Music for Autism
Abingdon, England - United Kingdom
www.MusicForAutism.org
www.osj.org.uk/osj-music-for-autism

There is More Inside

As a professional touring musician, I have had the privilege to play in many of the world's great concert halls with many of the world's greatest musicians. I can honestly say, that the power of music is never more apparent than while doing concerts for Music for Autism. To us, the musicians, what we do seems simple – just play beautiful music in an uncomplicated way. The effect this music has on the children is far from ordinary...it is truly amazing. To see children respond in ways that their caregivers and parents find hard to believe, is both heart-warming and inspiring for us. I can only try to imagine the effect that it must have on them. Music is clearly a fundamental aspect of our human existence. It seems not to matter what particular set of difficulties a child may have – music reaches out and unlocks something inside a person. It may be purely subconscious and short lived, but there is absolutely no doubt in my mind, that music is hugely beneficial.

Of all the many remarkable incidents that I have witnessed over the years, one stands out in my memory. If I remember rightly, we were in Chelmsford playing at a school with very severely impaired children – many in wheelchairs and several needing at least two caregivers each. Looking around for prospective guest conductors, our orchestra leader, John, settled upon a young lad and tried to encourage him to come to the front. His caregiver, however, was not so keen and assured us that it was a terrible idea - fearing he would destroy the instruments or start throwing something.

John didn't give up and with a "well, it's on your head', his caregiver let John bring the lad to the front, where he proceeded to conduct beautifully and sing his heart out - all the way through Eine Kleine Nachtmusik! The most moving part, was not that the lad was having such fun, though he clearly was. It wasn't that nobody at the school knew that he had any idea who Mozart was, never mind had the ability to sing an entire piece. It was the reaction of his caregiver that truly struck me – this young lad's performance, quite literally, moved her to tears!

Sometimes, it's good to be reminded that there is more inside these little people than meets the eye.

Duncan Ferguson – Violist
www.osj.org.uk/osj-music-for-autism

<u>Soothing Effects of Music</u>

I have been taking part in Music for Autism concerts for over ten years and have yet to do one that has not left me affected in some way. This can be manifested in various ways, starting with a continuous feeling of gratitude for the normal family life I enjoy. I often reflect on the amazing time, love and care the staff of the schools give to these children wherever we go.

I can remember one school in Broadstairs, Kent, where many young people are sent because there is nowhere else for them to go. We gave three concerts, the third of which, was for seniors. There were three 17 year old boys there. The school's Head Teacher came to observe and was almost in tears at the end of the 50 minutes - these boys sat quietly the entire performance, instead of tearing the room to shreds, which he feared they might do. 'The best day of my working life', he told us.

The most powerful example, however, came when a boy came into the hall where we were about to play, screaming like a parrot and jumping two feet in the air like a Masai. He continued this behavior until we began to play a very gentle lullaby by Mozart. The music not only seemed to soothe him, but actually stopped him from jumping and screaming for a full three minutes. His two caregivers were not only astonished, but close to tears, as was I on my drive home.

John Heley – Cellist
www.osj.org.uk/osj-music-for-autism

"Till I Am Myself Again"

The song '*Till I Am Myself Again*' by Blue Rodeo, seems like it was written for me. In late August 1995, I was involved in a serious car accident and suffered a severe brain injury. Driving back to finish my final year of university in Nova Scotia, I was ejected from a moving car at a speed above 100 km per hour (62 miles per hour). Not only did my confidence go missing, as the Blue Rodeo song speaks to, but ALL of the memories of my twenty two years on earth were now gone. After spending seven days in a coma, I returned, but unable to walk, name a colour, a shape or perform any basic human functions. Perhaps even more shocking, was that I awoke with absolutely no memory of anyone I had ever known, including my own family. I, literally, felt like an alien trapped within my own body...someone who had been instantly transported into an unknown world.

One day, one of my doctors suggested bringing music into my life. Uncertainty gave way to hope, as my family saw me mouthing the words to one of my favorite songs '*The Weight*' by The Band. My enormous reconstruction project had begun. Luckily, my youth and young adulthood were spent with an uncontrollable passion for music and, somehow, all of the musical memories were still intact. My first, and forever love, was there to save me from the wreckage.

Recovery was agonizingly slow. Between the hospitals and home care, it took a few years before I was "presentable" or kind of normal. I had full amnesia, as my entire twenty two years had been completely blacked out. Except for a handful of buildings and locations, there was no information there, except for (luckily) music, of which I forgot none. It seemed that any music I had ever heard was safely stored in my mind. From commercial jingles to anything I have had the pleasure of hearing, was stored and undamaged. I still have visual agnosia, which makes me unable to recognize anyone, including my own family, despite being re-introduced to them many times over. I, instead, rely on the sound of their voice to remember someone every time I see them.

Music became the life raft that helped carry me through the abyss of brain injury - whether it was listening to lyrics and looking up the meaning of "new" words to expand my vocabulary, to give me a slightly better understanding of language, to be my shoulder to lean on, my "get out of jail free" card or to comfort me. When you are thrown into a blender or rollercoaster of everything new, with nothing understood, you need something. Whether it was one of the Gods, a TV host or aliens in charge of this life, I appreciate them allowing me to keep the gift of music.

When frustrated, angry or sad at the hand I had been dealt, it was only a play button away from a better place. Music was my first love and will be my last. It has the ability to take me to a higher place, a safe place, somewhere far away from complexity and hardships that can show up without warning. Find the records that make you happy, inspired and willing to take on a challenge. Keep these close to you on your playlist and you will have a better life, I guarantee it. Happy listening.

Jonathan McMurray, Author of "Mind the Gap"
Georgetown, Ontario – Canada
www.JonathanMcMurray.com

"Rock to the Future"

Rock to the Future began 10 years ago when my wife Jessica left her job in financial services after winning The Turning Point prize from Women for Social Innovation, with the mission of providing student driven programs for Philadelphia children and teens at no cost. We help prepare the next generation for every stage in life by unlocking their fullest potential through the benefits of learning music. Starting with 13 students, we worked as volunteers for two years while growing and raising additional funds. With the support of dozens of team members, volunteers, board members, community, and families, RttF now provides programs in school, after school, during the summer and online for hundreds of youth each year who otherwise would not have access. We believe in teaching the whole child and take a holistic approach with programs that include tutoring in traditional academic subjects, mentoring, and college and career prep assistance. Since inception, 100% of our after school program students further their education after high-school and pursue professional career plans. Here are a few of the stories we would like to share from our experiences:

From Special Classes to AP

Ethan's mom, Karen, first came to us when he was in 6th grade after reading an article about Rock to the Future in the local newspaper. Ethan liked to play RockBand and she felt this would be perfect for him, even though he had never played a real instrument before. Ethan is on the Autism spectrum with Asperger's, which has a huge impact on his social skills and ability to make friends, but also has given Ethan the unique ability to hear a song and play it on any instrument. Being a part of RttF gradually helped Ethan come out of his shell, building his confidence and self-esteem. He began making friends and it wasn't long before everyone wanted to be in the band with him. It wasn't just that Ethan was becoming a better musician - he was transforming into someone that other students looked up to.

Due to Ethan's circumstances, his regular schooling consisted of mostly special education classes. After working with RttF and additional tutors at his high school, Ethan was eventually able to move to regular classes. In his senior year, he moved up to AP Literature, was on student council, and even made the Honor Roll. His experiences with us gave him the confidence to work hard and not give up.

During Ethan's senior year, he received a D'Addario Foundation scholarship and is now enrolled in Music Production classes. Ethan's mom had this to say:

"Growing up with RttF has made Ethan a good performer, self-sufficient, independent, social and a much better student. This experience also helped him to discover who he is, who he identifies as and what he wants to become. Even when situations weren't comfortable, Josh and Jessica stuck with him. RttF helped break down walls and opened doors for Ethan that we didn't know existed. Ethan is full of potential and I can now see him living a life without me one day, which is a huge accomplishment."

Rock & Roll Hall of Fame

When Nia first joined RttF as a middle-school student, she clearly loved music and had natural ability but had a hard time recognizing relationships. Initially standoffish and confrontational, she would often push the boundaries of acceptable behavior at RttF and in school. Her mother once asked, "Why do you care so much?"

We knew that Nia was also a bright student and eager to learn – what she needed was something that would challenge her. As she developed her musical skills on voice, piano, and guitar, she also developed into a young leader. She began supporting our summer camp programs where she would go the extra mile, helping to move and set up equipment for the performances. As she grew in the program, she became a team player, showing kindness to all with her evolving leadership skills.

Nia's RttF experience has seen her perform at the Rock & Roll Hall of Fame, Union Transfer and The Fillmore in front of hundreds, and sometimes thousands of people, and has collaborated with Chill Moody and Rogers Stevens (Blind Melon). This year's pandemic, however, has made her senior year less than ideal. But Nia is determined to make the best of it with an RttF class called "Ready For the Future". This is where we work closely with students to help them map out what they want to do after graduation. Whatever she decides, we will be there to support her and know she'll carry a love and talent for music throughout her life.

College Move-in Day

One family we have been privileged to work with had three girls – twins Alex & Sophia and younger sister Lydia. All were super bright honor students, often competing with each other to see who could do better.

They joined RttF in middle school and stayed throughout high school, building a community of friends, and being accepted into the colleges of their choice. We try to connect students to area colleges that are "within reach", based on their academic and financial situation. During the twin's senior year, their mom became sick. We knew girls and their father needed extra support with their transition to college, so Jessica and I helped move Sophia into Penn State Schyukill and Alex into Cabrini College to begin their college experience. Both Penn State and Cabrini were schools we had visited on our annual college and trade school visitation trip.

It has been inspiring to watch these amazing young women grow over 10 years as they pursue their professional dreams in journalism, education, and computer sciences. Music brought us together, creating friendships and community for us all to lean on in difficult times. We're proud to say that Alex will be graduating from Cabrini this year after studying Digital Communications and serving as editor of her college newspaper. She often comes back to help RttF with video work for events. Alex even gave the tour for current RttF students during a more recent college visitation. Sophia is finishing up her education degree at Penn State while Lydia has started at Community College of Philadelphia.

Pursuing Their Dreams

Destinee was with us the day we first opened our doors at RttF and over a period of 5 years excelled on piano, guitar, and voice. Upon entering high school, she struggled with depression and low attendance due to severe bullying. A caring and talented young woman, we provided Destinee with the flexibility she needed and also worked with her mother and contacted the school to provide support. Destinee thrived and wrote original music about depression and other teen issues, while building confidence to share her music and rock on stage in front of thousands of attendees. Through music, she grew into a confident young woman to take on the world. We were thrilled when Destinee began her college career at a Penn State to study psychology. Perhaps our proudest moment came when together with her mom and cherished friends, we watched Destinee walk for her college graduation in 2019.

"It's okay to fail, it's ok to cry, it's okay to take your time and it's okay to make mistakes. We live one life - learn, grow, love and rock." - Destinee

Joshua and Jessica Craft
Rock to the Future
Philadelphia, Pennsylvania – USA
www.RockToTheFuture.org

"Madison Square Garden to Washington D.C."

When I was a child, my journey in music started with the piano in concert band, playing symphonic and orchestral music. As I grew and developed my musical tastes, I added guitar to my tool belt and began to discover bands such as The Beatles. When I got to my junior year of high school, Trans-Siberian Orchestra had become a staple of the holiday season; packing arenas with their unique blend of classical music and heavy rock/metal guitars. With my background being mostly classical, TSO's music was a natural gateway for me to fully embrace rock and metal music. I quickly became an avid fan spending hours going over the prodigious guitar melodies that defined their catalog. That holiday season, I visited my family in New York and a group of us went to Madison Square Garden to watch them perform. I was absolutely overwhelmed by the experience – amazing high-energy musicianship paired with an incredible and immersive laser and lights show. I went home the following week, bought recording software and dedicated myself to a life and career in music.

Fast Forward to 2017 and my musical journey now includes supporting the music education efforts of the NAMM Foundation in Los Angeles area classrooms. For the first time, I also found myself going to Sacramento and Washington D.C. to support these efforts at a state and federal level. The first day in Washington, we held a Day of Service to teach music at a Title 1 school. Day of Service events, like the ones we do in Anaheim Elementary Schools each January, are some of my favorite outreach activities. Seeing the children's faces light up as many have a real instrument placed in their hands for the very first time is something special to witness and be a part of. During the course of a service event, we teach students the fundamentals of the instrument and then get together with the larger group at the end to play a song based on what we've taught them in the classroom.

As we all gathered in the auditorium for the Day of Service finale, my eyes grew wide as I saw Mark Wood, the original lead violinist for TSO, who I first saw in New York as a high school student. I went over to introduce myself, and told him the impact he and TSO had on the career path I chose, and how that ultimately led me to be in Washington advocating for music education. He was excited and thankful I shared my personal story with him and happy to hear about my journey in music to that point. He invited me to jam with him and his wife at the NAMM party later that week and I enthusiastically accepted.

A few nights later, I found myself on a D.C. rooftop playing bass against the backdrop of the United States Capitol building while jamming to "Statesboro Blues" with Mark and his wife Laura. The kid that watched him and the rest of the band play at Madison Square Garden could never have dreamed up a scenario as wild as the reality of that night. I was humbled, excited and overwhelmed at the trajectory music had set me on. None of us can ever know what musical journeys are ahead of us. All I can say is how grateful I am to have chosen a career that allows me to do what I love while also giving back along the way.

Justin Emord, Love & a .38 Bass Player
Los Angeles, California - USA
www.LoveAnda38music.com

"Musical Time Machine"

I was the Director of Choirs at Horizon High School in Scottsdale Arizona when our group traveled to Oahu, Hawaii to perform for the 70th Anniversary of the Pearl Harbor Attack. Our show choir put together a 1940s tribute show, complete with the girls in authentic period costumes and the young men in military uniforms.

When we arrived at Pearl Harbor, we took a tour of the memorial site, before our scheduled performance on the USS Missouri. We were told by security, that we were not allowed to perform or sing anywhere on the memorial site. We were also told to stay respectful and quiet as we walked around that sacred ground.

Because there would not be time to change clothes before our performance, our students walked about in full costume. It was like being transported back in time, seeing all of these young people walk around in period clothing from the time of the actual attack.

Near the gift shop, there were three older gentlemen, seated at a table signing books. We walked over and discovered they were actual survivors from the Pearl Harbor attack, and were there signing copies of a memoir they had written. When they saw the students, they were overcome with emotion and asked the students if they would perform for them. I told the gentleman that we were not allowed to perform in that particular area. Just then, I was interrupted by a young Navy officer, who turned to me and said, "With all due respect Miss, you can do whatever these gentlemen ask you to do." Our students circled around the table where the gentlemen sat and proceeded to sing "I'll Be Seeing You". The gentlemen took off their glasses and wiped away their tears as they listened to the students sing. Of course, many of the students were wiping away their own tears as well.

When the students who were on that trip graduated from high school, every single one of them said that the memory of singing for those American heroes, was the most impactful moment of their entire high school career. It gave all of us a newfound respect and reverence for the sacrifice that so many have made for our freedom.

The power of music to transport you through time, to summon memories, to encourage patriotism and to heal hearts, is simply astounding. Being a choral director charged with instilling this appreciation for music in young people, is an honor I carry with me every single day.

Kathrine Kouns
Carmel, Indiana – USA
www.CarmelChoirs.org

Never Stop Dancing to the Music in Your Heart
-Katrina Mayer (www.KatrinaMayer.com)

"What I wanted to be and who I am is a singer and a songwriter. I wanted to be onstage and I wanted the world to hear my music. The product of that is fame and the celebrity that goes along with it. But celebrity does not equal creativity."

Katy Perry
www.KatyPerry.com

"Shriners Journey to America's Got Talent"

My earliest memories are of growing up in a home that was always filled with music, from my dad's eclectic taste that ranged from Celine Dion to Dido and country music influences, to my mom's more traditional taste of Abba, Linda Ronstadt and Christian contemporary music.

I was about seven years old, when I began to sing all over the house and develop my own taste in music. I remember running down the corridors of our home singing the Spice Girls', "If You Wanna Be My Lover" to the shock of my poor mom!

I joined the children's choir in church and began to really enjoy singing, but for me, it was purely a recreational pastime... just something I enjoyed very much. When I was eleven, I went off to boarding school and carried on with my love for music, being part of singing shows and plays.

On December 10, 2005, I was involved in a terrible plane crash on my way back home for the Christmas holidays. I was one of only two survivors out of the 109 passengers and crew members. This immediately changed the trajectory of my life. I was flown, first, to South Africa for emergency treatment and then to the USA for reconstructive surgery and rehabilitation.

Following the plane crash, I was in a coma for five weeks. During that time, my mom knew music would reach me, even when she could not, so she bought a small CD player and several CDs of my favorite artists including Destiny's Child, Kelly Clarkson and Justin Timberlake. She would play them over and over again, especially outside visiting times, when she could not be by my side singing to me.

Even deep in my subconscious state, I could always hear my mom singing to me. In fact, when I woke up, I sang one of the songs she used to sing to me, back to her. It was a song I had never heard prior to the accident, because she had just learned it! That was how much of an impact music had in my life.

But, the greatest impact music had on me, was when it was incorporated into my rehab. While in Shriners Hospital in Galveston, I discovered music therapy. My physical therapist noticed I was always singing during our exercises and asked me if I would be interested in music therapy. I was very intrigued and agreed to give it a try. A whole new world opened up to me. From that day onward, physical therapy (as painful as it was), was bearable - it meant that afterwards, I would get to go on to the music room to sing with the music therapist. She found out what kind of music and songs I liked and, every week, we would have a new song with her playing an instrument.

In Shriners Hospital Galveston, the patients in music therapy held a concert for the staff and patients and it was a great hit! That was my first time performing in front of an audience, that was not just family. It was nerve wracking, but it gave me a taste of what it would be like to perform on a stage. From then on, I secretly imagined a time when this dream would become a reality. After that, I went on to be a part of the worship team in my church, (still am) and that is a level of fulfillment that brings so much joy to me. I also auditioned for various shows whenever I could.

Fast forward to 2017 - I was in college, just beginning my Masters degree while working on campus, when I received a call from America's Got Talent that completely changed my life. All through the competition, all I wanted, was to convey to the judges (and to America) how much I loved music and what it meant to me. I seemed to have succeeded, because I went on to be a finalist that year and also AGT: The Champions in 2019 - going as far as getting Simon Cowell's much coveted Golden Buzzer.

AGT opened up my world to new possibilities and gave me the courage to act on what I could not even dream about, prior to my accident. I now get to travel all over the world, performing in front of huge audiences. In 2018, I released my debut single, "Don't You Dare", and just completed the final details on my full album, which will be released in the spring of 2021.

So, what does music mean to me? Music is a part of me, a part that I literally cannot do without. I found that out the hard way, when I lost my voice on the very first day of 2020. I had overstressed my vocal chords and developed calluses on them, requiring me to rest my voice for a full month – absolutely no singing! It was, very simply put, a very dark period in my life. I could not even listen to music, because of the temptation to sing... The world became bleak. I was very unhappy. I had no joy and that opened my eyes to exactly how much music means to me.

Music is my rest, my joy, my healing, my peace, my happy place and my way of expressing things that mere words cannot convey...Music is my life.

Kechi Okwuchi
Houston, Texas - USA
www.KechiOfficial.com

"Full Circle"

My mother started me out on piano lessons at the age of 3 and I ended up studying with Sue Spataro for over a decade. I wrote my first piano original at the age of 7 and began singing with piano from there on out. I wrote choral arrangements for my high school choir and put out two unmixed albums by the time I was 18. When I entered James Madison University as a freshman, I was playing piano, the Hammond b3 organ and singing background vocals for a group called Georgia Avenue. We opened for The Roots, O.A.R., Dispatch, Blues Traveler, Wilco, Cowboy Mouth, Pat McGee and others. I was planning to transfer to Berkley College of Music in Boston, but myself and Ross Copperman (now songwriter for several country music stars including Keith Urban, Blake Shelton, Kenny Chesney, Brett Eldridge and Dierks Bentley) ran into John Mayer at Mac n Bobs in Roanoke, Virginia in 2001. During our conversation, John advised me to skip Berkley and just keep writing and asking record companies to listen to my original songs.

Ross and I are still friends today, although he is deep into the music business down in Nashville. Shortly after our chance meeting with John Mayer, Georgia Avenue broke up and I went into a deep depression. I had been living my dream, sharing the stage with major acts throughout the east coast and, now, I feared what was going to happen. That depression led me to make the biggest mistake of my life. I got behind the wheel of my jeep with my head in the wrong place, and got into a life-altering accident. Fortunately, no one else was involved in the crash, but I was pronounced dead on the scene and later shocked into a coma. After my family and friends were told I'd be lucky to come out of the surgery alive, let alone drive, perform music and finish college...a miracle happened. Dr. Yuschak and Abington Hospital performed extensive brain surgery and saved my life.

As I rolled my wheelchair to the second floor in Moss Rehab, I began to remember everything I'd ever written. While learning to walk again, I wrote the song "Miracle", as I sat in that wheelchair. Since the crash, I have fully recovered, with the exception of permanent hearing loss in my right ear and only partial sight in my right eye. I put out my own debut album called 'Something Better On My Side' and began to perform again, as a solo act. I completed a degree in English Literature at West Chester University and spoke at C.B. South for Mike Shaeffer's Health class, teaching kids to not feel invincible and make better choices. I also played a benefit at Moss Rehab with my uncle, Hal Robinson, from the Philadelphia Orchestra to help give back. Music has always found a way back into my life to help others. In 2011, I was the singer on a song called 'Miracle Heart', which helped raise money for Gary Onufer, who received an artificial heart that saved his life.

After college, I spent most of my time working in sales-related jobs, while still finding time to play music live and entertain people. When the Covid epidemic hit, I lost my day job and performance opportunities quickly disappeared. A speech pathologist I was close to, was working at a New York nursing home that was losing many residents and employees to the dreaded virus. As I listened to how deeply she was being affected on the front lines, I decided to pack my music gear into my truck and do what I could. I believe the date was April 9th. I drove to the Doylestown Hospital parking lot that day, plugged my piano and PA into the truck and started playing music for the medical staff to help lift their spirits. This was around the time everyone else was staying at home. I also broadcast the music live on the Quarantine Karaoke Facebook page, to help lift spirits of people watching at home. Nurses and doctors came out of the building in tears, thankful for the sounds of something positive. What happened next, was amazing. My good friend, Joey De Noble, heard me on the broadcast that day and asked if he could come join me. I set up over 100 shows at medical facilities and essential businesses all around to play. We would end up playing around 2-4 shows a day. Throughout the Covid tour, we received a multitude of messages from nursing staff, sharing their stories and heroic deeds. We also made a lot of new friends and landed good news coverage on 6ABC, Channel 69, CBS and others.

One day, our Musical Tour for Frontline Heroes led me back to Abington Hospital and, prior to the show, a close friend at Doylestown Hospital reconnected me with Dr. Yuschak. I told him I'd be playing 'Miracle', the song I wrote in Moss Rehab, for the facility and surgeon who saved my life nearly 20 years earlier. He said he was truly grateful that I called to thank him, but unfortunately, his schedule would prevent him from attending the show. Later that day, I experienced a flood of tears as I sang 'Miracle' for the first time ever at Abington Hospital...all the emotions from the past began coming back. While I was singing, someone yelled out to look to my left. There standing, listening to me sing 'Miracle', was Dr. Yuschak himself. He ended up staying for the whole show and we did a virtual hug and spoke afterwards. For me, this was truly a full circle, giving back to the man and facility that saved my life.

As the virus still trolls on and we learn new ways to fight it each day, I still play music live whenever I can. What a beautiful thing it would be to make a living off of my gift, but I still thank God every day for this gift, which he's given me to help bring joy and peace to others.

Keith Garner
Chalfont, Pennsylvania - USA
www.KeithGarner.com

"Survivor Girl Ukulele Band"

"I'm not alone anymore, I'm part of a band!!" said Raya, shouting with joy.* Her words made my eyes sting with happy tears. She and ten other girls had just given the performance of a lifetime. The audience was on their feet, and the girls were over the moon. They may have been beginner ukulele players, but today they were superstars.

In 2013, I started a small project in India called Survivor Girl Ukulele Band: bringing restoration and hope to survivors of human trafficking through the healing power of music and love. I bring a bunch of ukuleles to India and, for six months of the year, I work in a shelter home with girls who have been rescued from forced prostitution and other vulnerable situations. As part of my efforts there, I teach them how to play the ukulele.

Raya is one of those girls. She had been abandoned on the streets of Kolkata and had lived most of her life in a shelter home. I started volunteering as a ukulele teacher at her shelter home in 2015, and Raya was one of my first students there. Since then, she has not only performed many times, she has also helped to write a song and record ukulele and vocals for our CD. Once she reached the age of 18, she left the shelter home and has gone on to teach ukulele to private students and girls in another rescue shelter home in Kolkata. But, even more than that, Raya stays in touch with the other survivor girls from the shelter home where she first learned to played the ukulele. They are now family.

Teaching ukulele was not part of my plan. Not at first, anyway. Ten years ago, I didn't even know how to play the ukulele, but I was searching. Searching for a meaningful way to help girls who were survivors of human trafficking. Years before, I had been traveling in Nepal and learned that thousands of girls each year were preyed upon by traffickers who tricked their families with "offers" of well-paying domestic jobs in a nice home in India, only to be whisked across the border and sold into a brothel and raped ten to twenty times each night.

This bothered me. At the time, however, I didn't know of any way to get involved. The years went by, but the plight of those girls stuck with me. My computer held a sticky note with a quote from Ray Bradbury: "We need not to be let alone. We need to be really bothered once in a while. How long is it since you were really bothered? About something important, about something real?" And then, one night, I woke up with the words "rescue and restore" in my head. These words were about those girls. It was time to get involved.

First, I volunteered for short stints with a number of anti-trafficking organizations in India, hoping to find a place to plug in. Meanwhile, I started to learn guitar. It was a ton of fun and, soon I could crank out a few songs.

Then, volunteering one day in Delhi, the staff were off to a village outside the city to work with girls who were at high risk of being trafficked. My guitar and I jumped into the van and went along. After the team's presentation, I got to strumming on my guitar, and then it happened. The girls and I belted out "Twinkle Twinkle Little Star" and "Happy Birthday," and soon we had a full-fledged talent show on our hands. The guitar was a magnet, and the girls zoomed up to me and asked how it worked.

Their response lit fireworks in my brain. Could I teach girls to play guitar? Hmmm... not likely; the guitar is big, hard to learn and pricey. But, then, I remembered this musician I'd met on a flight a few months earlier. She had a ukulele, which she easily placed in the overhead bin, while I struggled with my massive guitar. When we got to talking, she said, "The thing about the ukulele is that it's easy to transport, quick to learn and inexpensive. You can have a lot of fun on a ukulele!"

Suddenly it hit me: I will learn to play ukulele, bring a bunch of ukuleles to India and form a survivor girl ukulele band! And that's my story. I get to bring the joy of creating music into the lives of survivor girls who live in a shelter home. We even made our very own CD! And if you could see the girls' faces when they hear themselves on that CD. Wow!

When these girls learn the basics of ukulele — can properly tune, find chords on a chart, play our beginner song list and read tablature — they earn their very own ukulele, tuner and songbook to take home.

One my students is a young woman named Preeti.* Like all the survivor girls, Preeti's story is complicated and difficult. If you met her, you'd notice her shiny hair, her prominent facial bones and that her arms are worryingly thin. You'd notice that she's the last one to make a fuss and that she plays the ukulele with a quiet confidence. Preeti is HIV positive and lives in a hospice. In that hospice, Preeti teaches the other girls how to make friendship bracelets and play ukulele. Here's what Preeti said: *"At first I thought ukulele was difficult. Now I think it's easy. And when I play, my mind is free."*

Salma, another a girl trafficked from Bangladesh, was in my very first class.* She taught me how to say "I love you" in Bengali: *"Ami tomake bhalobashi."* And then she said, *"Nothing good has ever happened in my life. And then you came. Why didn't you come sooner?"*

These precious girls have had very little education and opportunity and often feel powerless and worthless. But when they achieve new skills and practice and perform music, they find their voice and feel empowered. This is something they never imagined they could ever do. In learning how to play the ukulele, they learn *how* to learn and they learn how to work together and be a band. You should see them as they begin to teach each other. One of my dreams is to help more of these young women become ukulele teachers when they leave the shelter home.

I don't do this alone. Many people from around the globe have come alongside in support of Survivor Girl Ukulele Band Project. They send their love to these girls and make it possible to continue this rewarding work; I am so very grateful to those who support this project and for the opportunity I have been given to help these girls.

Laurie Kallevig, Founder
Survivor Girl Ukulele Band Project
Bellaire, Texas – USA
www.sgub.org
* All names have been changed to protect the girls' privacy.

"If I Had a Boat"

I've participated in countless Musicians On Call (MOC) programs and they're always very special for different reasons, but there's one experience in particular that sticks out in my memory.

I was performing for a patient who, I was told, was not responsive. One of the things I've always heard about patients who can't physically or emotionally respond, is that they usually can still *hear* what's going on around them. I was happy to play "If I Had a Boat" by Lyle Lovett for this patient, as it's one of my go-to songs during my MOC programs. It's just a fun song that usually gets a chuckle or a smile out of people.

Soon after I began playing and singing, everyone in the room was a little shocked and overwhelmed with joy when we noticed the patient's toe tapping to the music under their blanket.

That's how we knew the music was connecting. It was truly an unforgettable moment, proving once again the power music has to reach *beyond* what is thought to be possible.

Lindsay Ellyn, Musicians On Call
Nashville, Tennessee – USA
www.LindsayEllyn.com

Music is often the magical cure for what ails us

"All Because of Austin"

I come from a very musically inclined family. My six sisters and I grew up singing in the church folk group and ringing in the handbell choir under the direction of our dad, Sigmund Racki. I was always singing, but I wasn't a songwriter. That is, until the tragic passing of my nephew Austin, who lost his cancer battle just shy of his 2nd birthday in 2001. As you can imagine, it was the most traumatic event a family could ever endure. I remember one of the sweetest memories of Austin... I was visiting my sister and her family, right before Christmas. Austin heard my voice and ran the whole length of the apartment to greet me. His arms were outstretched - I picked him up and hugged him tight. I whispered to him, "you just gave Auntie Lisa the best Christmas gift ever!"

About a year after Austin passed away, I walked by his picture hanging on the wall. I stopped as his eyes met mine and said out loud, "I can almost feel your touch when you look at me". At that moment, I instantly heard a melody and lyrics in my mind and was compelled to start writing the song I would title "When You Look at Me". Writing became a grieving outlet for me and it gave my family a reason to smile again. The songs kept coming to me and I have been writing ever since.

In 2005, I recorded my first album of all original music in Nashville. When I formed a band, my sister Gail (Austin's mom), sang back-up vocals for me. It was so emotional for me to watch her sing, knowing what she had gone through, losing her child. Her strength was unbelievable and I realized that the music was also helping her to heal and honor Austin's memory. "When You Look at Me" was crowned the winner for an online international competition and I finally started to feel at peace with his loss.

I switched gears a bit in 2010, and wrote my first musical "Can't Bully Me Now". I got a call from my mother about a family member that was violently bullied. He was held down and punched on a school bus seat, all because they wanted to take his slice of pizza. I also suffered cruel teasing as a child. Kids laughed at my hair and my clothes and constantly picked me last for school teams. My ultimate hope, is to help educate youth about bullying and to bring back compassion and empathy. I'd love for schools to perform the musical, as I designed it with assemblies in mind. I was grateful to receive the first Peaceful Genesean award for the work I've done on the musical and my efforts to combat bullying.

In 2012, I was awarded a grant for the song "Everyday Hero" by the New York State Council on the Arts and GO Art. I wrote the song for youth who choose to live a drug-free life. Youth were selected to professionally record the song and be part of the music video. I was proud to receive the Drug Free Hero Award for the song by the Foundation for a Drug Free World.

I also wrote a special song entitled "Make a Wish" to honor the Make a Wish Foundation. During his brief life, Austin was granted a beautiful gift by this amazing organization. He absolutely loved "The Big Comfy Couch", a PBS show that gave him joy and comfort as he battled through so much pain. Loonette the Clown came to his home one day with Molly the doll and spent several wonderful and unforgettable hours with Austin. Our family is forever grateful to the Foundation.

It's amazing for me to sit back and think about all that has happened, all because of Austin! I'm incredibly sad that he's gone, but songwriting became a way for us to remember him with a smile. It's like he left me this beautiful gift! All because of Austin, thousands of lives around the world have been touched by the music. It has helped people heal, laugh, cry and smile. My goal has always been simple – to touch people's lives through music, in Austin's memory.

Lisa Barrett
Rochester, New York – USA
www.LisaBarrettMusic.com
www.LisasLyrics.com

"Don't interrupt – he's downloading another song."

Clearly this is before streaming became popular – Quick, somebody get Tweety bird a Spotify account!

"The Story of Lucy and Jack"

Many years ago, I released a web-based CD and my bio listed Mary Chapin Carpenter as an influence. Music is a difficult path. During one of my discouraging times, fate inspired me to continue.

In spring of 2001, I received a fan message from a man named Jack: *"I listened to your songs and absolutely loved them! Mary Chapin Carpenter is my favorite singer, because of the intelligence in her lyrics and great voice. I can see why you are inspired by her...you have many of the same qualities! Jack"*

I replied to Jack, who was surprised I responded and was intrigued by what inspired my songs. We began corresponding back and forth and, within one of those emails, he wrote:

"As far as identifying with a song, I love your song 'Madly in Love'. How heartfelt these words are:

"I am suggesting we wipe the slate dry,
the very next time we don't see eye to eye,
Before we go saying what we're thinking of,
We remember the times when we're madly in love"

This strikes right to the heart of most "discussions" among spouses. I identified with it so much, I printed it out and left it on my desk for the little woman!" Jack

A short time later, I then received a note from another fan: *"I don't know if you'll get this, but I had to tell you...I was clearing up my hubby's desk and found the lyrics to your song, 'Madly in Love'. Wow! I felt you had been looking directly into my heart. You wrote that we should all evaluate our methods of disagreeing with our partners", rest assured you have reached one at this end. Lucy".*

Of course, I started to wonder...could this be related to my correspondence with Jack. I wrote: *Lucy, This may be* the most important message I received since I released my CD! I attempted to share my thoughts with the world and hopefully make a positive impact.

She replied: *"Wow I guess these fan e-mails work. I'm not sure if I'm happy or embarrassed! Interesting, your favorite song writer is Mary Chapin Carpenter - she is my hubby, Jack's, favorite too!"*

Proof this WAS Jack's Lucy! We became friends around ordinary things and on Sunday Dec 22, 2002 I received this note:

"Dear Liz, with incredible sadness in my heart, I have to tell you - Jack - my one true love, passed Saturday at the Westchester Medical Center.

He was driving home Thursday when someone rear-ended him. He called to tell me, but was hit again and we lost contact. I called 911! Jack called, again, and said all was fine. The bumper was damaged, but HE was OK!

I never heard from him again. The police said there was no record of his accident. We checked the medical center and were told they had a "John Doe" in critical condition. We rushed to the hospital to find out Jack suffered extensive global brain trauma and was in a drug induced coma. Yesterday, I had to sign the DNR papers and withdraw medical intervention...he was brain dead. He went peacefully with his girls by his side.

I can't believe he's gone, it does not seem real...is it a bad dream? Please wake me up! This past year, we had found our love again and, to our surprise, it was deeper and more magnificent than we ever imagined it to be.

I wish I could write a song; I would tell all, the wonderful friend he was. Think of us. I think of you and that wonderful song that got us back on the road to rediscovering our friendship and true love. Thank You Liz, thank you from the bottom of my heart.

The accident that killed Jack was a high-profile accident that occurred on the New York Thruway on Thursday December 19, 2002. I told Lucy I would write a song about our shared experience that brought us together as friends. I wrote:

Here is the story of Lucy and Jack
To tell it correctly I have to go back
To a note I received from a stranger one night
After hearing my songs on an internet site
He said I was listening and loved all your songs
Especially the one about fights going wrong
When saying those things you can never take back
I just had to tell you and he signed it thanks Jack

So I sent a letter in answer to his
We began corresponding of that and of this
He printed the lyrics and left them in view
For Lucy to find during chores she would do

And now for the interesting twist to my tale
The computer soon chimed
You've received some new mail

It said I found the song left deliberately
Just wanted to share of it's meaning to me
Things have been tough for my husband and I
And lately we never see things eye to eye
But his leaving those words for me
Straight from his heart
Has given me hope we can make a new start

Could it be of the millions out surfing the web
This was Jack's one and only who'd written instead
It had come from a fan through my page MP3
And was signed all the best to you Lucy

Once more I penned my regards to a fan

And a bonding of friends over wires began
She told of how life never gives any slack
But mostly she wrote of how much she loved Jack
And Jack on occasion would write of his world
Of his feelings for Lucy and three growing girls
It all was apparent from Lucy and Jack
That love had survived and the clock had turned back

Since the story began it was almost two years
When I heard from Lucy and read through my tears
Of the tragic events leading up to that day
Now just before Christmas her Jack passed away

She told how their love it had grown more and more
Far deep and magnificent than all before
And if she could she would write him a song
And tell all the world of their love ever strong
A story of just how true love did unite
Through a song he had found on an internet site
How it's never to late to put it all back
The proofs in the story of Lucy and Jack

Lucy wrote: "Oh Liz! This is so special; I just can't find words to express what I'm feeling. If only my tears could explain it...I know Jack would feel so special knowing that he had helped inspire your song. He never ceased to be my one true love. Thank you my good friend for such a beautiful song, it touches my heart and soul more than you'll ever know. I know he feels the same. All my love, Lucy"

I'm grateful I took the time to respond to these people who encouraged me in my craft. A simple gesture of well done, the importance of a kind word and a note from a stranger became a lifeline for both the listener and artist.

Liz Rogers
Downingtown, PA – USA

"We're Made of Love"

Each and every time we bring music into a hospital playroom or to a patient's bedside in a Children's Hospital, we expect and experience miracles. We know music heals. Through a grant from Pickleberry Pie Hospital Concerts for Kids, my husband RJ and I get to use our musical abilities, intuition and sensitivity for the vast differences in illnesses, ages and situations.

We were looking forward to a San Francisco hospital visit in late October 2019. Usually, we go bedside, but today was different. The night before, my husband had a dream about a song. It came to him fully written - a melody that was complete with beautiful lyrics entitled, "We're Made of Love." A perfect song to add to our repertoire for our hospital visits.

In the morning, I typed up the words, printed them out and away we drove the hour-long journey to the hospital. The trip gave us time to figure out chords and harmonies. I play guitar, so I brought my Martin Backpacker.

When we visit this particular hospital, bedside visits of 5-10 rooms are not unusual and we always stay as late as we possibly can. We have to... we are there to be of service to the children and families who need us most. But today, no bedside...just a playroom visit. It's a new, beautiful playroom with mood lighting and soft colors in an artistically designed room.

The Child Life Specialist brought us in where we met with an Art Therapist working with a young lady, who was 18 years old...they were creating art on river rocks. The young lady was very ill and we could feel her pain. The Art Therapist explained that she was having a "not so good" day and maybe our musical visit would be too much. We understood and respected her wishes. However, as we made eye contact with the teen, I believe she felt we were genuine and came in to raise the vibration of the room.

She could only communicate with a little white board and wrote on it for us to "please stay", so we played several songs. And, indeed, we were the medicine she needed. We could see her spirits were lifting. She even smiled and clapped along to the songs. The Art Therapist and Child Life Specialist were dancing and singing along, raising the vibration even higher.

Then RJ said, "Let's play the new song." At first, I hesitated and made a joke saying, "What key was that in again?" The thing is, I wasn't kidding...it was so new. As we played the brand-new dream song, this sweet, lovely, young lady closed her eyes as the tears rolled down her face. She was in a blissful, contemplative and meditative state. We see the two therapists crying as well. We later found out this was the first smile and happy moment this young girl had experienced in weeks, due to her challenging condition and difficult treatments.

Our delicate patient, who can only write on a small white board, writes that she loved the song. All the while, during our musical visit, they were making acrylic miniature paintings and messages on river rocks to put on the new 5th floor Healing Garden. The Art Therapist said they were infusing it with our music and love.

We were all connecting with this emotional experience, but eventually it was time for us to leave. The teen then writes on her white board for us to please play "We're Made of Love" again. Of course! It was what we call a "miracle moment"...beautiful, heartfelt and meaningful. There is a word in the Sanskrit language for being 'moved by love' - it is Kama Muta. We left the hospital with new friends and floated out feeling like we were touched by the angels.

Skip to 9:00 the next morning. The head of Child Life at the Hospital calls me. Did I do something wrong? OMG, what? She called to let us know how profound our visit was. We lifted this girl's spirits, brought laughter, love and helped soothe her soul. The girl in the playroom is dying and probably will not make it through the month. I am speechless.

The young girl asked for a copy of the song - she loved it that much. Yikes! We just finished writing it. What to do? It's not recorded. What else could we do? We have a recording studio, so starting at 10 am until 5 pm that day, we produced "We're Made of Love." The song was sent to the Child Life Department Head to be presented to the young girl that evening.

About 15 minutes after having sent the song, I got a text saying that there was not a dry eye in the room. There were doctors and nurses, therapists and family in the patient's room at the time the song was presented and played.

We were told that our music, and this song, had such a positive effect on her healing. Within a week, they discovered that a new treatment became available for her condition and there was hope on the horizon.

One of the greatest gifts for us playing music for kids in the hospitals, is the unconditional love that we feel and give. We are grateful to the families and Pickleberry Pie to allow us to be of service through our music.

UPDATE: The new drug therapy is working! The young girl recently graduated from high school and is on a path to becoming a nurse.

"We're Made of Love" has since been passed around to numerous facilities and taken on a life of its own, bringing musical healing with it everywhere it goes.

Lori Moitié - Pickleberry Pie Hospital Concerts for Kids
Redwood City, California – USA
www.LoriAndRJ.com
www.PickleberryHospitalConcerts.org

Do something today that makes your heart sing

"Travesty to Triumph"

I was introduced to the piano as a five-year old growing up in Leningrad, USSR. I went through vigorous training throughout my school years, including Mussogrsky College of Music. I trained in music theory, piano performance and pedagogy.

In 1989, at 21 years old, I rewrote my destiny while in Rome, Italy, as accompanist for a choir from Leningrad. I was fascinated with American literature and culture and, on a whim, went to the American Embassy and filed for political asylum. It was granted in record time, just three days, although it took me a year to get airfare and tickets arranged. Patrons from Arizona State University met me at the airport and, soon, I was playing for the ASU Choral and Dance Departments. Later, I was also hired as accompanist for Ballet Arizona classes, where I met Patrick Swayze and Mikhail Baryshnikov.

Fast forward to 2008, I had two boys (3 and 11), my own private studio and was playing with a quintet regularly. On March 28, I was preparing to take a shower, when I collapsed on the floor of the bathroom. It happened so quickly, I couldn't understand what had just occurred. When I began to come to my senses, I heard my youngest yelling, "Mommy's dead! Mommy's dead!". I could hear everything around me, but I could not move at all. Nothing worked.

After our son's desperate calls, my husband entered the room to find me on the floor. He had just returned home to retrieve his wallet a few minutes prior. He picked me up, put some clothes on me and laid me on the bed. The paramedics arrived a few minutes later and announced I had a stroke. The only thought I remember is, "A stroke...at 40...ME!...NO!!!"

After I arrived at the hospital, I spent the next five and a half hours in surgery, cleaning up the mess in my brain from the burst vessel. Out of surgery, I still could not move at all. I was frightened beyond imagination. After a few days, the nurses had me walking, although I could only drag my right leg and my right arm was completely unresponsive. When I attempted to speak, I could only mutter and was devastated that I was unable to communicate at all.

I returned home from the hospital a week later. The doctors told me that my body would 'probably' return to order over time. The day after returning home, I struggled to put on a robe and went to the piano, dragging my right leg. I sat in front of the piano, held my right arm up and tried to play a simple scale. I could not move my fingers. My left hand was fine. I swore to myself, that I will practice a little bit every day. By the end of the first week, I could move my fingers just a little, but I was still far from being able to play a simple scale. I still could not talk.

My mother was living with us then, having moved her from Russia after my father's passing a few years before. I was so thankful for her being there, taking care of everything that I would normally have been doing. It allowed me not to worry about housework, cooking meals and caring for my sons. I was able to focus on my recovery with every ounce of energy I could muster.

I followed my piano routine for months, unable to talk or walk normally, until I could begin to play a simple scale. I would try to play simple pieces, but found I could hardly play them at all. My fingers just weren't responsive. I was depressed, but determined to play again. After a few more months of gradual progress, my cellist friend, Pat Fisher, offered to come twice a week and play simple duets with me. This generous offer to help with my musical recovery made a huge emotional difference for me.

In time, I began to notice I was getting a little better with being able to play familiar pieces, though my fingers still weren't completely functional. At one point, it seemed as if something else was coming alive, as if the music had some kind of healing power to restore my fingers. I suppose the familiar piano pieces were indelible in my brain from years of training and, somehow, my neurons were finding order again.

Over the next weeks and months, Pat continued to show up twice a week. Her support was amazing and I cannot express enough how grateful I am for her. I don't know what I would have done without her help. I may have recovered eventually, but it came much earlier with her support.

Over the next few years, I gradually felt like I was regaining my finger dexterity. I spent hours playing and practicing, often with other musicians. Although they never said a word, I could tell I was still not at the level of playing prior to the stroke. I began teaching piano again, though it was still a challenge to speak at times.

The gift of music and the tenacity of my sheer will to play again, eventually brought me back to full, or nearly so, ability to perform and play. I knew in the beginning that I would recover, but I didn't know how long it would take. Being able to play again was the most factor driving me to recover from my stroke. If it were not for the piano and the opportunity to play, especially the classical pieces that are so full of emotional range, I don't know that I would have ever fully recovered. Music means so much to me – the immense feelings I get when connecting to the minds of history's greatest composers as I play. I feel as if my life would be empty without it. I consider myself fortunate, indeed, to have the gift of music in my life.

I've never shared my story before and hope that, maybe, this story of travesty and triumph may help someone to overcome extreme, or even slight, impairments caused by unforeseen events in their lives. Music can truly heal.

Luba Brodsky-Benefiel
Chandler, Arizona - USA
www.Lubov4Music.com

"Just Keep Playing"

While attending an all-girls high school, I was the piano accompanist for several choirs and soloists. I would play for rehearsals and performances. Our director was a classically trained nun, who ran a very tight ship. She taught us to maintain our posture, breathing and self-control at all times.

The spring concert was finally here! All of the choirs were performing for the school first and then, later, for our parents and families. All went well for the daytime concert for our peers. The evening performance was going great, that is, until we were midway through a medley with all the choruses. My page turner started to sneeze...and, accidentally, knocked the keyboard cover onto my fingers!

Pain shot through my hands. But, the pain was overwhelmed by fear, as Sister Nancy looked at me with her well-known fierce gaze that said "KEEP PLAYING!!!"

I did. And managed to get to the end of the piece. Which, thankfully, was the finale of the show. Sister Nancy pointed to me to take a small bow as she always did. She then followed me out of the music pit to look at my hands.

"Well...you've got a bit of a bruise there. But you did a nice job!"

Sister Nancy didn't hand out compliments lightly. I went home with a smile.

Marcia Marino
Franklin, Wisconsin – USA
www.Twitter.com/MarciaMarino

"The Trail of Tears: A Spiritual Music Experience"

In Alabama, there is a memorial to an incredible, indigenous woman of the Yuchi people. Her great-great grandson, Tom Hendrix, built it from rocks taken one at a time from the river the Yuchi people know as the Singing River. As the water flows over the shoals, through a place now known as Muscle Shoals, the voice of a woman living in the river can be heard by the Yuchi people.

Te-lah-nay was forced to leave this sacred place and march to Oklahoma on the Trail of Tears, when she was but a young woman. She spent one winter there searching for a river that sang. She found nothing that would fill the hole in her spirit left by the absence of the voice from the river. She made the decision to leave Oklahoma and travel back to her home - back to the Singing River. It was against the law for her to return, so she hid under the cover of darkness, travelling alone at night. It took five years and the overcoming of many obstacles, before she finally arrived home.

On a December morning in 2015, my husband and I had the privilege of visiting the site of her memorial. We spent hours listening to Tom tell Te-lah-nay's story and the tale of how the Wichahpi Commemorative Stone Wall came to be. Wichahpi means "like the stars". Tom said his inspiration to build the wall came from the words of a Yuchi elder who said, "All things shall pass. Only the stones will remain."

It is hard to explain the feelings generated, while walking through this memorial pathway, bordered by this lovingly created stone wall. It is as if the rocks have absorbed memories that are shared as feelings with whoever walks among them. One part is straight to commemorate the path of the journey from Alabama to Oklahoma; the rest of the path is curved and circuitous, symbolizing her long journey home. The emotions evoked at various parts of the wall are remarkable in their differences.

Within this memorial structure, built on private land owned by Tom and his family, is a small, outdoor amphitheater. A gently curved part of the memorial wall is the backdrop. Stone seats are scattered throughout the tree-covered area, facing this section of the wall. Each seat has two stones for legs with one on top, forming the sitting surface. There is a red prayer ribbon, like one of the many hanging around the memorial site, swaying in the gentle breeze as Linda takes her place to perform her song.

We were visiting the memorial that day with a singer–songwriter friend, Linda McRae, who had researched Te-lah-nay's story and captured it in a song simply titled "Singing River." She hoped to share the song with Tom during our visit. It is early morning and our group of 6 are alone in the amphitheatre with Tom. Linda takes a seat in front of the stone wall with Tom sitting nearby, facing her. She lifts her guitar and strums the opening bars of the song she has lovingly crafted. Her voice lifts to tell the story of Te-lah-nay's journey. She is hoping for Tom's approval, hoping she has captured the essence of this woman.

The rest of us watch in rapt silence as the world fades to only Tom and Linda. Seeing him clench his fist and tap his heart, gives flight to Linda's strong voice, as it rises to the treetops and resonates on the stones of Te-lah-nay's wall.

Goosebumps form as the song moves on. They are not the usual goosebumps - they are, in some unfathomable way, magnified by the resonance of the environment in which we are ensconced. My heart clenches and a lump forms in my throat, as tears begin to fall.

Linda intensifies her voice as she sings "Singing River take me home." She adds percussion by striking the side of her guitar and stamping one foot in time to the music, mimicking the steps of Te-lah-nay, as she once, long ago, moved toward home.

Chills course up my spine and the hairs on the back of my neck stand at attention. Tom rises and hugs Linda, making the sign of the third eye on her forehead as he releases her. The third eye is an indigenous concept, suggesting a higher state of enlightenment.

Our own trail of tears flowed freely then. Tears for the journey of a brave woman, tears for the societal wrongs and tears for the song that captured it for future generations.

Music does that. It captures history and transmits it to future generations, ensuring no one forgets and hoping no one repeats the wrongs.

Marie Gage
Minden, Ontario – Canada
www.MarieGage.ca
www.LindaMcRae.com/track/881961/singing-river

"Music Healed My Soul"

Music has always been my therapy and my savior. As someone who's suffered from depression since childhood, in music I have found the most amazing creative outlet for my emotional struggles. I'm pretty sure it saved me from alcohol dependency and a life of absolute misery. At my shows, I often share how magical music has been helping me combat depression and overcome difficult periods of my life.

Last summer music performed yet another miracle for me. After giving birth to my first child, our little Violetta, a severe case of Postpartum Depression (PPD) set on. From the day I gave birth, I cried (sobbed, more like) almost every day. Sometimes for no reason at all. I could be in a middle of a sentence or at a grocery store. That's PPD for you. I had the worst of thoughts and was down most of the time during what should have been the happiest of chapters in my life.

If you don't know much about PPD, it's a common thing, but sadly, not very much talked about. Moms are supposed to be thrilled with joy with their new baby, right? Which we are. But... it's life, and things are never simple. PPD is triggered by severe ongoing sleep deprivation, raging hormones, recovery from deep physical and mental trauma that is giving birth (which can cause PTSD-like symptoms) and a complete and sudden change of lifestyle with a newborn baby. Sprinkle some baby crying to the mix (baby crying recordings have been used as a torture technique) and you have yourself a very difficult situation.

So, for 2 months after giving birth I was in a fog of sorts, in a state of shock. I was truly depressed, feeling like a ghost of someone I used to be, with no hope in sight. To make things worse, I felt an overwhelming amount of guilt for being depressed. But like with other types of depression, it had nothing to do with love you have for people around you - I absolutely love my little girl and my husband (who's my co-writer/guitarist) more than anything in the world.

During those first 2 months, I didn't have time or energy for anything outside of my mom duties. I just about had time to shower and take little walks. There was no time to play the piano and sing. But then I took a leap of faith and made a commitment: I scheduled an online concert, streaming live from our living room. Online concerts were something I started doing on regular basis at the end of pregnancy, since I knew we wouldn't be able to tour for a while.

I was such an emotional mess, I could barely pull myself together for that online show, but - with support of my husband - I did. And after performing for 2 hours (to an audience of loving fans from around the world), being in the moment, singing my songs and even crying on camera, I was myself again. The music has healed my soul once again. Just like that!

After that day my PPD was gone. It still rears its ugly head once in a while, but in a very mild way. I just have to make sure I carve out time to write and play music and schedule my online concerts on a regular basis. That's how music will continue being my healer and savior every day.

Marina V
Los Angeles, California – USA
www.MarinaV.com

"Beyond My Wildest Dreams"

Before there was music for me, there was baseball, lots of baseball. From the time I got home from school until dark and every spare minute on the weekends growing up in Syracuse, New York in the 60's. I couldn't dream bigger than playing shortstop for my New York Yankees.

For my first year of junior high, we moved from Syracuse to Binghamton, New York and, pretty soon after, life threw me a real curveball. I had a problem with my right kidney. Surgery followed to try and save it without success. Another surgery followed to remove it. Both times I spent a long time in the hospital and with what seemed like endless recovery time. I had experienced this before at around 6 years old with Rheumatic fever - another long spell in bed.

While I was healing, right around February 1964, my original dream made way for a new, even bigger one ... The Beatles on The Ed Sullivan Show! So many of my songwriting and musician friends have the same story. From that Sunday night on, their path was set. Over time, the baseball glove was replaced by a bass guitar that sat propped up on a pillow, on my stomach, while I was healing. Music is a powerful pull, almost impossible to explain. You have to give yourself to it completely. And I did. I started bands in school and began trying to write my own songs soon after. Life was never the same. It was better.

Over the years I've been able to play with, and write songs for, many of my musical heroes including a few I watched on other Sunday night TV programs; Joe Cocker, Diana Ross, Chaka Khan, Tina Turner and more. Music has taken me all over the world, from writing in castles in France to having a number one record in the UK, home of The Beatles. I even met my wife Kathy playing music one night in Indianapolis, Indiana. It's been hard work with sacrifice, rejection, lots of rejection, more strikeouts than home runs, but a powerful pull. Writing a song still feels like a magic trick, something out of thin air.   When you hear from someone who was moved by something you created, it's an indescribable feeling. Music has the power to reach people's hearts and souls, shape their path, change the world and even to heal.

Music gave a sick kid a way to get outside himself and reach for a whole world...beyond my wildest dreams.

Mark Cawley
Nashville, Tennessee – USA
www.IDoCoach.com
www.MarkCawley.com

"Under Table Ballet"

Some years ago, I was at a live music event by a musician I knew named John D'Amico. The venue was a really nice restaurant and everyone was seated at tables. During the upbeat jazz numbers, I could see the man sitting next to me dancing from the waist down under the table. His feet and legs were moving non-stop all around his seating area. He was doing a lot more than just tapping his feet in this under table ballet. When intermission came, I was shocked to see this man reach for his crutches and, with substantial difficulty, raise out of his seat and slowly move away from the table. While he was engrossed with the music, I never would have guessed he had any movement issues at all. He clearly absorbed great energy from the music, enjoying it thoroughly and giving his body a reprieve from his level of incapacitation. I was greatly struck by this experience and have always remembered the healing power of music.

Mark Seidman
Philadelphia, Pennsylvania
www.InspireArtSpace.com
www.SeidmanFluteTechnology.com

"Magic Music Time"

Music changes lives and it has, most definitely, changed ours. Our fairy tale began in 1968 when my, now husband of nearly 50 years, asked me to dance, at his Junior Prom.

Music has always been important to me and I am very grateful to have it in my life, especially when difficult times have presented themselves. A few years ago, I suffered a bleeding aneurysm. My doctors call me a walking miracle and say I should not have survived. What some may not know, is that brain development is stimulated by music and movement. My career consisted of teaching preschool music and creative movement and, throughout my life I was also a Ballroom Dancer, Square Dancer and Country Round dancer. This combination of constant music and motion left me with a reserve of brain cells that marched in and took over when the aneurysm struck. Not long after, my husband lost his left arm in an industrial accident. Had I not survived that aneurysm, I would not be here to care for him. How different his life, and that of our children, would be.

Since his accident, our lives have been filled with weekly doctor visits and occupational therapy sessions. To cope with all of the surgeries and lifestyle changes these events brought about, I surrounded myself with people and experiences that make me feel good. My daily early morning walks listening to songs that inspire me, have brought a smile to my face and helped me make it through all this turmoil.

On top my aneurysm and my husband losing his left arm, I recently developed an inoperable neuroma on my left foot. This made many of my favorite activities like baking, shopping and dancing all but impossible. One of the songs that has kept me going during this time, is "I Believe" by Scooter Lee. Even when I can barely walk, I can still teach and do The Swing and The Cha Cha and more...because I dance on my toes!

Our fairy tale continues with the birth of our ninth grandchild on New Year's Day, little Miss Hailey...it's a whole new world! You just can't wipe the smile off my face, since Hailey's birth and having celebrated our second honeymoon at Paradise Stream (in the heart of the Pocono Mountains in Pennsylvania), where we first stayed in 1972.

I'm a firm believer that we make our own happiness. Music was my answer to keep believing and has enabled me to face each new day and challenge. The magical power of music will always give me hope and belief in better days ahead!

Mary MacPherson Kelley
Magic Music Time
Pembroke, Massachusetts - USA
www.Facebook.com/MagicMusicTime

"How Music Kept Me Alive"

Music has always been a big part of my life. When I was a little girl, I could be found organizing neighborhood children into small groups to sing for our parents. Throughout school, I sang in various shows and church choir, but was still unsure what path I wanted to take after high school. I ended up enrolling in junior college for two years, where I took mostly music classes. After graduating, I took a music teacher's job at a small Catholic School. While there, I made the decision to dedicate my life to teaching music, so I enrolled in a music program at the College of NJ.

As I prepared to start working on my music degree, I began not feeling well and realized I was losing my singing voice. A visit to the doctor and some blood work gave me an answer, an answer I did not expect. I was diagnosed with Lupus and told that I would probably never sing again. There were a lot of other things in that diagnosis, however, the not being able to sing was something I could not accept.

My doctor advised me to move somewhere with a more consistent climate. I was told that the chances of having children or getting my voice back were not good. They also said I might have ten good years ahead of me. Taking that as a challenge, and not a definite, I moved from New Jersey to Florida where I focused on life and music.

I taught in the school system in Pinellas County for 3 years, until my daughter was born (Yup. I did that). Wanting to enjoy the child I was told I may not have, I resigned my position so I could stay home with her. My daughter sat with me at the piano as soon as I could hold her there. She would often sit in her baby seat while I played guitar and sang. When she was older, we would go to playgroups where I would sing and dance with all the babies. The parents eventually asked me to create music classes for them.

While teaching the classes, I ventured into producing a local TV show, doing workshops for teachers and recording the songs I was making up. This led me to researching the therapeutic effects of music on the brain. Although I did not realize it at the time, I now know that music played a HUGE part in my survival. According to most medical data, I should not be functioning as well as I do, or even still be alive. For me, that was never an option. Lung disease caused by the Lupus should have disabled my ability to sing. Yet, I still sing. In fact, I sing in a rock band belting out Janis and Gracie. Music is what keeps my brain and muscles functioning at a higher level than what is expected with Lupus. Music is a gift that I literally owe my life to. Thanks to music, my days are far more numerous than what many medical professionals expected, and for that I am forever grateful.

Maryann "Mar." Harman
Music with Mar - Founder
Palm Harbor, Florida - USA
www.MusicWithMar.com

"Sing with Your Hearts"

For 40 years, I have been amazing audiences of all ages as "Myklar the Ordinary, the only magician good enough to call himself 'ordinary'." One of the hallmarks of my performances, has been the music I have chosen, music which comes from a panoply of cultures and genres, from oriental to rock to jazz to hip hop and gospel. One of God's great jokes, is that He gave me an incredibly eclectic appreciation of music and absolutely no music talent. My love of music has opened many doors and sparked many post show discussions with folks who wanted to comment on music I had used during the show. Over two decades ago, one such incident etched itself into my heart forever.

I had just finished a show at a Washington, DC elementary school and was packing up my equipment. As I was packing, a children's gospel choir had been called into the auditorium for practice. The song they were practicing was Kirk Franklin's "I Sing Because I'm Happy". It was not a happy song, as the children just could not get the melody and the harmony to match. It was definitely not "music to the ears". I stopped gathering my things and went over to them and said, "You know why you can't get it together?" They were not offended, because I was the "magic man" they loved. They asked, "Why?". I said, "because you are only singing with your mouths. Try singing with your hearts." They smiled - that smile that only little kids can smile and thanked me - with that "thanks" that only little kids can thank.

I went back to packing, with my back turned toward the choir. All of a sudden, I thought angels must have come down from Heaven and taken the choir's place. Now THAT was music! The innocence and beauty of those wee voices must have made God smile. I smiled, because I was happy and I was happy, because I had made them smile. The next time you see yourself in the mirror, smile. You will notice that smiles are circular. Oh, yeah, and meant to be shared.

Mike Russell
Ft. Washington, Maryland – USA
www.Facebook.com/michael.e.russell.792

"Still Kickin'"

A middle aged lady came up to me at one of our shows...very excited to share a story that was clearly dear to her heart. As she began telling me details about her father's health, I wondered why she insisted on sharing this with me, and not someone that she actually knew. But I continued to listen as she spoke of how several doctors gave her dad two weeks to live, at most. One day, she decided to bring a CD player into the hospital to play our CDs for him. He could barely talk, but she knew that our music was something he enjoyed. She was trying to comfort him in his last days in any way possible. Over and over the music played. She looked at me with tears in her eyes and said "Michelle, that was 2 years ago and my dad is still kickin'! There was no magic medicine or procedure...we just listened to your music! You have no idea how much he loves your music and how music can heal people! Thank you! Please don't ever stop playing music! The doctors can't believe it!"

Michelle Jerabek
Oshkosh, Wisconsin – USA
www.CopperBoxBand.com

MUSIC helps to make every day sweeter...

"Kerry's Ten Penny Wash"

Many years ago, I was a new Kindermusik instructor struggling to learn the program and attract families to classes, while also balancing motherhood for the first time. One of the classes I held was on a Thursday night with just one child registered to attend. This was the only time slot the father was able to join us, so I chose to continue the class with just one family. Their little boy was just 14 months old, suffering with some health issues, and had missed the last two classes while in the hospital.

Up until this point, this little boy had experienced only a few classes, one of which was with a visiting family where we danced to Kerry's Ten-Penny Wash. When the family was finally able to return for the Thursday night class, the boy's mother was not feeling well and couldn't find the strength to hold him while dancing, once again, to Kerry's Ten-Penny Wash. For those unfamiliar, this song features a fairly long dance with lots of movement. Having already danced to other songs that night, I suggested sitting down and bouncing to the music.

The little boy would have nothing to do with that and quickly got off his mother's lap and walked over to me. He put his hand up in the air, as we do in the "clap" part of the dance. I clapped his hand and he moved back, stepping side to side, smiling all the while. He repeated this several times, while I continued to bounce my "baby" in my lap. The little boy then bent over to my shoes and put both of his little hands on them, pushing on the right and then the left. He made it very clear to me, without words, that he wanted me to move my feet. I got up and said, "Okay, I'll dance with you." He smiled and began stepping from side to side and walking up to clap my hand. Still I wasn't moving, only standing in place and

waiting for his return. He again stopped, and bent down to my feet, pushing down on one and then the other.

I responded by saying "That's right, we are supposed to be dancing". We continued walking up and back, clapping in between, until the end of the song with his parents watching in awe.

This experience is one I will never forget and I don't think his parents will either. That one night inspired me to continue pushing through the struggles and led to a rewarding career bringing music and movement to young families for the past 20 years.

Nancy Jones - Sing With Nancy, LLC
Tuscon, Arizona – USA
www.SingWithNancy.com
www.SingWithNancy.kindermusik.com

"The Subway Saw Lady"

All my life, I dreamed of being a dancer. I was a trainee with the Martha Graham Dance Company of Contemporary Dance, a tap-dance teacher and earned a living performing in musical theater. In short, I was a happy dancer, until... one day, on my way home from Lincoln Center, I was hit by a speeding taxi-cab as I crossed the street. The accident left me suffering with permanent damage to my upper spine and instantly ended my dance career. Needless to say, I was devastated. I had dedicated my entire life to dance, and now what was I going to do?

To cheer me up, my parents took me on a trip to Austria. As a kid, I absolutely loved the movie 'The Sound of Music', having watched it 14 times! So, thinking it would elevate my spirit, my parents decided to take me to the country where the film was made. While there, we attended a show for tourists. One of the acts was...a musical saw player! I had never seen, nor heard, of a musical saw before. This was completely new to me and the experience totally blew me away. I thought the sound was phenomenal – spiritual, angelic and different from any sound I had ever heard before. What really appealed to me, was the visual – not the fact that it is a carpenter's tool, but the fact that the whole instrument moved when being played, and the sawist's upper body along with it. It was almost like a dance! The musical saw is one of very few instruments where the entire instrument moves, constantly changing shape as you play it. This is unlike a more traditional instrument like the violin, where the bow moves, but the body and shape of the violin remain fixed.

After the show, I went backstage to talk with the sawist and asked if he would give me a lesson. His answer was a flat and resounding 'No'. Of course, I said I would pay him and asked how much he wanted, but all he would offer is that I didn't need a teacher. "Pick up a hand saw, hold it the way you have seen me do on stage and figure it out" was his instruction. As a "bonus hint", he said the more expensive a saw I get, the better it would sound.

Armed with these instructions, I borrowed an old saw from a friend. It was rusty from age and woodwork and after some experimenting, I discovered it was capable of playing just 6 notes. So, I took a trip to the local hardware store, which turned out to be quite an interesting experience. At first, the owner was furious about the "whistling" sound someone was making in his store. He was later puzzled, when he saw where the sound was actually coming from. Once he realized I intended to purchase an expensive saw, he let me continue to test all the saws in his inventory.

Indeed, the Austrian sawist was right. I did figure it out all on my own and went on to play the musical saw with orchestras, on movie soundtracks and numerous television appearances. I am very grateful to him for having given me the satisfaction of being able to say that 'I did it all on my own'. Along the way, I also discovered that I loved being the 'Saw Lady' and I don't even miss dancing anymore!

In addition to playing regular music venues, my passion is playing in the New York City subway. I never planned to be a busker, it sort of just happened. I used to have a job selling souvenirs at a Broadway theater. I had a lot of free time during that job, because I only had to work when the audience walked in and out of the show and during intermission. The rest of the time, I could do whatever I wanted. So, I began bringing my saw to work and taught myself to play, as I sat outside the theater in an adjacent parking lot. I figured, if I practiced in the parking lot, no one would be disturbed.

One day, a guy and his son came to stand by me. They listened to me play for a while and then the guy took a $5 bill out of his pocket and gave it to me. I asked him why he was giving me money and he said they really enjoyed listening to me and wanted to show their appreciation. I thought that was wild, so I told my co-workers, who then insisted that I play in front of the theater during intermission...that's when buskers come to play for the audience that goes out to smoke. I didn't feel ready to perform, but my friends wouldn't take 'no' for an answer. They dragged me out in-front of the next door theater prior to their intermission, put an empty box in front of me and stood back to see what would happen. The people who smoke, came out of the theater, so I had no choice. I started to play and people gathered around me. They were smiling, applauding and proceeded to drop money into the empty box. By the end of the 10 minute intermission, there was as much money in the box as I was making at work that day. After that, I figured it would be silly to continue practicing in the seclusion of the parking lot.

So, that's how I got to be a busker. I first busked on the side street of my theater. When my confidence grew, I moved around the corner to the big street: Broadway. It was so much fun, that when winter came and the weather forced me inside, I decided to give the subway a chance. The acoustics in the subway were so amazing, that it became my favorite space to perform. While playing in the NYC subway, I've also witnessed many acts of kindness that stem from music. One of my favorites was while playing at the Times Square subway station. During my performance, a blind man joined a group of passers-by gathered around me. The blind man's face lit up to the sound of my music. It was clear he truly loved what he was hearing. A lady from the crowd, unrelated to the blind man, also noticed his joy. She came over to me, bought one of my CDs, walked over to the blind man and put the CD in his hand saying, 'This is the music you are hearing now. This is for you' and she gave it to the blind man! To think that, in a small way, my music was the impetus for such a beautiful, selfless act of kindness between two strangers – simply priceless!

Like most buskers, I also have a career off the streets. I've had the opportunity to perform at Carnegie Hall, Lincoln Center, Madison Square Garden and on many movie soundtracks, but busking is extremely addictive: even if I get to be a millionaire or win an Oscar award, I would still want to busk. My soul was kidnaped by busking.

Natalia 'Saw Lady' Paruz
New York, New York - USA
www.SawLady.com

"Something for Me"

Our family's world was tragically altered when my oldest son suffered a catastrophic brain injury in a car accident many years ago. I resigned my position to take care of him at home and, after a few years, I decided that I needed to find something for me. I loved music and decided to take a couple voice lessons. All my life I loved to sing, but not in front of anyone. So yes, I'm the one singing my heart out in the shower.

When I went to my first lesson, I brought a tape of me singing, because I had never sung in front of someone. The song was The Colour of My Love by Celine Dion. I'm not a Celine wanna-be, but the words resonated with me and our commitment to our son. When the teacher listened back to the recording, she had tears in her eyes. The academy was having a concert with all their students and she asked me to do this song. Unfortunately at the time, she did not have the accompaniment for it, so I had to sing this to Celine's version with the words all but muted. It was the worst possible way to attempt to sing when trying to stay in pitch and be in time with the tape... what a nightmare! However, I wrote it off as an experience... good, bad or ugly.

Two years later, I sat at my computer and, within half an hour, I wrote a song for my son - the melody took a little longer. I ended up writing another one for my younger son, one for my hubby and when my girlfriend's son died, I wrote a special song for her from one mother to another. All of these writing experiences were very cathartic.

That is pretty much the sum total of my musical 'career' and trust me, I use that term loosely. My son was 22 years old when his accident happened and I was one month short of my 42nd. birthday. He is 51 now and I'm 70. My hubby and I still look after him at home. Music has been a blessing and, when I sing songs that I use to sing when he was younger, he will turn his head towards me...he does not take his eyes off me until I stop. Those moments are precious.

Nicole Moore
Carleton Place, Ontario - Canada

"Slaithwaite Philharmonic Legacy"

Music runs in my family and I feel proud to know I am keeping the tradition alive. My great great grandad, John Taylor, worked in the mill in Yorkshire from the age of 9, as his father had been injured in a mill accident and was unable to work. He was so tired at the end of each working day, that his mother would come down the long hill where they lived and carry him home on her back. Somewhere, somehow, despite being very poor, he acquired a cello and found his passion. Later on his son, John Herbert Taylor, took up the cello as well. Together, they helped set up the Slaithwaite Philharmonic orchestra, in 1891. At the time, Slaithwaite was a small village of a mere 4,000 people. It was said that John Herbert was always willing to teach the youngsters to play, so that they could be part of the orchestra. The orchestra is still running today with a book celebrating their first 100 years entitled *"An Improbable Centenary"*, written by Adrian Smith.

John Herbert Taylor had 7 children with his wife Hannah. Though there was barely enough food to go around, any child who wanted to learn an instrument, was given the opportunity. When he took his son John Taylor out of school for his clarinet lesson, the teacher tried to put a stop to it, saying that he wouldn't be able to earn a living playing music. John Herbert told him that his eldest son, Beaumont Taylor, was indeed doing such a thing playing cello for a cinema in Scunthorpe and earning far more than him! His son, John, also went on to earn a living playing music by teaching clarinet and saxophone.

My grandma, Maggie Wilkinson nee Taylor, was the youngest of the Taylor family's 7 children. She played piano and would help local singers by playing for them at her home. Her only child, my mother Peggy Housley nee Wilkinson, also played piano and, later in life, played violin and now sings in Exeter Choral Society. As a single mother, she didn't have much money to spare, but once you have your instrument, the rest is free! I loved falling asleep listening to my mother playing a medley of Salad Days, creating pictures and scenarios to match the music.

I played piano from the age of 7 and fell in love with it very quickly. At secondary school, I played trombone. We couldn't afford to buy one, but the all-girls school I went to was so pleased to finally have a female trombone player, that they bought one for us to play.

In my late teens, I joined an all-female band - Frantic Spiders - playing bass guitar. We all came from similar backgrounds; working class, no money to spare, buying the cheapest instruments, but determined to have a go. In the back of my mind was one of my favourite bands, the Sex Pistols, who couldn't afford ANYTHING, so stole what they needed! Thankfully, we weren't quite as broke or gutsy. Inspired by the DIY Riot Grrrl scene of the time, we produced our own EP and organised our own gigs.

As an adult I had a reasonably good job in insurance, but later developed repetitive strain injury (RSI) in my hands and was unable to type. My income went down as I had to leave my job, but my love of music continued. I thought a life in catering was all that I had to look forward to, until a friend asked if I would teach her, as she wanted to do things that her current teacher didn't cover. At the same time, another friend asked me to teach her daughter who was getting nowhere with her teacher at school. And, so, began a career in teaching piano, keyboard and brass, which I absolutely love. And just this week, I offered a discount to a mum who can't afford the usual instrumental teacher prices. I don't want to price children out of playing, when I know the joy it brings. Amongst so many other benefits: there's a reason middle class families encourage their children to play instruments.

I am not famous, I am not rich, but I am rich for having music in my life. It is my life and happiness.

Bec Housley
Exeter, Devon – United Kingdom

"Learning to See by Teaching the Blind"

Two years ago, I had the biggest *aha* moment of my life. As a professional singer, I'm often asked to go to schools to sing or talk to students about my career. But, when I was asked to visit the Academy of Music for the Blind and sing duets with some of the students there, I was surprised. A music school for children who are blind? I'd never heard of such a thing." Within a week, I had my visit planned: the kids had requested a few specific songs and I was prepared to perform and teach them.

A tiny five-year-old wanted to sing "Time to Say Goodbye" and a seven-year-old wanted to sing "A Whole New World." Andrea Bocelli AND Alan Menken in one morning? Sign me up!

I walked into the first classroom where the five-year-old boy sat next to his walking cane. The teacher said, "Gavin, this is Rena and she's going to sing "Time to Say Goodbye" with you. The music began, I started my verse in my best fake Italian and my light soprano voice. Gavin's face lit up with a huge smile and, although his eyes had been darkened by blindness, they expressed something that lit up my heart. Gavin's mother sat behind me and I could hear her audibly gasp. Then, he began his verse in a childlike, fun Italian, but hit every note perfectly. We sang together and finished the song, each holding out our high notes till we ran out of breath and broke into uncontrollable laughter. I laughed, because if I didn't, I'd break down and cry. This sweet boy's voice penetrated my heart with a smile that healed any pain I'd ever been hit with. I turned to his mother. "I think I just saw my son fall in love for the first time," she said to me quietly with tears in her eyes. The feeling was mutual.

I went home and did what any normal person would do after a day like that...I cried. How had I never known the depth to which music could reach into a person's soul? I cried, because I felt like I had been leading such a self-involved life up till now. I cried, because I wasn't appreciating my own sight every single day. I cried, because...well...because...I had just met a group of kids who showed me the true power of music.

Two months later, the Academy asked me if I wanted to become a regular voice teacher. "The students have really taken to you," the director told me.

"But, I don't know how to teach voice to blind children? What do I do? I can't do that?" My response was fearful. But, despite my insecurities and doubts, I said YES! I knew that I needed these kids in my life. I finally felt like I had found deep purpose to living in Los Angeles and fighting the fight to be a professional actor.

Why do we sing? Why do we use music to heal? To teach? To communicate? Every week, through my work with the Academy, I feel like my life is enriched and the lives of my students are changed. I challenge them to sing though their fears and connect to what they're saying.

During my first week teaching at AMB I had a student, Jenny, who was 14 years old and had gradually lost her sight due to glaucoma over the past year. She walked in, as shy as could be, her eyes facing the floor and her hands often covering her mouth as she spoke.

"What would you like to sing?" I asked her after doing a soft and easy vocal warmup. "I don't know, I guess 'Part of Your World' from 'The Little Mermaid'. That's what I'm singing in school". And, so, she began. Her voice was tiny, quiet and disconnected. "Look at this stuff, isn't it neat?" she sang.

I stopped her. "How do you feel?"

"Ok, I guess. I don't know. Fine."

"Do you like singing this song?" Do you feel the same way Ariel feels in the movie?"

"Not really," she softly answered.

"I'd like you to go home tonight and listen to someone named Alanis Morrisette. She was really pissed off in the 90s and I have a feeling you might like her. I am giving you full permission to be pissed off in class, OK?" A tiny smile came across her face, but her hands were quick to cover it. The next day, I received an email from her. "Wow! Alanis is amazing! She says some bad words, but I really like her. Can we sing 'Ironic' next week in our lesson?'

The following week, she walked into my room and I swear she had a smile on her face, like she had a secret. 'Are you ready to sing?" I asked. Her eyes faced towards me and she started. "An old man turned 98, he won the lottery and died the next day...". Her voice was steady, strong and had a power that I didn't know she possessed.

Then came the chorus: "It's like rain on your wedding day..." Her voice soared over the keyboard and her head was raised high. Her fists clenched as she got out her own frustrations though this song. She was singing from her heart and I was brought to tears. Her grandmother ran into the room with tears in her eyes, "Was that Jenny? Oh my god! We haven't heard that voice in years!"

Jenny needed to be pissed, to scream at the top of her lungs that losing her sight as a teenager wasn't fair. Once she did that, she found her voice. We have since sung "Isn't She Lovely," "What's Up" and yes, we've even gone back to "Part of Your World."

The best part of all of this, is that, I never have to stop being a singer in order to teach. Not only am I singing in my classes with the students, but I've opened up AMB to the world of public performances. These events serve to raise awareness of blind youth music programs, while greatly boosting the kids' confidence by being on stage and hearing the sound of applause.

At least once a month, I take the stage with Gavin and we hold hands and sing "All I Ask of You" or sometimes revive our now-classic rendition of "Time to Say Goodbye." Other performances, I share one of the truest moments when I sing "For Good" from Wicked with my beautiful student Danielle, who asked me to sing that song with her because of the changes she's experienced in her life. I've even passed on my favorite song "Don't Rain on My Parade" to 12-year-old Dorothy, who once told me "Ya know Rena, so many people at school say I can't do things because I'm blind, but I tell them that's not true, I can do anything!"

My stories of these kids could fill a novel, but I'll leave you with this. These kids have made me very proud. And I'm honored to be part of *their* world.

Rena Strober
Los Angeles, California – USA
www.RenaStrober.com
www.OurAMB.org

What's that one song that gives you goosebumps every time?

"Ricky Remembered"

I grew up in a small town where receiving a strong music education was not only valued, but essential. The music teachers were given an almost celebrity status. The decision to become a music educator felt obvious to me. In fact, it felt like more like a calling than a choice. Even after moving away, I have stayed in close contact with most of my former music teachers.

Several years ago, our choir's tour itinerary had us performing an evening concert in my old hometown. Immediately, I reached out to all of my former teachers, to let them know that I would be in town with my choir. The morning after the concert, we had several hours of free time before we would need to depart for the next destination. I filled this time by confirming a performance at a local nursing home.

As expected, the evening concert was emotional and it gave me great pride and joy to introduce my students to my former teachers. These teachers had taken a special interest in me at an early age and, as a result, had empowered me with confidence and direction. During post-concert discussions, I mentioned that we would be singing at the local nursing home the following morning. I was told that Mrs. Tarbell, my junior high choral director, was a resident there. I was also told that I shouldn't expect a grand homecoming, as she was suffering from the late stages of dementia. I prepared myself and my students for this.

When we arrived at the nursing home, we were escorted to the performance area and told they would be bringing the residents in within the next 20 minutes. When I entered the room, I discovered she was already there - sitting in her wheelchair, looking just as elegant as she did 45 years ago. She had snow-white hair and a face that encouraged and made you want to perform at your highest level. This was the woman who put me on a stage to sing my first solo. This was the woman who saw great potential in me. It occurred to me that, had it not been for Mrs. Tarbell, I wouldn't be standing where I was.

I knelt down and took her hand. "Mrs. Tarbell, my name is Richard Nickerson and I was a student of yours right before you retired." She barely acknowledged my presence. Instead, she stared blankly off in the distance. She said nothing, nor did she show any expression. She was completely detached from the moment. It didn't matter. Even if she didn't know me, I knew who she was. It saddened me to think that, while she had influenced hundreds of young musicians, her life was now confined to a wheelchair - a prisoner of her own mind. I had been through this several years earlier with my own mother, so I knew not to take anything personally.

When the concert finally started, there is nothing that could have prepared me for what followed. From the very first note, Mrs. Tarbell came to life. She was smiling, moving and singing along (to a piece that was in Latin)! I could sense the surprise in my students' faces and it wasn't long before tears were falling.

At one point, Mrs. Tarbell yelled out, "Oh, Ricky, this is wonderful!" I had introduced myself as Richard. Ricky is what she called me 45 years earlier.

For the next half hour, she was engaged and fully aware. After the performance, I went over to her and we had a discussion that I will never forget. While she was very complimentary of the choir's performance, it was how she articulated it to me that was so impressive. She talked about tone quality, intonation, repertoire selection, dynamics and other musical elements. It was, as though, I was having a discussion with a colleague. Just 30 minutes earlier, she didn't know me. I have heard of the power of music on people suffering from various forms of dementia, but to see it unfold in such a dramatic manner, was an experience I will never forget.

Eventually, I made my way back to the tour bus and saw my students had already boarded. When I entered, I noticed that many of them were talking on their phones. So many, that it made me wonder if everything was okay. I found the choir president and asked what was going on. Through tears, she told me that they were all on the phone with their grandparents.

In my 35 years of teaching, this may have been the most significant concert I have conducted. I don't remember how the choir sounded. I don't remember what we sang. In truth, it doesn't matter. On this day, we learned first-hand, what the power of music really is.

Richard Nickerson
Windham, Maine - USA
www.RichardNickerson.com

"A Unique Challenge"

A & G Central Music has been serving students and schools in the Detroit area for over 50 years. One day, we were presented with a unique challenge. We became aware of a student who was struggling to play the clarinet in her middle school band, due to tremors caused by a recent medical condition. Her mother, believing her daughter could never play her beloved clarinet again, asked if she wanted to leave band. The determined young girl steadfastly replied that leaving band was not an option. Inspired by her resolve, we decided to see what we could do to help.

After getting a better understanding of her condition, we brainstormed a bit and came up with a custom modification to the clarinet. We physically redesigned and rebuilt the section where the right hand controls notes on the clarinet in a way that enabled her to still play. We also recommended she begin using a neck strap for added support while playing the instrument.

The following is a letter from her middle school band teacher:

"I cannot thank you enough for what you did for one of my students, after a medical condition left her with a tremor in her hand. Doctors were unable to treat the condition. Her mother, knowing her daughter could never play the clarinet again, asked if she wanted to leave band. When my student said that's not an option, you guys got to work.

After all of the rebuilding you did to alter the right hand of her clarinet, along with the suggestion of using a neck strap, she was so beyond excited to play her instrument again! Donating this new instrument to her family was just over the top. She is, once again, able to play with her friends in band and will have many wonderful memories for years to come, in spite of her uncontrollable condition. Words cannot express how grateful they are."

We are always looking for new ways to connect young music makers with the wider music community, to which they belong. Another time, we heard a number of students were chosen to perform in the Detroit Symphony Honor Band Program, but couldn't afford to participate. We just knew we couldn't let these kids miss out on such a great opportunity.

First, we began our fundraising efforts by asking students from affluent areas to help sponsor one of their peers. Second, we sought out donations from our over-the-counter customers. Anyone making a donation, was encouraged to write a note of support, to be shared with the student who would benefit from their kindness. Our store matched all donations made and we used our social media platforms to help to spread the word. Before long, we were able to help 35 deserving students to participate in the program.

In the end, the connections made between the students from very different backgrounds were, perhaps, even more important than the money raised. Music, once again, proving to be a sturdy bridge able to connect people regardless of their age, gender, socio-economic background or race.

Robert Christie
A & G Central Music
Madison Heights, Michigan – USA
www.SchoolMusicOnline.com

"Saved by Rock'n'Roll"

I was coming home from college to do my laundry, toting a sack of dirty clothes the size of Santa's bag. The sack occupied a seat of its own on the trolley, but it wasn't yet rush hour and nobody complained.

One of the things you have to know, is that I wasn't really a college student. Sure, I was enrolled in classes. Sure, I tried to earn good grades. But, I'd bought a Les

Paul with my student loan, was already playing with my first band and we'd already released our first single. I was no college boy. College was just a place to tread water until I could figure out how to make a life out of writing, recording and performing music.

The trolley stopped in front of St. Anne's School and it was almost time for dismissal. As I ascended the hill and reached the stoplight, sack slung over my shoulder, I saw Mrs. Flynn - the crossing-guard - awaiting the rush of kids. She saw me and had a story to tell.

"Bobby," she said, "Pat (her husband) and I had David hospitalized. He was going to turn eighteen and we just couldn't, in good conscience, allow him to become a legal citizen without trying to find out what's going on with him and trying to help."

David was her youngest, a troubled kid, but not a bad kid. The kind of kid to climb the Columbia Gas tower (drunk in the middle of the night), the kind of kid to ride down the hill on a bicycle with no brakes, the kind of kid to steal his mother's car and crash it through a storefront because she wouldn't drive him to a party. A fun-loving, reckless kid who was given a diploma by his high school, so they wouldn't have to deal with him for another year.

David was prone to mood-swings and acts of rebellion. The hospital in question, was a psychiatric hospital. David would later say, "They put me under ninety days of surveillance."

Mrs. Flynn explained, "Bobby, he just seems to hate everyone and everything. We asked him if there is anybody he likes, anybody he would want to be like and he said YOU. Bobby, he admires you so much."

I have to rewind a little bit here. When I was about fifteen, my own family disintegrated. During this time period, my dad was a violent drunk and my mom ran off to escape. Some of the kids in the neighborhood had seen me get into serious fistfights with my dad. I was a good wrestler and he was always drunk, so I always won - but that isn't something a kid should have to go through, you know? This led to a time when I isolated myself. I lived in a room above my grandmother's garage, avoided people at all costs, missed a lot of school and spent the bulk of my time alone in my room, playing my guitar.

I walked out of school one day, went to the mall, paged through the music magazines at a newsstand and came across a photo of Lou Reed and Miles Davis with a caption about an "underground legend." Intrigued, I bought a Lou Reed album with lunch money I'd saved and, when I got home, I heard a song that said, "Her life was saved by rock'n'roll."

Hey! Me, too! My life was saved by rock'n'roll. My friends abandoned me. My family abandoned me. My church couldn't have cared less. But, I could live in this little fantasy world - me, my guitar, my records and my dreams. When I had nobody and nothing, I had music.

And now, here I was accomplishing something with my life, in David's eyes, at least. I'd come through the dark times, was playing in a band, doing my own thing in my own time and I'd become somewhat of a role-model for David.

A few months later, my band did a show at a public square in downtown Pittsburgh. David took the trolley to the show and we let him come up on stage for our encore, a version of Lou Reed's Sweet Jane. David played my Les Paul.

That was a long time ago. David passed away recently, God rest his soul. Mrs. Flynn's confiding in me that day at the stoplight set off a chain of events: I understood that I had a responsibility to look after my young friend. In years to come, I would continue to write and play music, David would be part of our "inner circle" and he would eventually buy a Les Paul of his own (now in my possession). David went on to teach himself how to paint, his signature - DAF, short for David Allen Flynn - affixed to his paintings. Every time he had an opening or was part of a gallery show, he asked me to perform.

Throughout his life, David had numerous breakdowns. He'd find himself back in a psychiatric ward, sometimes delusional. I visited him one time and the nurses warned that he'd been mechanically restrained in his gurney, because he'd been throwing things and threatening violence.

"Can I see him?"

When I entered his room, David calmed. I could see the wheels turning in his head as he tried to force himself into lucidity and find the words to greet me. He was silent for a few minutes then said, "I shook Lou Reed's hand!"

The nurses observed. "We won't be needing these anymore, will we," one asked as she removed the restraints.

"No, I'm not going to hurt anybody," David assured her.

I lost count of the number of times David suffered a mental collapse and had to restart his life with nothing. People would say he should live in a group home, but David told me, "I don't want to end up playing Pictionary with a bunch of schizophrenics."

David had a plethora of health-issues. Dizzy spells led to falls, fractures, infections. One time, doctors warned that he would never get out of bed again. They said he'd never again eat solid food or walk. But, the kid was dang-near indestructible.

About a week before he died, he called me. He didn't have much to say, having been somewhat of a shut-in for most of the preceding year. I set the phone down and played a little concert, all of his favorites, songs that might be too abrasive or too personal for the average listener, but healing and sustenance for people like David and me.

I hope someday you get to see some of DAF's paintings. Beautiful, tortured, honest. I'd like to think the same could be said about some of my music. Music saved my life and, maybe my music helped to save his, at least for a while.

None of us will live forever, but maybe some of the art will stick around to show how we toughed it out, survived and did what we could with the time and talent we had.

Robert Andrew Wagner of The Little Wretches
Philadelphia, Pennsylvania - USA
www.LittleWretches.com

"Learning to Live in the Moment"

Heat. Humidity. My hands are slipping on a cart loaded with boxes of ukuleles. I've arrived at the Francisco Bangoy International Airport in Davao del Sur, Philippines.

I barely make it past customs. Why so many instruments? My pleas in English and my mother's bossy Visayan, interspersed with the English word "Donation! Donation!", cause the customs agent to relent. The agent looks about nineteen years old. Outside, there is a small convoy of relatives to pick me up in true "pinoy" style.

We drive through the congested city of Davao and into the country. The ride to my mother's house in Digos takes over an hour. Coconut trees. The ocean. The beauty of the land is juxtaposed with the poverty I see all around. Condensed shacks on the waterfronts with rusty, corrugated steel as the roof. Piles of trash burning in front of homes. Children playing with tires in dirt lots strewn with discarded plastic.

This is my mother's homeland and where her heart will always be. And it is the place where I have brought instruments to teach children how to play. I have very little time to be there, so the class will take place the next day.

15 kids are present in the first group. They wear their best clothes. I suspect that some of the ill-fitting dresses have been borrowed from others. Some have walked. Some have squeezed onto each other's laps in motorcycle taxis. One child arrives on the family motorcycle, firmly wedged between his father, who is driving, and his mother, who is holding an infant. None are wearing helmets.

The things we call necessities in the United States are luxuries here. With most families earning only a few dollars a day, even a budget ukulele would cost a family two to three weeks worth of wages. In this country, "cancer" is called the "rich man's disease". The rich know when they have it, because they can afford a doctor to diagnose and treat it. The poor simply die.

"I don't know how you're going to teach all these kids at once" my mom says, looking concerned. She arranges and rearranges chairs. I don't know how to explain it. It's our universal language... music.

"Mom, this is what I do."

Once the children are all seated I hand out the ukuleles. I remember each donor and try to match the donor with a child I see. The smiling, mischief maker gets the ukulele donated by a gentleman with sparkly eyes from the uke club. A quiet, withdrawn child gets a uke donated by another thoughtful student from San Diego. The children clap and cheer as each one is given away.

Now, the learning begins. I lead the children through call and response, making funny noises using my voice. *"Whhheeeeee!"* *"Whhhoooo!"* *"Chug-a-chug-a!"* They're locked in. We move to the ukes. This string *"TWANG!"* That string *"TWANG!"* I just need three notes and we've got "Mary Had a Little Lamb."

I work my way around. I put them into groups. The ones who are quick to learn get separated first. Their little shoulders square up with pride as they move to the more advanced "Happy Birthday" song. The others work hard when they see what's happening. Soon, they are all in their own groups. My ear picks up a child attempting a few chords on the music photocopy I provided. I look and see the child showing the others what she's found. There we go.

It really came down to those few hours. From here, they will learn from their friends and teach the others, each child discovering something new and sharing it. Teachers are only the guides. Here is the path. Here is your instrument. Go.

In the days after the class, my mother and I walk through the city market. There are the eggplant sellers, the banana ladies, the boy hawking fruit from the back of the family truck. Seller after seller has their product out on sheets. Tarp, if they're lucky. They offer okra, onion, oil in plastic bags, used clothing, dried fish. Some of the more prosperous merchants have wooden booths. Fruits and vegetables are colorfully displayed. Charcoal is sold in small plastic bags.

The market stretches on and on. There is no shortage of places to buy rice, fish, or fruit. It's late at night and the marketplace is still alive. Motorbike taxis clog the roadway and young people are hanging out with their friends. Although it's a school night, children are huddled on the sidewalks near their parent's stalls.

I wonder about these children, the ones in the marketplace late at night, the ones playing with tires in empty lots. Driving past their homes, my mother explained how large families live in bamboo huts. The word "America" is said in reverent tones by many of the children. America is where you can earn money and buy things.

In my mother's country, there are many people who don't think much beyond the day they are in. Why bother? Who knows what will happen next week? Today we need rice. Today we have no meat. Tomorrow is far away.

So, when a child here receives a ukulele, all their thoughts and feelings are focused on the music. The child is not thinking about whether there will be rice tomorrow or if rain will come through the roof at night. The child is living in the moment with their instrument, each note completely engaging all their senses as they learn to play. All that matters is now. All that matters is music.

This is the lesson given back to me. To be present. To be mindful. To enjoy each note as life sounds it out. Not yesterday. Not tomorrow. Only today.

Robin Jean Sassi
San Diego Music Studio
San Marcos, California - USA
www.SanDiegoMusicStudio.com

> ## *Playing music helps us live in the moment...*

"Gifts"

The purpose of life is to discover your gift.
The work of life is to develop it.
The meaning of life is to give your gift away.
—David Viscott

Music Seeds International uses music to empower youth affected by poverty, war and disease. It continues to change my life and the lives of all those we connect with. How did it happen? Gifts.

I spent the 80's singing in bar bands before taking my bow in 1987 and moving into TV production. I remember a moment twenty years ago when I stood in a TV studio thinking, "the world is on fire and I am standing here making episodic television that I am not going to watch".

In 2001, I traveled to South East Asia with a camera and an idea for a TV show. 'Earthscapes' would showcase interesting people, in faraway places, doing extraordinary things. I met and filmed a group of entertainers who were travelling around SE Asia doing shows for disadvantaged youth - Dr. Penguins Magic Circus.

I arrived back in Canada to realize two things. One, I didn't have the footage I needed for Earthscapes and, two, I had some amazing footage of a man teaching kids how to juggle, twirl fire and ride unicycles. That man was Steve Groh.

Steve had created the Youth Circus Foundation, a program for street kids at the Mercy Centre in the slums of Bangkok. A place kids could escape to, if just for a few hours, and leave feeling like they could do things they never dreamed of. He was on fire with passion. It was his gift.

As a videographer, I knew what he needed. Without telling him, I created a promotional video for his foundation. My gift.

Later that year I gave him the CD, telling him it was just some footage from my previous trip. He called me soon after, thanking me profusely. "This is exactly what I need to show people my work." From that point on, whenever I transited though Bangkok, I was a welcomed guest and friend at his home. Steve would wake up with the energy of a man possessed and come home sweaty and dirty with a smile on his face as wide as the Mekong River. I wanted what he had.

In late 2006, Steve called me to ask me if I would like to come to Kamandu, Nepal. A philanthropist had discovered his work and wanted to fund his program as part of their educational work there. I jumped at the opportunity and asked if I could I help with his circus program.

He agreed, adding, "why don't you create a program of your own; music perhaps?" I hung up the phone. My life was about to change in ways I could not yet know. I sat down and began designing a music program for kids. Another gift.

In early 2007, Steve called to say we were going. We landed in Kathmandu in May and began our journey at Shree Mangal Dvip (SMD), a boarding school for Himalayan kids whose villages lack schools and electricity. Steve introduced me to the Director, Shirley Blair. I told her my plan and explained that I had never tried anything like it. She said, "don't worry, the kids will know what to do". She called a girl over that was playing nearby. "Sri Jana, this is Ross, he is here to do a music program. Could you please find some students for tomorrow?"

The next day Sri Jana brought thirteen girls with her. The school accountant Niraj, also a music aficionado, asked if he could join us, and altogether there were sixteen of us. While I had an outline of what I was going to teach, I surrendered to whatever powers might guide us.

So, we began. The students chose a topic and a language to write in. The lyrics began appearing on the white board. With a little guidance, the students began writing a song that would become an epic hit at the school - 'Bring Back Peace'. After 10 years of civil war, this was the message they wanted to share with the world. Their gift.

Each day, I left the classroom on cloud nine, continuing to write out class plans that went mostly unused. The information I needed to convey was streaming from a source unseen. The music for 'Bring Back Peace' came to me effortlessly and, when I played it, the students were thrilled. As we worked out the melodies for them to sing, the excitement ramped up.

I will never forget the day the students sang their finished song, as I played guitar and sang along. The stillness when it ended as they glanced at each other - that triumphant instant suspended in the room. For a moment, no one believed it and then, at once, all of them realized it. Realized they had created something very special from nothing. Then we sang it again, again and again. Their gift.

The magic continued.

A man I met at a local restaurant found us a recording studio that donated its' space and time. After a few more days of rehearsal, we piled in a van and went on one heck of a field trip. Steve videotaped the day and, once we saw the kids singing, we knew there had to be a music video - not just a song. A woman I met in Thailand a few months before, sent money for DVD's to be printed. A radio DJ played the song on her show, so the kids could hear it on the airwaves. When they performed it for the school, their mentor from Roots 'n Shoots Nepal, Jane Goodall, was in attendance.

Steve met his sponsor in Bangkok months later and insisted he watch the video, before anything else was discussed. That day, the first funding for Music Seeds International appeared from a man whose mission was to share the gift of education with the children of Nepal, Mr. John Cook.

Over the last 14 years, Music Seeds International has created 35 music projects in eight countries, all available on our website. The most recent project was the creation of an after-school guitar club at SMD and the students' latest song 'Pray for the World'.

"To know the value of music, imagine a world without it. "

Ross Green
Music Seeds International
Calgary, Alberta - CANADA
www.MusicSeedsInternational.com

"Fulfilling a Commitment to My Parents"

We are enrolling more and more adult students in music lessons. I always like to know more about their story and what was the catalyst that caused them to act on their musical interest. Recently, a middle-age man called to enroll for drum lessons. Later, I bumped into to him at a local restaurant and asked him what caused him to pick up the phone and call about lessons. His response was jaw-dropping. Here's what he told me:

'I decided it was time that I fulfilled a promise I made to my parents. When I was a teenager, I begged my parents for drums and promised that I would learn to play. They kept their end of the deal by providing me with the drum set, but I never followed through on my end of the agreement. Even though that was 30 years ago, I decided I needed to honor my commitment to them. I also needed to do this to show my son the importance of being true to your word and faithful to the promises you make to others.'

That was a 'Drop the Mic' moment.

This Too Shall Pass

My earliest memories center around singing. I'm not sure if I actually remember being four years old and making the living room my performance stage, or possibly it's the old black & white, 8mm home movies I've seen so many times. Either way, singing has always been my favorite musical expression.

I also remember, as an 8 year old, being outside mowing the yard while singing my favorite gospel hymns from church at the top of my lungs. It didn't matter the place or the audience, I loved singing! It seemed as if I just couldn't contain the song that was in my heart. I...just...had...to...sing.

To supplement singing, my parents provided me with piano lessons. I was ok at piano, but passionate about singing, at least until puberty hit. Initially it didn't matter when my voice cracked or when I had discovered some lower notes I didn't realize I could hit. I was ok with who I was, until some girls from school made a comment that almost changed my life forever. They said,:

'Russ...we've got some good news. We've actually found someone who sings worse than you do!'

My heart sank, my confidence was shattered and even as I write this story 50 years later, my eyes fill with tears as I re-live the pain and devastation of how those words made me feel.

At that moment, I vowed never to sing in public again! I walked away from the joy of singing and substituted my love of singing with my mediocre piano skills. Sure, piano was still fun and rewarding, but it never filled the void left in my heart that singing had always filled.

In middle school, I opted to participate in band rather than choir. Little did I know that the instrumental skills I was developing would prepare me for my future. All I knew was that I was substituting instrumental music for my true passion for singing.

Three years on the other side of puberty, fast forward to my freshman year of high school. I will forever be indebted to our school choir director, who also happened to be the music director at my church, Mr. Don Davis. For some reason, he identified some untapped potential in me and invited me to audition for the high school choir. I was terrified. Would I actually have the courage to let someone else hear me sing and risk the possible disappointment of being labeled as a 'terrible singer' again? In a moment of 'all or nothing', I signed up for an audition.

Much to my surprise, he not only accepted me into the choir program, but I was only one of two incoming freshmen that were placed in the Select Mixed Choir. From there, I auditioned for the All-Region Choir and made it. Next was the All-State Choir try-outs and to Mr. Davis' surprise, as well as mine, I was the first freshman boy from our school to ever make All-State Choir.

After that came the opportunity to audition for the America's Youth In Concert, All-Nation Choir. I'll never forget coming home from school and meeting my mom at the door. In her hands was an envelope with the audition results. Upon opening it I read these words, 'You have been accepted to join 500 other vocalists and instrumentalists....'. I honestly don't remember what the rest of the letter said. All I knew was that I finally felt validated. I realized that I had a voice that could draw people to my music rather than repulse them away. This afforded me the opportunity to sing with some of the best singers in the USA and in some of the most prestigious concert venues in NYC, Washington, DC and throughout Europe.

My destiny was sealed....music was what I was meant to be, to do, and to share with others. After high school I went to college as a music major followed by graduate school where I received a master's in music as well. Throughout my adult life, I have continued to use the vocal and instrumental skills that I learned earlier in life to sing solos, direct choirs for children, teens and adults, and organize community choir programs. I now own a music studio that provides private and small group lessons to over 500 individuals weekly.

I cannot imagine there ever being a time in my life where music will not be at the center. I especially have a tender spot in my heart when I hear of young boys who are dealing with the uncertainty of their changing voice. It's my desire to encourage them to keep singing and realize that 'this too will pass'. I often think about all the personal joy and satisfaction I would have missed if I had listened to the negativity, rather than believing in myself. The doors that have been opened to me through music are memories I will cherish forever. Knowing I can offer the same types of opportunities to others is the best reward of all.

Russ Porter, Director
Rockwall School of Music
Rockwall, Texas – USA
www.RockwallMusic.com

"Handel's Largo"

As a child, I lived in a small town in rural Australia. Like many country folk, we used the radio for news updates and general entertainment and it was pretty much on all day.   A regular program on our local station was the funeral notices. The announcements were bookended by a portion of a musical piece that was referred to as 'Handel's Largo'. Over time, I grew to love this piece and its mournful, haunting nature.

I was well into adulthood when my mother died.   For some reason I could not bring myself to cry when it happened...instead, I felt strangely numb. Some months later, I attended a ceremony to commemorate the 50 Year Anniversary of the end of World War 2. After the names of those who had lost their lives in the war had been read, the music 'Handel's Largo' began to play. Thirty years had passed since I last heard that familiar melody. I suddenly began weeping uncontrollably for the loss of my mother and the grieving process began. Such is the might and power of music...I love that piece to this day.

Sally Shurte
Queensland, Australia

> # *Farmer in the Dell holds his annual board meeting.*

"Wind Beneath My Wings"

In many ways, my best friend in high school was my ninth grade social studies teacher, Mrs. Metz. Music was woven into her classes, with Billy Joel's "We Didn't Start the Fire" released my freshman year, and The Scorpions "Winds of Change" becoming the name of an elective she taught two years later.

The artist she heard me talk about the most, however, was Bette Midler. I had recently seen, and loved, the movie Beaches - a movie that was all about friendship and also featured an incredible soundtrack. I would talk about how much I loved the song "Wind Beneath My Wings", but most of all, how I longed for a friendship like the one depicted in that movie. Although I excelled academically in school, I never had a large social network or a close group of friends.

High school would have been so lonely without Mrs. Metz. She not only embraced my friendship, but also reciprocated it. I looked forward to visiting her classroom after school, the way most students look forward to hanging out with friends during their lunch period. In fact, that classroom became my home at Great Neck North High School. It was a place I could always count on being greeted with a warm smile and, as time went on, a big hug.

After I graduated, Mrs. Metz and I kept in touch regularly and Bette's music was often a part of the connection. When I finally met Bette Midler, after sneaking backstage after a concert, Mrs. Metz was the first person I called. When I met Bette Midler again, and finally got a photo together, Mrs. Metz kept that photo on her classroom desk - telling me whenever she heard Bette on the radio, she thought of me.

Our correspondence continued and intensified throughout my college years, particularly my final year away, as she battled ovarian cancer at the young age of 49. When she died a few months later, in December 1997, I asked my parents if we could have dinner at the restaurant where we occasionally ran into her, as it was too late in the day to stop by my high school.

I remember sitting in that restaurant waiting for a sign which, to me, was going to be a song. I waited and waited as other tables finished, my hope for a musical connection diminishing as our meal progressed. Until finally, we were the last ones left in the restaurant. We were just getting up to leave, when "Wind Beneath My Wings" came on the radio. Twenty three years later, I still get tears in my eyes remembering that moment, genuinely believing she sent me that song as one final gift.

The following week, when I spoke at her memorial service in our high school auditorium, I quoted that song's lyrics. And for years to come, whenever I heard Bette Midler on the radio, I felt the gift of connection to my dear teacher-turned-friend-turned-Wind-Beneath-MY-Wings.

Sally Wolf
New York, New York - USA
www.SallyWolf.com

"What Was Lost Is Now Found"

In 2010, the Caribbean nation of Haiti suffered a devastating earthquake. In the densely populated capital of Port-au-Prince, everyone lost something and some lost everything. Over the course of multiple volunteer trips to Haiti with J/P HRO (now known as CORE: Community Organized Relief Effort), I came to know some of those people who lost so much. But what struck me the most was not the sense of loss, but rather the demonstrations of strength and resilience.

One of those people is a girl named Abigaëlle Jose. Jose's life is not only defined by what she lost, but also by what she found: the healing power of music.

When the earthquake struck Port-au-Prince, Jose was just seven years old. At the moment the Earth began to tremble, Jose sat reading her Bible with her brother and sister. Amidst the chaos of the powerful 7.0-magnitude earthquake, Jose's mother acted quickly, grabbing her children and rushing them outside to safety, just as their home collapsed behind them.

Like many families in her neighborhood of Delmas 32, Jose's family lost their home and nearly everything with it. After spending the night at a local church, unsure of what the future might hold, Jose and her family moved into a makeshift tent city on a golf course in Delmas. Conditions were difficult as the camp's population ballooned to nearly 45,000. This transitional plan seemed all but permanent. Her family's precarious life in the tent city continued for three years, until at last Jose's family moved into their rebuilt home.

But just as life began to regain some normalcy, tragedy struck once again. While Jose was at the playground with friends, she began to feel a pain in her heart and immediately ran home. Her neighbors had gathered outside her home. Embracing Jose as she approached, one of her neighbors told her that her mother suffered a heart attack and died. "I never saw my mother again," said Jose.

The twin losses of home and family grew too heavy to bear, and Jose withdrew into herself. Her easy smile faded, and dark days passed.

But one day, she heard about after-school music classes. Drawn by the promise of learning to play music, Jose signed up and immediately gravitated to the piano, enchanted by its sound. Slowly but surely, she regained her smile. For Jose, the music lessons were transformative. "At school, I learned geography and history, but what I learned during the music lessons was far more important. I am optimistic again, and I have a lust for life."

I'm happy to report that Jose is now 17 and thriving. She says that music creates positivity and takes away sadness. She has committed her life to music and one day dreams of attending a conservatory and running her own music school. Jose's story, like so many others, inspires us every single day. I can think of no better way to illustrate the purpose and impact represented by the work we do every day at Music Heals International.

Adapted with permission from an interview and story by Karel Van Mileghem, featured in the book "Paradise City: Healing Cities Through Music"

Sara Wasserman
Music Heals International
Mill Valley, California - USA
www.MHInternational.org

"Music has always been incredibly cathartic for me, whether it's writing my own stuff or singing other people's music; it's very freeing."

Sarah McLachlan
www.SarahMcLachlan.com

"Forever in the Air Tonight"

Two days after our annual DRUMSTRONG event to BEAT cancer in 2010, I received an email from a Nashville session drummer, who had recently moved to Charleston, South Carolina. He told me about a young student of his who was a great 11 year old drummer and was dealing with his 5th cancer battle. He relayed that Ryan had real heart and skills, but the disease and treatment protocols had adversely affected his muscles and memory. And that his time with us was very limited.

I immediately called Ryan's teacher Daniel, who said he was sorry that the family had missed the main event. He also said Ryan knew about DRUMSTRONG, so maybe he would gain some comfort knowing that we were supporting him with our rhythm and, perhaps, have me send a DS cap, t-shirt or sticks.

Before I even got off the phone with Daniel, I was packing the truck with drums and began organizing a family, friends and neighbors drum circle at their home several hours drive south of Charlotte. I called Ryan's dad, Charlie, to ask who the young drummer's fav tub-thumper was, hoping I could possibly get them to acknowledge Ryan somehow. Finally, I rearranged my family's trip to 'get-away-from-the-crazy-28+ hr-non-stop-festival' we'd just completed and prayed Ryan would be there. My loose plan, was to facilitate a fun family picnic/drum circle and have his dream drummer call him at noon.

The answer to my fav drummer query was "Phil Collins" and I'm thinking, "Crap, how am I gonna get to Him?!" So, I start the ask. Luckily, through Peter Erskine (on our Board of Advisors), Pat Brown, John DeChristopher, to DW drums, to Zildjian, to ProMark, to Steve Orkin, to Chester Thompson, to Phil...he got the message. Phil didn't call, but he emailed this message for Ryan:

'Hi Steve, got your messages from a variety of sources!!! Chester Thompson for one. I can't call Ryan, but please pass this message on to him, from me':

"Dear Ryan, they say a person can be measured by the friends he has. If that's true, then you are a very, very nice young man!!! I've heard about you from quite a few of my friends and fellow drummers. I've heard that lady luck has not dealt you a fair hand and you're in ill

health. I also hear, that you are a formidable drummer! One of my " spies" also tells me that you are a bit of a fan of my music. This is very brave of you to own up to such a thing! So, I would like to take this opportunity to thank you for listening and spreading the word.
You must feel very proud to be so young and to have so many good friends all rooting for you. I want you to count me in that list of friends.

Although I can't be there in person at your Drum Circle on Sunday, I will be there in spirit. I'm currently rehearsing in Switzerland (where I live) for a few shows in late June, therefore, I'm tied to the spot.

It's obvious that you've been incredibly strong these last few months and, for someone your age, that is doubly impressive. I wish you a fantastic Sunday Drum Circle and may all your days be spent with a smile on your face, knowing how many lives you have touched.

For news of you to have reached me in the darkest outback of Geneva...you know you're cool!
Hang in there buddy and know we're all praying for you."

Your friend always...Phil C

A number of calls and emails went back and forth, between Ryan's parents (Charlie & Jackie), myself and all those who made it possible:

From Charlie on June 2nd:

"THIS IS AWESOME! I just read the letter to Ryan with one of Phil Collins' CD's playing. He was absolutely amazed that he received it. Of course, Jackie and I were both crying our eyes out as I read it. When I look at the list of names attached to this e-mail trail, I truly do realize a lot of people took this to heart, to make it happen. The Post family will always be grateful to all of them."

Sincerely,
Charlie, Jackie, Charlie III and Ryan Post

Ryan passed 5 days later.

From Charlie on June 8th:

"Scott, I don't know if word has reached you, but Ryan passed away yesterday at home with his family around him. We are so glad he had the opportunity to meet you. The drum circle at the house was one of the highlights of the last few days he was with us."

From Jackie:

"I can't express the joy that email brought Ryan. I truly wish I had a camera pointed at him when he realized who this email came from! It was the best smile ever. It brings a smile to me every time I hear a Phil Collins song and every time I remember you all coming over and drumming with us. You put it together in such a short time. I will always treasure those moments! "In the Air Tonight" was the last thing Ryan heard before he left us."

Scott Swimmer – DrumsForCures
DRUMSTRONG Co-Founder and President
Charlotte, North Carolina - USA
www.PlayMoreDesign.com
www.DRUMSTRONG.org

"My Friend, Maria von Trapp"

Sometimes I just want to pinch myself to see if things are real! Like the time I got to work with the real Maria von Trapp!

I remember seeing "The Sound of Music" when it first came out, in 1965. I was going to Temple University at the time, studying to be an early childhood teacher. When I saw the film, I loved the music, I loved the story, and I decided: I want to be just like Maria when I'm a teacher. In fact, when I became a teacher in the fall of 1967, the very first song I taught my kindergarten class was *"Do Re Mi."*

As life continued, there was always an ongoing thread for me – my love of kids and music. My journey took an unexpected path after I stopped teaching and became a mom. I volunteered at Please Touch Museum, Philadelphia's children's museum and learned the field of public relations. In fact, I was hired as their first PR Director. After that, in 1984, I started my own business with Sesame Place, America's only theme park based on Sesame Street, as my first client. That relationship lasted 26 years. It was such a joy for me.

In 1992, Franklin Mills Mall in Philadelphia hired my firm to do PR. They wanted us to publicize an artistic exhibition called "Vienna in Concert". I remembered the von Trapp family had lived in Salzburg in Austria, not far from Vienna. I also knew they now lived in Stowe, Vermont and thought 'how amazing it would be if a member of the family was our special guest at the opening'. We sent them a letter inviting them and, I couldn't believe when Wilhelm von Trapp called and said he couldn't make it, but maybe his sister Maria could come! Sister Maria? That confused me, until I researched and learned she was the second oldest daughter of Georg von Trapp. Another Maria! The names in the play and film were changed to avoid confusion about two Marias. I was so thrilled when Maria said, "Yes".

The day of the event arrived and my client asked me to hire a limousine to pick her up at the airport. We talked a bit while driving, and I got up the courage to ask her about her stepmother, Maria. I remember like it was yesterday. I asked, "Were you close with your stepmother?" She said, "Maria was a genius ... and you know how geniuses can be!" ... (Um, I really didn't know, but it was a clue about their real relationship.)

We arrived at Franklin Mills Mall, and my client handed Maria two dozen red roses. They were beautiful. I introduced her to people at the reception and then we were asked to be seated. During the program, five members of the Philadelphia Opera Company sang selections from "The Sound of Music". My brother and I always loved the song, "Edelweiss" and there I was, sitting next to Maria Van Trapp listening to a beautiful rendition. When they finished, I turned and whispered to Maria, "Do you like this song?" She said ... "Not really." (I laugh just remembering that.) Then, I had the idea that Maria should thank the singers. She said she didn't like to speak publicly, and would only do it if I came with her. So of course, I did.

I said to the singers and the crowd, "Maria loves your voices and she would like to give each of you a rose." (She was still holding all those roses!) So, she handed each singer a rose and thanked them individually.

When the event was over, Maria wanted to go to her hotel and relax for the night. The next day was Sunday, and it was my "job" to occupy her time until she took a 4 p.m. plane to Baltimore. No burden there!

Sunday was another magical day. It started with brunch and Maria and I were joined by my daughter, Hope, 17 at the time and now my business partner, and my brother Barry Stupine. We talked more about her family and we learned some of the REAL story of the von Trapp Family. Ready to hear? First, Maria - her stepmother - was not responsible for bringing music into the house. They always had music. She does get credit for teaching them part-singing. Second, her father did blow a whistle for the children, but only because the gardens were so large, not for discipline purposes. Third, and I hate to tell you this – they did NOT climb a mountain when they left Austria. They took a train. Fourth, Do you know why they left? While their father was definitely against the Nazis, they left Salzburg because their American agent booked them to perform in America. Do you know where? In Philadelphia!

Now the story gets more interesting. Brunch was over around 11 a.m. and we had so much time before Maria needed to be at the airport. Maria had a request and said, "I'd love to find the house where we lived. It was in Merion, Pennsylvania. Could we try to find it?" Since I love a good adventure, I was happy to go. Hope and I went.

I grew up in West Philadelphia, a section called Wynnefield, directly across from Merion. When she told us the street, I knew exactly where it was. We drove to the street where she lived and we found the house. There were actually two homes owned by Merion lawyer Henry Drinker, Jr. – one where was his mother lived before she died and a larger one across the street where the Drinkers lived. Mr. Drinker lent his mother's house to the von Trapp family with one stipulation. One Sunday a month, they had to perform in his ballroom. That was no problem for the family.

When we found the house, Maria was so excited to see it. Her family lived there from 1939 to 1942, 50 years prior. We knocked on the door and the current owners were home. They were so gracious and seemed to know the von Trapp Family connection to their home. They invited us in and gave us a tour. As it turned out, they were art collectors – I saw pieces of work I studied in art history and more contemporary art I had admired in museums.

When we got to the ballroom, my daughter exclaimed, "Mom, it's the keyboard from the movie 'Big!'" And, it was. The owner is an attorney and represented the designer of the keyboard, Remo Saraceni. There we were, Hope in her jean shorts and Maria in her housedress staring at that oversized keyboard on the floor. It didn't have much impact on Maria. She hadn't seen the film. But, the vision was priceless. There was also a grand piano in the room. She remembered many Sundays when her family sang there.

After that incredible experience, we took Maria to the airport. I was so sad to say, "Goodbye." I felt like we had become fast friends. She actually gave me a copy of her book about her family and I gave her a copy of one of my books.

I have always loved Broadway, musical theater, and was fortunate to have the Merriam Theater as a PR client for 16 years. We publicized their Broadway tours. In the year 2000, the "Sound of Music" was being presented at the theater starring television and film idol Richard Chamberlain as Captain Georg von Trapp. Richard is also an artist, so I thought he and the cast might like to visit the home where the von Trapp lived in this Philadelphia suburb. I actually called Maria and asked her to visit, but she wasn't available. She sent me a note and said, "You are the best representative our family could have." Can you imagine? We had that special visit with the cast and Richard Chamberlain and, this time invited the press! The Inquirer did an exclusive print story on it. Television came as well.

A few years later my family went skiing in Stowe, Vermont and my daughters and niece came with me to visit Maria. She was as wonderful as she had been during her Philadelphia visit. She died last year at the age of 99. She lived a long, fruitful life.

It is totally surreal for me to say, "Maria von Trapp was my friend."

Sharla Feldscher
Feldscher Horwitz Public Relations
www.FHPublicRelations.com
www.KidFunandMore.com

"The Sound of Music"

When my daughter was 3 years old, we were driving in the car and, instead of listening to *Radio Disney* or the Beatles (who she thankfully delighted in), I decided to introduce her to a genre of music she wasn't yet familiar with: Classical. First song up was Samuel Barber's "Adagio for Strings," performed by the London Philharmonic Orchestra.

It was extremely quiet in that back seat for a while. But soon, my toddler inquired, "Mama, what kind of music is this?" *Ah...*I thought. *Good. She's paying attention.* I said, "This is called classical music, honey."

As we drove a little farther, I thought I heard whimpering coming from behind me. When I turned around, I saw tears streaming down some very red cheeks. *What had happened in-between last we spoke and now?* "What's the matter, honey?" I asked. She was sobbing. "Oh mama, classical music is *so* sad."

Yes it is my girl. Yes, it is. She was clearly overwhelmed and bewildered, having just discovered something new and intense about the world and its offerings — sound and harmonics are powerful.

Out of respect for the full experience, I let the piece conclude, and then switched the station to something less provocative: Radio Disney.

It's never pleasant to see your child cry. I was, however, relieved that she was receptive. That even at the tender young age of three, she had the capacity to be moved so deeply. This is what we *want* art to do for us all.

When she calmed down, we had our first of what would be many spirited conversations about what music is, how it colors, shapes and enhances our mood. How it can bring us pleasure or make us cringe. How it allows us to express and receive passion in a language without words.

It's no wonder Samuel Barber's "Adagio for Strings" is the piece that often accompanies the televised footage of the falling Twin Towers. It's not like we needed to be any sadder or more horrified than we already were. But, if there *was* to be accompaniment, this was the quintessential solemn piece that could usher us through what had happened on 9/11 and help us connect with, and therefore process our grief.

Music shifts us. Changes our perspective. Opens our eyes. Our hearts. It elicits feelings we've only been on the verge of. After a song is over, we feel differently than how we felt before it started. Whether it be wanting to dance, laugh, scream or cry.

I'm listening to "Adagio" as I write this, not because I'm writing about it, but because its essence is tugging at my heart and, therefore, it's easier to express myself.

I know just how my (now 23-year-old) daughter felt that day in the car. I don't regret choosing that station. Over the years, we've shared many a genre with each other while driving together...Sheryl Crow, Vance Joy, the score to *Cinema Paradiso*, the soundtrack to *Les Misérables*, Motown, my favorite '70s playlist, Bon Iver and Taylor

Swift - we've co-experienced the gamut of emotions these various selections have brought forth.

That said, I'm concerned for the next generation of Samuel Barbers and Sheryl Crows. How lucky, that in this modern age, technology has made it possible to listen to as much music as we desire. It's like an all-you-can-eat buffet...whenever and wherever we want it. But, technology is a double-edged sword. The digital business model has been catastrophic for the creator, hijacking reliable income streams. Songwriters are paid a micro percentage of a penny on a stream. Music delivery services exist because of music and, yet, the composers who create it are being thrown under the bus.

As someone who has made her living from penning pop songs for over 25 years, it's been painful to witness fellow colleagues throwing in the towel, because they're no longer able to sustain themselves and their families. Where does this leave those of us who have put in our 10,000 hours, survived ruthless rejection and struggled for decades to make it?

Organizations like SONA, (Songwriters of North America) are passionately fighting back to preserve the value of music and the people who make it, so that future "Adagios" can be written - so that young children in back seats, whose little hearts are just waiting and willing to be moved - can hear their parents explain what a powerful force is the sound of music.

Art is like a flower. If we don't water it, nurture it, support it and respect it, it will perish. Of course, we could exist without music. But life would be as bland as food without flavor, sex without love, or a rainbow in shades of gray.

Shelly Peiken
Los Angeles, California - USA
www.ShellyPeiken.com

Happiness is finding that perfect song...

"Assumptions"

In the Summer of 2011, I was invited to bring our band The Slants to the Oregon State Penitentiary. The Johnny Cash fan inside me was so excited, I immediately began planning an outfit that would be all black. That excitement overshadowed everything else, not thinking twice about the waivers we were required to sign in order to perform. They were filled with "hostage disclaimers" to ensure we wouldn't sue if we got shanked, killed or maimed while there. It never crossed my mind, that the idea of sending an all-Asian American band into a prison with one of the largest populations of white supremacists, could be a dangerous one. I mean, I signed similar forms just to perform at high schools.

Things began to change as we arrived and were handed bright orange vests to wear over our clothes. Our singer, Aron, asked if we could take them off mid-concert since our own suits could get quite warm and it was a very hot day. "Sure," the guard said, "but, if something happens out there, those vests let us know who not to shoot." "Yo, can I get two of them vests?," I asked, "I want a backup in case I lose mine."

We continued through security with significant precautions taken at every step. There were bars and armed guards everywhere. The clanging of the doors would echo loudly every time one would open or shut.

Obviously, the place was designed for containment, not comfort. The only thing I knew about prisons, was what I learned from books, TV and movies. But this was before the hit show Orange is the New Black began its run so, at the time, I didn't see the prison industrial complex as a way to perpetuate white supremacy. I only thought about the kinds of people that were sent to a maximum-security prison: drug dealers, murderers, rapists. Was this a good idea?

Eventually, we stepped onto a large field surrounded by tall concrete walls. They called it "The Big Yard." I looked up at the sentry towers, placed strategically around us, with searchlights and mounts for weapons. There was a large running track with a grassy field in the center. At the end, was a small stage with a thin line of plastic police tape stretched across the front. I read the words POLICE LINE DO NOT CROSS. This flimsy plastic tape was the only thing that was going to separate us from nearly two thousand convicted criminals.

"Um...I don't know if they follow those kinds of instructions" I told the guard. "I mean, that's kind of why they're in here, right? They can't follow instructions." He told me not to worry. They had a plan. He said if anything happened, we should drop everything and run through the opening in the chain link fence behind the stage. "Our guys will be stationed there, so once you're through, we can secure the fence." "Ok, let me get this straight", I said. "If something happens, run. You'll be on the safe side and, if we make it through, you'll lock the fence behind us." Did they get this plan from the Walking Dead?

As we started our set, a small crowd began to assemble in the front, while the rest continued to walk around the yard - getting the only hour of outdoor time they'd have for the day. As we continued playing, more inmates began gathering closer to the stage. As we launched into our cover of "Paint it Black," hundreds of prisoners jumped and cheered. It was incredible, watching a sea of orange and blue ripple in front of us. Our little 45 minute set turned into a two-hour marathon of music.

At the end of the concert, I was standing near the edge of the police tape (on the safe side, of course), when a group of shirtless white men began walking towards me. As they got closer, I could see the words emblazoned across the chest of the man in front: WHITE POWER. He and his companions were completely covered in swastikas and white pride tattoos. The man in front walked up to me, blocking out the sun in the process. He seemed nervous as he handed me a piece of paper with a small, sharp pencil.

He asked me for an autograph. I didn't know what to do. I was completely frozen. But, then, he said four words that cut right through me: "It's for my daughter." I turned over the paper. It was a makeshift flyer for our show in the prison. He wanted to tell her that he had met the band. My band. "I know what you must be thinking", he said. "I've made a lot of mistakes in my life and they're ones that I don't want my little girl to make." He wanted to show her that he could learn, that he could change his heart and mind, even if he couldn't change what was stained into his skin.

This was one of the most powerful moments in my life. I went in with all kinds of assumptions, but that all changed with that one brief conversation. For the rest of our time there, I walked around on the other side of the police tape, listening to the men behind bars tell their stories. The music we shared that day truly helped to open them up. The other band members had similar exchanges as well.

I started The Slants, because I wanted to change people's assumptions about Asian Americans. Assumptions can be powerful. However, this deliberate act of claiming an identity was something the government considered to be disparaging, initially denying us the trademark to our band name - something that I fought and won, at the United States Supreme Court.

The government thought they were protecting the public from harm but, instead, they were erecting walls designed to discourage people from mobilizing for social justice by using language to re-appropriate ideas. They used walls to divide us, both within our own communities, as well as outside of them, pitting us against other marginalized groups. They weren't protecting us, they were trying to keep us complacent. They didn't stop to think that art, like glass, can provide crucial social mirrors and serve as a window into what is possible.

Against all odds, those walls came down. But, it all began with a name - and music - worth fighting for.

Simon Tam – The Slants
Cincinnati, Ohio - USA
www.TheSlants.com
www.SimonTam.org

"Human Kind"

When the mayor of Los Angeles ordered a city-wide lockdown in March, due to COVID-19, I assumed it would last only two weeks and everything would be back to normal. Since the shutdown meant that the Hollywood club where I worked as a hostess would be closed, I decided to visit my family in Iowa. In addition to spending time with my newborn niece, I figured I could also wrap up all my pending projects. I had a lot of writing I needed to finish and a protest song I'd been trying to record for months. A fortnight felt like more than enough time to kill two birds with one stone.

Two weeks of abundant quality time with family morphed into long dreadful months of paralyzing anxiety, as the corona virus infections grew to a global pandemic. My productivity level dwindled from writing and singing every day to binge watching episodes of *The Vampire Dairies, Desperate Housewives* and *Law & Order: SVU.* When my eyes needed a break from the screen, I turned into Martha Stewart and spent many evenings in the kitchen, perfecting my meatloaf, scallop corn casserole and baked mac 'n' cheese recipes.

Despair threatened to swallow me whole every time I watched the news or perused social media. Between this explosive election year and increasing deaths from COVID-19, I questioned if I should even bother completing my projects. What was the point? All live events were cancelled indefinitely, so I couldn't perform anywhere. And with the club I worked at still shut down, I had no money to pay for studio time. Even if I did manage to scrape a few coins to spring for a recording session, I felt people were too financially strained to spend money on music. And, besides, I argued with myself that I should have been saving every dollar I could find, in case I got infected at a time when I had no health insurance. I continued to spiral, one harrowing thought after the other. Somedays I felt so defeated, that I spent all day in bed and all night watching TV.

When it seemed as though I was destined for more depressing months, a silver lining popped up in my email in the beginning of September. At first, I thought it was yet another PSA encouraging people to vote or more COVID-19 updates, but it turned out to be a song contest. The organizers of the competition were seeking music with a 2020 theme. I didn't think I had a chance of winning, but I figured working on a record to submit for the competition would help me regain some enthusiasm to complete my forsaken projects.

I abandoned my religious binge-watching routine and made creating a new record, from scratch, my new mission. My screen time turned into hours of producing fresh beats and searching my soul for lyrics to best describe 2020. I allowed my songwriting, pop-singing and lyrical rap skills to travel to places I didn't know lay in my heart. Topics like police brutality, children in cages and deaths from the corona viruses were hard to write about, but I felt empowered singing about them. I chose to name the song "Human Kind", because this year reminded us, that no matter what we go through or how stark our differences may be, the one thing that unites us is that we are all human.

I added a Kiswahili verse as a reflection of my Kenyan background, and also to shed light on how other countries are dealing with the pandemic. I assembled a make-shift studio at my parents' house with only my laptop and a very old microphone. I recorded four drafts of the song on *GarageBand* before I felt it was ready for a studio.

As luck would have it, I was forced to fly back to Los Angeles to handle a few things that had gone unattended due to the pandemic. Though I was running around doing a million and one errands, mask and sanitizer in hand, I was able to find a safe studio. I followed every single precaution: wearing a mask, ensuring the recording booth was sanitized and keeping a safe distance at all times. I recorded into a microphone that smelled like it was doused with an entire can of Lysol. The long journey of the song left me drained, but also proved to be a cathartic experience. The defeat looming over my head for months dissipated and was replaced by hope.

Since then, I've finished all my projects, started posting home recordings on Instagram, entered more contests and made efforts to stay connected with other artists through social media. Even though live performances won't start anytime soon, I've begun rehearsing, as if I have a show to prepare for. I don't know when the world will ever get back to some semblance of normal, but keeping focus on my music is helping me stay strong.

Sonia Grace
Los Angeles, California – USA
www.SoniaGraceOnline.com

"It's Never Too Late!"

I am one of the countless people who really cannot sing. Now, I realize that with some training, I probably could be decent at it. But this is where the story begins.

I was so far off in grade school that the teacher would ask me to not sing, so I wouldn't throw off other singers in the group. I loved music, but even I could hear I was "off key" by a lot – I just didn't know how to correct it.

So, my love of music turned to listening only and enjoying music from a variety of artists in a variety of music styles. Nothing wrong with that.

I started a business career, but did not have a college business degree. I was told, repeatedly, that I was either at a disadvantage or even worse "you won't go far in business with your background."

Well, one thing I discovered about myself at a young age, was that I was driven by challenges of any kind. When I first began my career in business, I was playing soccer and told I was too small or did not have enough playing experience and so on. Sounded like the same old messages to me. So I worked hard, got good coaching and became a college all-star and semi-pro soccer player.

As my business career took off, against all the "odds", I sought out other areas of interest I wanted to explore. First, I wanted to be published and found ways to do that and become a best-selling author. Next, I wanted to do public speaking, no matter how scary it seemed. Again, I sought out help and put in the effort and practice. In less than a year, I was doing a paid keynote address to one of the biggest companies in the world at their annual management conference. It was a real thrill to speak to thousands of people, one I will never forget.

Fast forward, I decided I did not want to continue working for others and started my own business. Again, most people said it was too risky. But I did it, even though I had no idea exactly what I was going to do.

Then finally one day it hit me - I really want to learn more about music. But I wasn't really interested in singing, possibly because of my earliest experiences or maybe not. Either way, I had this internal urge to learn the bass guitar. I loved rhythm and saw the bass as a foundational instrument.

You can guess what I heard, "aren't you getting too old to do that?"

By then, I knew that you are never too old to do anything, so I went after learning the instrument with all my energy. I set a goal (always a good thing to do) that I wanted to be able to play well enough to be in a band in less than 2 years. I found a fantastic instructor and made sure my goal was achievable.

Not only did I achieve that goal, but I even started my own band. I began writing music, generating social media publicity and indie radio station airplay. I love to practice, play, and write music, even though I was "too old" to start, or so people said.

Music is so much fun and affects people in so many positive ways and is now the passion I will follow until I can do it no more.

My message is simple, it is never too late to start anything you want to do! Find your niche in whatever it is, set goals and go after it. And **REPEAT.**

Most of us have hidden talents just waiting to be discovered. *What talents do you have that are waiting to be discovered?*

Maybe it involves Music.

Steve Burgess aka Papa B.™
Southern Oregon – USA
www.facebook.com/DelphiRavens
www.DelphiRavens.com

"Creating Connections in a Pandemic!"

In October 2020, I had the honor and privilege to teach Bollywood dance workshops to visually impaired and blind students. Under normal circumstances, we would have gathered together in one room. But, given that we were in the midst of a pandemic, we needed to connect in the virtual world, via Zoom. Of course, my first thoughts were a mix of excitement and trepidation! How could I make meaningful connections without being in the same physical space with the students?!

The school for the blind had about twenty-seven students, including both children and adults. They were spread out into pods of three students each, along with their teachers and aides, while a few students joined from their homes. The workshops were held twice weekly and lasted for eight weeks. On day one, we settled in with a warm-up routine, and I slowly guided the students with my voice, giving detailed movement cues. Then, we put on music and, immediately, the energy shifted!

The upbeat, foot tapping Bollywood music created instant joy! It didn't matter that the students couldn't understand the words in Hindi; their bodies understood the universal language of beats and rhythms in music! Our warm-up routine became more energizing, all thanks to the music.

After the warmup, we would work on our Bollywood dance choreography. I would provide descriptive verbal cues and occasionally close my eyes while describing a movement. It was humbling to realize that a seemingly simple gesture of hands, folded in the Namaste/prayer position, is unclear unless I could mindfully guide the students to bring their hands in front of their face, palms touching, fingers open and straight.

Once we worked through the mechanics of the dance steps, we put it all to music! Our second Bollywood song was a catchy number the students really enjoyed dancing to. I called out the students' names often, celebrating their progress and cheering them on. Their aides used the power of touch to guide them through some of the movements. We also included dance adaptations for those using wheelchairs. The music even had the teachers and aides dancing!

The most joyful and surprising segment came one day, when two of the students continued dancing, beyond our choreographed routine and began free-styling to the music! The sighted group among us all broke into cheers, while these two enjoyed showing off their moves.

Another beautiful moment was when one of the students, we'll call her J, felt inspired by the music to create her own four-step dance routine, ending with a curtsy. I followed right along and J agreed it would be wonderful to incorporate her piece into our choreography for the virtual holiday recital.

At a time when the pandemic has so many of us feeling isolated, Bollywood music helped cut through all barriers and weave new connections. I remain grateful and awed by the power of music and dance to connect us all!

Swati Chaturvedi
Swedesboro, New Jersey – USA
www.CommunityBollywoodDanceProject.com

"Tracking Down My Musical Past"

My entire childhood into early adulthood consisted of me singing, whether it was at church, on stage at a New York City club or in theaters across the country, when I did my first National Broadway Tour. My family would always wonder where my vocal prowess came from, but I always kind of knew it had to be from my estranged birth father's side of the family. So, in my mid-twenties, I set out in search of him. He left my mother in the early 80's after she told him she was pregnant - even gave a fake middle name on my birth certificate so I could never find him. The good old internet solved that one for me. Found him, emailed him and headed on a flight from New Jersey to Florida to meet him.

After a long, emotional day of meeting my birth father for the very first time, he told me his parents were still alive and were also living in Florida. On the way to meet his parents, he also informed me that my birth grandfather was "a singer". As soon as I walked in the door and locked eyes with my grandfather, I knew he was something special. His broken English had that old time Hollywood flair to it and his smooth tone and the twinkle in his eye told me he was more than just "a singer." He took me to his bedroom and showed me his collection of old records and 45's and played some of the most beautiful music I'd ever heard- boleros. Turns out, my grandfather was a well-known Latin nightclub singer in New York City back in the 40's and 50's. He was invited to sing on the radio with live Latin bands and performed in popular clubs throughout the city with Tito Rodrigues, Tito Puente and many more. The songs he recorded made my heart sing and my eyes water - so emotional, I could barely stand it. I'd always been drawn to the old Broadway standards and show tunes, but this style of live band music moved me in a whole new way.

After returning home, I went into the recording studio and remastered two of his beautiful ballads. I rearranged them as a duet so I could sing along with him on the recording. I learned to sing in Spanish and emailed the recordings to him, as a gift. He absolutely loved them and told me how what I did was very brave - to find the family - and that he was very proud of me. I was very sad when he passed away last year, but I often play his songs to relive the musical memories. They take me to another place – one where I was able to connect with a grandfather I barely knew. I'll never forget him, but will always have his voice. And his music.

Theresa Fowler Pittius
Millstone Township, New Jersey – USA
www.ThePrepNJ.com
www.SocialSidekickMedia.com

> **It's never too late to start playing a musical instrument, and once you do, the LOVE of MUSIC will be with you forever...**

"Forever Our Muse"

John Ryan Pike is the person you thought couldn't possibly exist. Thankfully, for us, he did. We were lucky enough to have known him, to have been inspired by him and finally, to have loved him. He was the perfect balance of compassion, talent, humor and intelligence - all wrapped up in one great package with an infectious smile as a bow.

John passionately pursued all his interests and excelled in many, especially musical composition. He took advantage of every opportunity presented to him and created many of his own along the way, including becoming a founding member of the rock band Ra Ra Riot.

To put it simply, John was a gift. His sudden and tragic death was felt by an entire community of neighbors, supporters and fans. John was an extremely talented musician and songwriter, but for his family and friends, he was so much more. Everyone who knew him felt the need to do something in his memory and to share his gift and love of music with our community. John is, and will always be, the inspiration and driving force behind The Musary. Forever our Muse.

John got his start on the drums at age two! His parents quickly realized his talent as he "played" the pots and pans throughout the house... never just "banged." As a toddler, he graduated to his first Noble & Cooley kit. Everyone thought giving a two-year-old a drum set was a crazy idea, but they quickly changed their tune, once they heard him play. He constantly had music in his head and was fortunate to have such a supportive family that would help his talents soar. This foundation of family support helped lay the groundwork for what The Musary would later become.

Drums weren't John's only calling, as he could play just about any instrument you gave him. He excelled on guitar and piano as well, all self- taught. He was an extremely talented musician, but an even better person. His accolades and accomplishments could fill a novel. He fit more into 23 years than most could even comprehend. At the time of his sudden and tragic death, John had written and recorded over 400 songs! His music can still be heard on the radio today.

John also loved accumulating knowledge and having access to information. He taught himself multiple instruments, graduated Magna Cum Laude from Syracuse University's Newhouse School and even won a blue ribbon at the Topsfield Fair for brewing his own beer. Side note about the beer - he wasn't yet 21 years old and had only read about how to do it. He grew his own ingredients after digging up his mother's garden and, then, won the contest at the oldest agricultural fair in the country - no small feat!

John loved access to knowledge and learning so much, that I'd be willing to bet he was the only rock star on tour that carried a library card. Cross country tour? No problem - every city and town has a library and access to information and activities for learning. Performing on the Late Show with David Letterman? Let's swing by the Guggenheim first or Museum of Modern History. European tour? Let's do this thing internationally! In fact, John once missed an important meeting at a record label that wanted to sign the band because he was at a museum in London with passes he got at a local library.

After his passing, it was clear that the perfect tribute to John would be to combine his two loves - music & the library - The Musary was born in 2008. John has always been and, will always be, the driving force behind our mission - forever our muse. At its core, The Musary is a musical instrument lending library, we lend instruments to anyone in need - no strings attached.

Over the past few years, The Musary has grown tremendously, working to fulfil its mission to spread John's love of music in our communities. After lending only 3 instruments in our first year, we have now reached over 25,000 patrons in over 60 Massachusetts communities, 11 states and 2 continents! Every single one of our patrons has a story that inspires us to keep going. It's the patron that finally has access to the right instrument and doesn't give up; the special needs students at the Beverly School for the Deaf, that fall in love with music; providing instrument opportunities for the most vulnerable members of our community, keeps us going. The idea that, one day, one of our patrons will win the Grammy award that John was destined for - keeps us going.

The Musary was founded on the belief that music belongs to everyone, but we know that certain barriers exist when getting started. The Musary works to motivate, cultivate and inspire people in our communities to get involved in music. Just like John did. Currently, The Musary has a wide variety of instruments looking to be played by some up-and-coming musicians and is always looking for more! We would love nothing more than to spread the passion for music John exemplified to everyone in our communities. So, if you want to help us make some noise, then all we have to say is... Play On!

Thomas Jones
South Hamilton, Massachusetts - USA
www.TheMusary.org

"Who Needs Luck if You're a Gifted Gambler?"

My brother and I learned, at an early age, that nothing in life is free. Something extraordinary can only be achieved through hard work and perseverance. Little did we know, that a lucky chain of events and a night of good fortune, would one day change our lives.

Rainer and I were both classically trained, he on guitar and myself on piano. In addition to our traditional music teachings, we also loved classic rock. Our dream was to make quality rock music at the highest level and, one day, present it on the world stage. "Music without borders", we called it, meaning no external influences to retain creative freedom. We ignored the cynics and naysayers around us, left school and dove head-first into the music business.

Before long, we landed an opening slot for an international artist on tour, adding two friends on bass and drums to complete our lineup. The tour provided us invaluable experience, but we quickly realized good would never be good enough. Virtuosity was required for the level of success we were envisioning. Not only for writing and recording, but for live performance as well. We then set out to find the best musicians we could, who would also share the same passion for our "vision", without losing sight of the importance of family. Honest, hard-working and willing to put integrity of the music before ego. After searching, our music finally founds its voice with Mark, an American rock singer living in our home, Germany. Our band of brothers was completed with Nils, whose taste for hard rock and metal drumming talents, made him a perfect fit.

The next challenge came when we realized that without a budget, producing a recording at industry standards would be especially difficult. We decided to pool our resources, as best we could, and prepared for a long road ahead. Then, just as it seemed as if our path was set, we were faced with a major personnel crisis - one of us needed to relocate due to family health issues. We had come to a crossroads and had to ask ourselves: "Is this it? Must we quit before it begins?"

For weeks, we tried to find a solution. With no answer in sight, we decided to get out of the studio, to blow off some steam. While out, we tried to relax and kept joking about "I bet", a running gag we often shared during rehearsals: "I bet you break a string during the solo", or "I bet you can't sing that an octave up" or "I bet you can't double time that on the hi-hat". As the night drew on, we decided to go to a casino just for the fun of it...this time joking "I bet we win"– and win big, we did!

The next day we all met with clear heads and renewed faith. Taking this amazing event as a sign, we committed to use our winnings to invest in new equipment, complete our studio and give us breathing room to concentrate on the music. We held to our dream, building our own microcosm: self-supporting, efficient and self-contained. With lady luck by our side, for one night, we were able to do it with no label and no producer - retaining the creative freedom that was important to each of us. Any doubts held on to by our naysayers were silenced with the success of our first single and, to date, our music has been streamed on Spotify over 5 million times. A vision first brought us together and faith in our music and each other carried us through. We're more than friends and band members – we are a band of brothers – a family. Despite our one crazy night, we still don't believe in luck. But, we learned from one twist of fate, that you cannot fail if you are a Gifted Gambler.

Thomas Krupka – Gifted Gambler
Neuss, Germany
www.GiftedGambler.com
www.facebook.com/GiftedGamblerMusic

"Kamikaze Karaoke"

Ever since I was a child, I loved to sing. Unfortunately, singing or playing a musical instrument was never permitted by my parents. Attending church became one of my favorite places, because I was allowed to sing there. When karaoke became popular in the 1980s, I began venturing out whenever I could, to sing my favorite songs and watch others perform. As I gained more confidence, I began doing what is referred to as Kamikaze Karaoke. This is when the singer allows the DJ to pick the next song, which may or may not be something you are familiar with. Doing Kamikaze karaoke has allowed me to sing over 6,000 different songs, since I first began.

In 2013, I lost my wife to cancer. To help take my mind off how much I missed her, I began going out to karaoke nights more often. Singing karaoke and watching others perform went a long way towards helping ease my grief. In the winter of 2017, I decided to make karaoke an every-night mission. I started researching venues in the Lansing, Michigan area that offered karaoke on a nightly basis and began making regular rounds. I also became religious about documenting every song I performed. As soon as I finished singing, I would get my logbook out and record the song title, date and location. My karaoke friends and I also started a Facebook page called 'Oke on the Town,' to let everyone know where we'll be each night.

I managed to perform karaoke for 135 consecutive nights before ending the streak on July 5th. I had begun not to feel well and had developed a really bad cough. I ended up spending 24 days in the hospital and, before I was discharged, doctors decided to send me to see an oncologist. In October 2017, I was diagnosed with stage four non-small cell lung cancer. As anyone who has experienced a cancer diagnosis knows, the treatment can be a physical roller coaster. Still, I continued to sing karaoke whenever I felt well enough to go out.

On April 3, 2018, I made the conscious decision to start another streak. With the continuing cancer treatments, I was beginning to feel a little better. From April to November that year, I had no trouble finding a karaoke venue each night. But, with the holidays and winter weather coming up, I was starting to wonder if I would be able to keep going. Then, after Channel 13 in Grand Rapids ran a story about the streak on the 13 ON YOUR SIDE program, a woman from Sparta, Michigan invited me to join their Thanksgiving feast. As it turns out, their family has a karaoke tradition every Thanksgiving. Thanks to their kindness and generosity, the streak was alive. As the weather got colder, it became more and more difficult to keep the streak going. Venues would close down some nights due to the weather, while others stopped offering karaoke, as less people were venturing out to sing. I began to travel much further on some nights, driving as much as an hour away and often in whiteout conditions. The streak, along with my passion for karaoke, kept me going until I finally made it to the Spring of 2019. All the while, my cancer treatments were continuing throughout.

By the time the streak hit the one-year mark on April 3rd, 2019, I began to feel tired. Keeping up the energy to go out every single night to perform, was draining me. I finally made the difficult decision that I needed to voluntarily end the streak before my health forced me to stop. On Sunday, April 7th, I reached out to 13 ON YOUR SIDE to let them know I was ending my streak the next night. They had played a big part in my journey with multiple news stories and I wanted them to be a part of it.

After 372 days, I ended my karaoke streak at The Avenue, a bar along Michigan Avenue in downtown Lansing. Since the streak began, I had sung 1,788 different songs. For my sign-off song, I elected to sing a repeat: "I've Gotta Be Me" by Sammy Davis, Jr, one of my favorite singers growing up. This felt like just the right song to sing that night. The entire streak had been about allowing myself to be me, despite the difficult health journey I was on. A little after 9 PM, I took the stage that night and sang with all the energy I had remaining. And with that, the world's only known consecutive day karaoke streak was officially over at 372 days. All records are meant to be broken and, whether anyone will ever choose to break this one, I don't know.

Tim Beam
Lansing, Michigan – USA.

"Mankind has been drawn to music ever since our primitive ancestors huddled around a campfire. And we still do that same thing today! It touches the soul in ways that are almost impossible to put into words.

Whether it's a melody or phrase of a lyric today, or a flash of a distant memory and experience upon hearing a piece of music, we are inexorably tied to the need to listen to, and enjoy music."

Tim Russ
@TimRuss2
www.TimRussWebPage.com

"Keeping the Beat"

Fifteen years ago, I was pregnant when I was teaching piano. I always kept a strong beat going for my students to practice scales. Suddenly, I became aware of my stomach moving. My little fella was kicking in perfect time to the beat! I tested it out so many times and, each time, the same thing happened.

A few months later, our little Leo was born and diagnosed with Down Syndrome. Starting with his in-utero rhythmic beat, music has been a huge part of his life. He absolutely loves singing, dancing...and playing piano! When Leo was twelve, he played piano and sang on the most popular TV show in Ireland – he brought the house and the whole country down. My little star in so many ways.

Check out Leo's 15 seconds of fame and watch to the end for a good laugh:

Leo Javaherian performs *"We Wish You a Merry Christmas"*
On the Late Late Toy Show:
www.youtube.com/watch?v=aPMJd6MpMuU

Tina Hynes
Kildare, Ireland

"What Will Be Your Defining Moment?"
(excerpted with permission from Todd Rundgren's 2017 commencement address at Berklee College of Music)

The one thing I did know when I was growing up, was that I was a musician, and it was apparent to everyone around me. Unfortunately, I grew up in an environment where that was not necessarily a priority. I was a horrible student. I only wanted to do things that interested me. As soon as I lost interest, I was disruptive and that continued for pretty much my entire so-called academic life. I barely graduated out of high school and found myself on the street. At that point, I had two things I could possibly do. I could try and get a job to make enough money for engineering school so I could learn how to program... that was the other thing I was interested in. Or I could just take my chances on the street as a musician. Fortunately, I found my way into a band in Philadelphia. At the time, I was a guitar player and guitar was my obsession. Literally my obsession, it was the only thing that mattered in my life. I didn't think about songwriting, I had yet to write a song. I didn't feel qualified to be a front man or a singer. The guitar suited me well and I was able to develop enough technique to impress the people around me and got a job in a local blues band. That band didn't last very long, so I started a band called The Nazz, which lasted about 18 months.

By the time I found myself on the street again, I didn't even have a guitar anymore. I was still a musician, but I didn't even have an instrument to play. I took any job I could get. I wound up designing lights in a discotheque and living with clothiers in the west village, which later affected my sense of style by the way. Fortunately, I had left a trail of some good work and was asked to join the Albert Grossman organization, which essentially was a repository for some of the greatest acts in the world.

Albert Grossman was the world's premier manager and they were just starting to get into the record business. They asked me to come in and interface with a lot of older folk acts, who had yet to get updated to the 60s. I got paired up with acts like Ian & Silvia, James Cotton and all of these old legacy artists, as well as some new artists. My big breakthrough was when I was involved in the production of Stage Fright, The Band's 3rd album and, from there, I became a very successful producer.

At one point, I got the bug to make a record of my own, a vanity project. I had no intention of becoming a performer. I just felt I had earned the right to make a record for myself. I was still writing, I was still learning how to write, actually. I made a record that had a minor hit, called "We Gotta Get You a Woman". But, I had no idea what it was like to go out, take my music on the road and perform it for people. When I first performed, I couldn't get through a 20 minute set without blowing my voice out. That's how far behind I was on the performance curve. But I persevered at that, and I persevered at songwriting and, eventually, I had a breakthrough album called "Something/Anything?". And while it had several hit singles on it, the biggest thrill for me was when I met Wolfman Jack, who had a half million watt radio station broadcasting out of Tijuana. He became my champion and that helped me a lot, because he could reach Chicago from Tijuana, which wasn't legal for any American radio station.

So "Something/Anything" was a big boon for me but, then, people started referring to me as the male Carole King. I was a Carole King fan, but it bothered me being compared to somebody else. You don't want to be compared to other people. You want other people being compared to you. So, I went into a complete 180 degree direction on my next record. It was called "A Wizard, A True Star". I was pilloried by the label, as well as the critics, for not following up on the success of "Something/Anything". But, there are two things to keep in mind here. I was a successful record producer, so I didn't have to fret about the success of my own records. And secondly, I started to see music as something different than what I had previously assumed. Up until then, I was writing what everyone else was writing. I had plumed a broken relationship I had in high school for 3 whole albums. And I suddenly realized, that I didn't care about this girl anymore. What am I doing? I also realized there were a lot more things in my head musically, from my experience. My dad hated rock and roll, so we would never have it played in the house. But, I would get to hear Revel and I would get to hear Bernstein and Gilbert and Sullivan. A broad range of stuff, that maybe you didn't get exposed to when you were especially young. But it all got stuck in me and I never realized until that point, that it was all a significant part of my musical make up. And, that I was writing like a hypocrite. So, I made this crazy record "A Wizard, A True Star", and I threw out all the rules of record making. I decided that I would try to imprint, as much as possible, the chaos in my head right onto a record, without trying to clean it up for everyone else's benefit. The result was a complete loss of about half of my audience at that point. Much later, Trent Reznor and other artists have cited that record as being a major influence on them. I have a special pride, for what essentially, was my act of tyranny after having achieved commercial success and this became a model for my life after that.

The irony was, that I never learned anything in high school. But, when I got out of high school, I learned to learn. And, ever since then, I have absorbed anything that can be put in front of me that is of interest. And, so I've learned not only how to expand the range of my musical expression, but I've also learned things like computer programming, video production and other sorts of things, which any of you could easily absorb if you don't leave here thinking that your education is finished.

Today, this appears to be the end of something, but it's really the beginning of something for you. I recognize there's great loss associated with this ceremony, as well as, great triumph. You are saying goodbye to friends who you might never see again in your life. But, the most important thing that you can take advantage of in the world of music, is to see yourself. I eventually got to the point where music meant self-exploration to me, more than anything else. I could objectivize my ideas, listen to them and realize if I was full of crap or not, or whether I might be on the right direction. I encourage everyone here to be brave in that respect. To be fearless in that respect. I have lost the ability to be insulted by critics. You never know the actual impact of what you do today and how it will actually turn out in the future. That album, "A Wizard and a True Star", which was such an abomination to everyone when it came out, eventually became the signature moment in my career. I hope everyone will feel the freedom, and the fearlessness, to undertake that when the time comes, because you may find that that's your defining moment.

Todd Rundgren
Kauai, Hawaii - USA
www.Todd-Rundgren.com
www.SpiritOfHarmony.org

MUSIC is the SECRET sauce
we ALL need in our lives...

"Spread Music Now"

I was recently given the chance to join SpreadMusicNow as Executive Director, a wonderful opportunity that I am very grateful for. I've always admired their mission to help fund high-quality music education, both in and out of the classroom. Our ultimate goal is to help put underserved students on a path to college, career and life success. We are proud to support many organizations committed to improving the lives of our youth and success of our communities through the passionate delivery of music education.

Below are a few student stories from organizations we are proud to partner with. The first is provided by Jess Hogan, a general music teacher at E.B. Kennelly School, which is part of the Hartford Performs program.

Kwaku Darko comes from an amazingly supportive family, who bravely emigrated to the United States from Ghana when Kwaku was just 4 years old. While in Ghana, at the age of just six months old, Kwaku underwent many surgeries for his eyesight. To this day, he is visually impaired - unable to see, except for a tiny tunnel of light. Yet, he has never let this hold him back from doing anything and everything that he sets out to do. I have watched him blossom from a quiet, timid first grader (with a paraprofessional at his side) to a confident, self-sufficient and musically talented young man.

Over the eight years in which I taught Kwaku, he shined as the quad soloist in the school's drumline, while also mastering (with precision) the parts on snare and bass. On his own time at home, he has learned to play the bass guitar, acoustic and electric guitar AND can play piano by ear; he can sit and play any song after just hearing it on the radio! Kwaku also plays saxophone in a brass band at the Charter Oak Cultural Center located in Hartford, Connecticut. This past summer, he gained a full scholarship to attend the renowned West Hartford Summer Jazz Program, where he shined on drums. For fun, Kwaku searches YouTube to sharpen his ear training skills. He'll also spend time creating layers of music tracks on the computer and then plays his guitars or piano along with the tracks; he eats, sleeps and breathes music!

Our second story is about Little Kids Rock alumni, Vincent Molden, a rising 9th grader from Chicago, who credits the organization for helping him land a lead role in the U.S. tour of the 1st National Broadway tour of "School of Rock the Musical".

In 2018, Vincent learned of an open audition for the tour through his Little Kids Rock teacher, Paul Gilvary. At the time, 12 year old Vincent couldn't imagine he would land such a prominent role. Prior his Little Kids Rock experience, he had never been on stage and this would be his first time in a play. He had so much gratitude towards his fellow classmates and teacher, that he offered to donate his entire salary to the organization - a gesture they refused. Vincent persisted and committed to a sizable contribution to the program, as well as donating instruments to his peers.

Vincent credits his Little Kids Rock participation and his experience in Chicago's All-City Modern Band program as vital to his getting the role. Of choosing to donate to Little Kids Rock and the impact of the organization has had on his career, Vincent says: *"I'm going to donate to Little Kids Rock, so that other kids can have the same experience that I had...where you can learn real instruments that can take you somewhere in life"*.

Tom Baggott – Executive Director
SpreadMusicNow
Colchester, Vermont – USA
www.SpreadMusicNow.org

"Christmas Surprise"

Music was present every day in my childhood home. My parents loved listening to records, especially music from the sixties and seventies. I was brought up with The Beatles, The Byrds, The Stones, CCR, Led Zeppelin, Uriah Heep, The Eagles...you get the idea. But, it wasn't just listening to records, my parents were very musical and would harmonize together, especially when I was a kid. They would also talk about the artists they dug. I loved the stories they told. I remember them so vividly: Brian Jones drowning, Elvis serving his country, Brian Wilson using his pool as an echo chamber, The Beatles playing in Hamburg. I was excited as one can be, listening to the stories in my early teens - learning about these legendary artists and, most importantly, about their music.

However, if there was a time when music had an even bigger presence in our house than on your usual Friday, it was Christmas. My parents started playing Christmas tunes in the beginning of December and wouldn't stop until New Year's Eve. One Christmas when I was 17, I remember them playing the heck out of "Happy Xmas (War Is Over)" by John Lennon and "Driving Home for Christmas" by Chris Rea. However, this is not the only reason why that particular Christmas stands out in my memory. The other reason, is the prank my father played on me.

To appreciate this story, what you need to know is that I've always loved giving and getting presents. Even as an adult, it's still very difficult for me to wait until it's time to open them. My parents knew me well enough to know, that if I could get my hands on anything that had my name on it before Christmas, I would somehow find a way to figure out what I was getting. This was one of the reasons they never left any of the presents at home, but instead stored them in my dad's office until the day before

Christmas. They did this until I was sixteen, at which point, my mom felt that being nearly of age, I was responsible enough not to touch the presents before the 24th. And, so, for the very first time in our family's history, my mom and dad stored the presents in our attic a week before Christmas.

For the first few days, I was able to resist the temptation. Then, one day after school, when I was home alone, I made my way to the attic - just to check how many presents I was getting. After all, what was the harm in that? I was only going to take a look. I collected all of mine in one big pile and noticed two, in particular, that interested me. Judging by their size and shape, these were CDs. "I'll just check these two," I thought. So, I ran downstairs to fetch some Scotch tape, scissors, string and matching gift wrap – I had to cover my tracks, after all. I can still remember my heart pounding as I began unwrapping the first CD-shaped present. My expectations ran high that year. The first ever Beatles box set, containing their entire catalog, had just come out. "Perhaps my parents had just wrapped two of the CDs," I mused. Much to my chagrin and surprise, I pulled out an empty jewel case that had a large Post-it Note on it that said:

YOUR MOTHER IS NAÏVE; I AM NOT.
DISAPPOINTED? WELL, HERE'S A LITTLE WISDOM TO
HELP WITH THAT: DON'T BE SAD WHEN A BIRD CRAPS ON
YOUR HEAD. BE HAPPY THAT, IN REAL LIFE, REINDEERS
CAN'T FLY. LOVE, DAD

Dad passed away a year and a half ago and not a day goes by that I don't miss him or his sense of humor. He was a riot to hang out with. He got old and sick over the years, but he never lost that spark in his eye. However, as sharp as my dad was, I could never truly see the connection between the wisdom and the prank – still, I kept the note for some reason. I still have it, in a box that has a few of my dad's things in it, along with the picture of the two of us in front of the Christmas tree, posing with that Beatles box set I had my heart set on. The Christmas note and Beatles box set remain two of my most valued treasures I hold on to. Oh, and although you were never very comfortable hearing this, I love you Dad.

Tom Tikka
Helsinski, Finland
www.ImpersonatorsMusic.com
www.TomTikka.com

"Sing Louder Than the Music"

My name is Tra Cee and I am a singer/songwriter, record label co-owner, radio station owner, daughter, aunt and mother. Of all the titles I possess, there is another that I still identify with - foster child.

When I was in my second foster home, my foster mother would tell me that she didn't want her son - who was younger than me - to feel as though I was smarter or more talented than he was. To that end, she would tell me that I could sing in the house, as long as the radio was playing and my voice could not be heard over the music. So for years, I hid my voice and tried not to be heard by others. I always felt like someone would either resent me for it, or be irritated by my singing.

When I got into high school, I had friends who would walk up to me and tell me to sing in the hallway. At first, I was too shy, but eventually I did. It took years for me to find my voice. I still struggle with feeling comfortable singing in public, but I am working past that.

That is why I came up with my personal message to anyone who has been prevented or discouraged from following their dreams. There will always be someone who doesn't want you shine brighter than they do - someone who wants you to stay in your place.

But, in spite of them, find your voice and always...sing louder than the music!

Tra Cee
Detroit, Michigan – USA
www.Tracee.co

"Music Doesn't Recognize Human Disabilities"

My adventure began with a phone call from Rory's mother saying, "My 10-year-old son has Autism. Would you consider teaching him to play the bagpipes?" Of course, I responded adamantly, "Yes, I would love to!"

After all, I have a grandson who has Autism and I hope others would do all they could to help him. Though I don't know everything about children with Autism, I do know they are special, and often very bright and intelligent. Children on the spectrum may have challenges expressing themselves outwardly, but inwardly, they have the same wants and needs as every child.

I admit, even though I was eager to begin teaching Rory, I knew the challenges I faced. I wasn't 100% sure I could keep him interested, as children with Autism can have a very short attention span, along with sensory overstimulation issues. I also wasn't sure he would be able to grasp the complex fingering movements required to play the bagpipes. All I knew, was that I was willing to do my very best to help him become a bagpiper.

At first, it was very slow going, but I was quickly impressed with his desire and determination to work hard and learn all that was required. I was fortunate, because at that time, my wife was an elementary school teacher for children with special needs. We often had conversations about Rory and how I could best teach and inspire him. She was able to offer many teaching techniques that she utilized with her school children.

Rory is what we call "high functioning." Within a short time of working together, I discovered several abilities that Rory possessed. One was a determination to learn. The second strength I recognized, was his ability to watch and mimic what I was teaching him.

After a while, it became clear that Rory exhibited a specific pattern of learning. When shown a new fingering technique for the first time, he would struggle and be unable to accomplish what I showed him. When I demonstrated the technique for a second time, he was able to struggle through, and in a rough form, accomplish what was needed. Then, almost without exception, once I showed him for the third time, he was able to successfully demonstrate the technique. That was the teaching and learning procedure we continued on for the next year and a half.

Finally, the big day came. How amazing it was, seeing Rory stand on stage in the spotlight, all by himself. Approximately 400 spectators reveled and cheered, as they watched Rory play the bagpipes for his first public performance. Shortly afterwards, the part I played in Rory's travels to become a bagpiper ended when I moved to another state. I said goodbye knowing that Rory, a young boy with Autism, showed the world what he was capable of. I learned never to underestimate or sell short, anyone with a desire to learn to play and enjoy music, in any form.

Rory is now living in New Zealand, helping his mother care for his grandfather suffering with dementia. His piping skills continue to grow and he is starting to enter solo piping competitions. He recently received first and third place honors in his age group. When asked about his bagpiping experiences, Rory shares that playing the pipes makes him feel calm.

Rory's Mom Ruth, recently shared her observations: *"Learning the pipes has been a positive experience for my son. Not only is he learning a great instrument, but as a child with a disability, he is receiving amazing support and encouragement from the members of the local pipe band. Rory looks forward to the day when he can don his kilt and represent the band at piping events."*

I look forward to the day when I will, once again, see Rory and be able to play our pipes together, not as student and instructor, but simply as fellow bagpipers!

Van W. Frazier
Colorado Springs, Colorado – USA
www.BagpipingByVan.com

"Brass is in Session"

It's well-known that some of history's most talented and exceptionally gifted musicians needed a helping hand in the early stages of their careers to stay motivated. Recently, I connected with a family who had a very specific need. A church pastor I met at a school district meeting referred me to the grandmother who said her 11-year old grandson, Malachi, was in need of a trombone. Malachi told her he had been listening to jazz and wanted to be able to play it on a trombone. I later came to discover that

Malachi suffered from anxiety and depression and, due to a financial hardship, had been using a borrowed trombone while playing with the school band.

Upon hearing Malachi's situation, the F2F Music Foundation felt compelled to help. I reached out to my friend, national recording artist and fellow board member, Paula Atherton, for assistance. During many phone calls and emails between Paula, myself and David Benedetto of the musical instrument manufacturer, F.E. Olds, we reached an agreement with F.E. Olds to donate a new trombone to Malachi.

We later discovered that a heart condition added to Malachi's obstacles, when his doctor suggested he stop playing the trombone, believing it might exacerbate his condition. This resulted in Malachi being removed from the school band, leaving him with no access to a trombone. After much discussion, we decided to proceed with donating an instrument. We didn't want to increase any potential anxiety Malachi might experience over being removed from the band and losing access to his borrowed trombone. I am also happy to report that we now have two instructors (the Director of Bands for the University of Charleston, along with another national recording artist) ready to provide free trombone lessons to Malachi when his family says he is ready.

I believe this new trombone will be the inspiration Malachi needs to achieve better health - mentally, physically, emotionally and spiritually and that his music studies will help him achieve a higher level of academic success.

Vel Lewis, F2F Music Foundation
Houston, Texas – USA
www.F2FMusicFoundation.org

"Surviving the Music Business Takes Pulling Strings"

So, I was asked to write something interesting, something heartfelt and memorable to share amongst musicians and maybe soon-to-be musicians. Let me go way back and start at my beginning. For starters, growing up in Collingdale, Pennsylvania (a small suburb outside Philadelphia), and learning a musical instrument in the 1960's was challenge No. 1 in itself. Having little to none when it came to funds, puts quite a strain on a kid who can feel the music in his bones, but with no meat on those bones to get the party started.

My parents were both musicians. Mom, then Mary Wayne, sang with the Tommy Dorsey Big Band when she was a teenager. Pop, Joe, was in a three-piece jazz band playing first fiddle, along with guitar and accordion. They would pound out their songs in the living room, while we listened from upstairs. I was already singing, but insisted I wanted to play the guitar. Mom and pop promised me a guitar, but made me take piano lessons until I was 12, before they would buy me my first electric guitar. What did they know about music! They insisted with a stick and a belt. That was called "training" by Italian parents back in the day.

And that became challenge No. 2. Five years playing an old, upright piano they bought out of a newspaper ad for $25.00 was not my idea of rock and roll. Those piano keys stuck more than the Milky Way Bars we ate on Halloween. I was taught by a little 'ale nun who swore (Ooo, I made her swear), because I wasn't reading the music, I was memorizing. Anyhow, shortly after, she died. Guess you could say my piano playing killed her. Did I make it to 12, you ask? Yep! And on my 12th birthday, my dad sprang for the electric guitar. That took pulling some strings.

Here's where the plot thickens, like Mueller Spaghetti sticks to the pot on Sunday afternoons. This guitar beauty was made by a well-known All-American manufacturer...also known for washer machines, dryers, fine furniture, bedroom slippers and apparel. That's right folks, Sears Roebuck! It came fully equipped with a guitar cable and W' wide strap that, ultimately, found itself neatly embedded into the groove in my shoulder. But, hey, I had an electric guitar.

Okay, now the sentimental part. I took guitar lessons for a couple of years from my Uncle Charlie. He was an original George Benson kind of player. Shortly after that, Uncle Charlie died. Guess you could say my guitar playing killed him.

Anyhow, when the local 14 and 15 year olds around the corner found out that I had finally gotten my music rig, we decided to put together a "combo." That's what it was called back then folks, a C-o-m-b-o. Only, we needed some songs, a name and we needed to practice. It took constant straining to hear our favorite songs playing on my transistor radio with the tiny 3" speaker, which I bought with my newspaper route money. I recorded them onto my tiny 3" reel-to-reel tape recorder that I begged for and got on my 10th birthday (more string pulling).

Here's where challenge No. 3 arrives. (So, who's counting?) While trying to babysit 2 kid brothers and 2 kid sisters, listen to the radio and jot down the words to The Beatles' "She Loves You" and The Rolling Stones "Get Off of My Cloud", while some non-stop, motormouth AM Radio DJ talked over the beginning and ending of every song, we finally put together our first (and only) set of songs and the band "90 Pruf" was born. What a great name for a bunch of 14 and 15 year olds that couldn't even spell proof, let alone drink.

So, you ask, 'Why did you need this song set?" Thanks for asking. We got our first gig, the city block party. All the neighbors were there, complete with kids, popcorn, cotton candy machines, a bunch of sisters from the convent down the street and a grease pole climbing contest. Yes, a grease pole. And the show began. Somebody from the Catholic rectory built a rickety platform for us and set it up right under the street light, of course, and across from the grease pole. We played our twelve songs over and over again throughout the night. Not sure if the crowd could even hear my guitar, since pop made my amp from an old 5 watt Hi-Fi home amplifier, but the crowd sure loved us. They screamed and cheered. To this day, I really don't know if they screamed and cheered for us or for the idiots trying to climb that grease pole.

All of this is my sentimental memory and the beginning of my music career. Is anyone envious yet? That was 54 years ago. Please, stop doing the math! That first gig exploded our careers and we were soon off doing Collingdale High's Sadie Hawkins Dance. Here's a bit of first-hand professional musical advice, dudes: If you want to get the ladies, learn to play the guitar! People often ask me, to this day, how I got into the music business. I swear I always reply, "*You mean how do I get out of it?*"

But, that's the truth. Being in cover bands, original bands, managing bands, worship bands...I think I performed at every wedding, bar mitzvah, fire house banquet, back yard birthday party and stinky, smokey night club in Philly, Jersey and Delaware. So, where's that most memorable part? Honestly, the most memorable and consistent thing about all those years of performance... making about $50 bucks per man, per night and still hungering for it 54 years later. The music is in your blood. When you want it bad enough, your heart will beat to 4/4. You'll memorize every piece of music you get your hands on and beat the dashboard of your '66 Chevy Malibu to every song: Beatles, Stones, Zeppelin, Hendrix, Doors, 4

Tops, Miracles, Steely Dan, Frampton, Doobies, Eagles and the like.

Now, after all these years and having owned several music studios, an indie record label, a music publishing company, a radio advertising agency, a CD/DVD duplication facility and an audio/video restoration company, you can see that I've pulled some strings to get to where I am today. The reward: my hardly-known, local Florida based oldies band does many of our gigs for...wait for it...for free. That's right: senior citizen facilities, houses of worship, children's church, Christmas parties, special needs kids events and the like. Even Covid-19 couldn't keep us down. We perform twice a month for our beautiful and very special needs audience on Zoom. And the crowd still cheers!

Yes, you might say I've come a long way to get to where I am in my music career. Would I do it all again? You bet I would. Would I do anything differently? You bet I would. I would have worked a little harder on reading the piano charts I was supposed to learn back then. But, what did my parents know? The high points? Doing what I know and do best and making a career living off these blessings. I guess penning the Philly City Song, "Philadelphia" was quite a feat. I do have to let you know, that it all came through the blessings and never-ending graces of my Lord and Savior, Jesus Christ. And none could have been accomplished without the loving support of my wife and best friend, Rhonda, and our fantastic family. They grew up listening to countless hours of smashing drum recordings and screaming guitar solos coming through the floors of my home recording studio in Jersey, while they were attempting to fall fast asleep in musical dreamland on the second floor above. Sound familiar?

Vito Fera - Network Sound & Video, Inc.
Longwood, Florida – USA
www.NetworkSoundAndVideo.com

"Silence Room"

"Sound exists only through time. Even if the silence is less than a millisecond long, it is essential for hearing the separation of the notes in a musical composition or in a sound arrangement. The importance of silence for sound or music, is substantially less explored than sound itself. Silence is before sound starts, it is there again at the end and it is in the middle, when tones change." This statement was part of a performance proposal for a sound festival held annually in San Pedro, California, a city at the southern end of Los Angeles County.

A good friend and fellow industrial punk sound maker, Tom Zear, and I produced the "Silence Room", an original idea to counter sound. We wanted to demonstrate that silence is an essential part of any piece of music, sound or even noise; unfortunately, not recognized as such by most music lovers and listeners.

Each participant was seated alone in a dark and well insulated "silence room" behind closed doors for one or two minutes. The total darkness of the room tremendously contributed to the sensorial experience, emphasizing the aural perception.

Our goal was to achieve a solemn space of quietude within the otherwise noisy festival installations. Since the room was a huge industrial freezer, which we clothed in red and black, we knew it would create a lot of curiosity. We were prepared and handed out educational information about hearing, listening, silence and its contribution to music, coupled with a questionnaire.

Right from the start, there were waiting lines up to 100 ft long. Some enjoyed the experience so much, that they came out of the "silence room" and went right back to the end of the line. It was a huge success, unexpected and a welcomed experience in a festival of highly thought out sound compositions. A rest for the ears. Out of hundreds of participants, only two became frightened and wanted to get out of the sensory-deprived room before their time was up. 92% congratulated us for the idea of a contrapuntal silence installation at a sound festival. Most were stimulated by the questions we asked and each and every one began to think about how much silence contributes to sound. Our provocative statement, that *silence is a defining factor of music*, created the starting point of a new listening perception experience and a wealth of debates when the show ended just before midnight.

Wolfgang Gowin
Temecula, California – USA
www.Wolf-Gowin.de

> ## *Perhaps the most beautiful music comes from nature itself...*

"Don't Listen to Your Mom"

I'm easily the worst musician in my band, Yosi & The Superdads. Just ask those guys: I speed up. I don't know how to play leads. At best, I have a character voice. But none of that matters. I've been exceptionally lucky to make a career out of performing and recording children's music for nearly 25 years.

As a young boy in Israel, I enjoyed singing along at the top of my lungs with my little record player, while my grandma and sister giggled at my earnestness. I had my fist up to my mouth like a microphone, as if I was on stage in front of thousands. I made up little tunes for my younger brother. I played the recorder terribly.

We moved to the U.S. when I was 9 years old, due to my sister's asthma. I discovered The Jackson 5 and School House Rock on TV, along with many jingles and musical cartoons. I asked my mom if I could get a guitar. My mom, being an eternal pessimist, responded "What are you going to do? Play it once and then hang it up on the wall?" I guess she never heard of lessons.

So with no instrument other than my voice and tunes playing in my head, I tried out for the middle school play and got the part of Nicely Nicely Johnson in Guys & Dolls. I actually got a standing ovation for my performance of "Sit Down You're Rockin' The Boat!" That was a defining moment. I was bitten by the show biz bug. I performed in every school play, always as a comic actor; never the serious lead. I joined the high school drama club. Meanwhile, I was writing songs and poems in my bedroom. I told my mom I wanted to be an actor. Her cynical response was, "What are you going to do? Wait tables all your life?" I guess she noticed a lot of out of work actors.

I was strong in math and enrolled in George Washington University in Washington, DC to become an engineer. My mom's idea, not mine. I failed miserably in the first year, which was a blessing, but I began to attend punk concerts and was fully immersed in the irreverent and irrepressible sound of punk music. I returned home and enrolled in a 2-year college with no idea what I would do. In a creative writing class, I met up with my high school friend, Scott, who suggested to his buddy Pete, "let's back up Yosi in a joke hardcore band." A few days later, I was in the hatchback of Pete's Ford Pinto with an old amp, some guy named Mike and, along with Scott, we started a punk band. I bought a cheap acoustic guitar and showed Pete basic notes to a punk song I wrote. He transformed those notes into power chords and riffs that kicked butt! Before long, we were writing angry songs and playing whatever venues would have us. It was a great way to release frustration and angst, plus learn how to craft a song. My mom said "I can't understand a word you sing, err, scream." The rest of my family and old friends thought it was a funny phase. But, I was energized and determined. Over 5 years, I slowly taught myself some basic guitar chords and listened to tons of new wave, punk, industrial and indie music. I also poured over lyrics, played every venue we could and kept writing better tunes.

The band broke up and I attended a master's program to become a therapist. I was still writing and recording songs on my own, but no longer performing. I got married, had a respectable counseling job, and we had a daughter who enjoyed hearing me play the guitar for her. Life was calm, normal and sweet.

When my daughter Hannah started preschool, I decided to bring my guitar one time to her school to play some songs like "Wheels on the Bus" to her class. This was a one-time only event. Hannah and other preschoolers, enjoyed the songs. I figured I did my little good daddy deed and was done. However, the director of the school said, "I like what you just did. Would you return twice a month and perform at all the classes for a tuition reduction?" How could I refuse? More time with my daughter, plus playing for little kids and a tuition reduction! It seemed like a good idea.

I quickly discovered that traditional preschool songs by various artists (Raffi, Barney, etc.) were syrupy and not at all fitting for this former punk. So I decided to write my own rebellious, quirky and funny punk-style songs ...and the kids loved them! I realized kids are natural punks: they dance and sing with abandon. Plus, kids love that I bring something lively and real to them. I'm no great guitar player. My voice is not beautiful, but I can bring joy and energy to others. I'm not conventionally good looking, but kids love me - moles, wrinkles and all!

Isn't this what I was rebelling against all these years? My mom's negativity. My friends and family's condescension that I am just "going through a phase." Society's ideas of what is prudent and financially rewarding. My own insecurity when I've been told time and again that my ideas were too lofty, wild, foolish and impractical.

But life has a way of bringing the truth out, if you're open to it. Before long, I was performing daily at schools, parties and various stages. I recorded award-winning albums and had a few hit songs on the radio! I quit my job as a psychotherapist and performed 400+ shows a year. I had press, a rockin' band and lots of tiny loyal fans. I know my mom was not being purposefully mean. She just got caught up in her ideas of financial security. In her own natural way, she posed a challenge and I'm glad I didn't listen to my mom.

Yosi Levin
Island Heights, New Jersey – USA
www.YosiMusic.com

"88 Ways Music" Beneficiaries

Musicians On Call has brought live and recorded music to the bedsides of patients in healthcare facilities for over 20 years. MOC Volunteer Musicians have performed for more than 800,000 patients, families and caregivers at facilities across the country. Musicians On Call is the nation's leading organization delivering the healing power of music, serving individuals in facilities ranging from children's hospitals to adult facilities, VA hospitals and hospices. *www.MusiciansOnCall.org*

Hungry For Music has collected and placed over 14,000 instruments into the hands of aspiring musicians; serving children whose trajectory has been altered by the uplifting and life-changing gift of music. They have delivered everything from guitars and trombones to violins and xylophones to kids in 49 states and 30 countries. *www.HungryForMusic.org*

Rock To The Future provides student-driven music programs in a safe and supportive environment at no cost for Philadelphia youth. Our program serves hundreds of students every year through the MusiCore after school program, MobileMusic in-school classes, Rock*A*Delphia and GuitarStars summer programs, and community events. We prepare the next generation for every stage. *www.RockToTheFuture.org*

Keep Music Alive is the founder of Teach Music Week (March) and Kids Music Day (October). Their mission is to help more children and adults reap the educational, therapeutic and social benefits of playing music. Each year they partner with over 1,000 music schools and stores to offer free lessons and hold special events for children playing music. *www.KeepMusicAlive.org*

Previous "88 Ways Music" Beneficiaries include:
Guitars in the Classroom, Spirit of Harmony and
The Mr. Holland's Opus Foundation

"KEEP MUSIC ALIVE"

<u>Some ways you can help keep music alive:</u>

- Support music education in your community – Let your local politicians and school board know just how important music and art education is for your children AND for our collective future.

- Support up and coming artists and local venues that offer live music. Bring your children out to events that feature music. Let them hear live music themselves and you will see how these experiences help positively shape your child's development and future.

- If music is not currently offered in your schools, find alternate ways to introduce music education to your children, whether it's outside music schools, private teachers and even Youtube offers a wealth of free tutorials where you can learn how to play almost any instrument under the sun.

For more information and resources, please visit www.KeepMusicAlive.org

To share your inspirational music story, please visit us at www.88WaysMusic.com